"Reading a collection of Royko's columns is even more of a pleasure than encountering them one by one, and that is a large remark for he rarely wrote a piece that failed to wake you up with his hard-earned moral wit. Three cheers for Royko!"
                                        —Norman Mailer

"A treasure house for journalism students, for would-be writers, for students of writing styles, for people who just like to laugh at the absurdity of the human condition or, as Studs Terkel said, for those who will later seek to learn what it was really like in the 20th century."
                        —Georgie Anne Geyer, *Washington Times*

"A marvelous road map through four decades of America, from the Freedom Riders in Alabama to the Persian Gulf War to the failings of the Cubs."
                        —Elizabeth Taylor, *Chicago Tribune Books*

"Mike Royko wasn't just the best columnist this town ever produced. He rates a spot on the short list with Ernie Pyle, Red Smith, and Murray Kempton as among the greatest of all American newspapermen. . . . *One More Time* [is] a wonderful collection of his best work. . . . This collection of his work is a powerful reminder why he had such an enduring hold on this town for more than 30 years."
                        —Steve Neal, *Chicago Sun-Times*

"It's been over two years since Mike Royko died, so it's easy to forget what he wrote to earn his reputation. . . . *One More Time: The Best of Mike Royko* is a refreshing reminder. . . . Rereading the columns makes one irony clear. Despite his influence (almost every journalist over 35 claims him as an influence), there's no one remotely like him out there today."
                        —Ben Joravsky, *Chicago Reader*

"The full range of Royko's writing talents are on display in *One More Time*. . . . Any reader of newspapers will find *One More Time* a more than adequate addition to their personal library. . . . For those who always wanted to cut out Royko's columns and put them up at work, or even on their refrigerators, *One More Time* is the next best thing."
—*Sun Prairie Star*

"The columns in this collection are remarkable on many levels and are representative of the breadth of [Royko's] coverage and the moods of his writing."
—*Abilene Reporter-News*

"On nearly every page of *The Best of Mike Royko* are lines that glisten long after the day's news has been forgotten."
—*Journal*, Franklin, IN

"*One More Time* offers a final taste of Royko's work with a selection of columns spanning his 30-year career. All the classics are here. . . . But there are also lesser-known pieces that are just as good or better."
—*Gazette-Mail*, Charleston, WV

"A superb vehicle to remember [Royko's] work."
—*Laporte Herald-Argus*

"*One More Time* is excellent. Every student of journalism should read the book. It describes the culture of the last quarter of the 20th century through the eyes of one of the outstanding observers of the era. To those of us who did not have access to the columns written by Royko through the years, *One More Time* will help us learn about one of the truly great writers of the century."
—*Forsyth County News*, Cumming, GA

"Royko was an expert at finding universal truths in parochial situations, as well as in the larger issues—war and peace, justice and injustice, wealth and poverty—he examined. Think of *One More Time* as one man's pungent commentary on life in these United States over the last few decades."
—*Booklist*

"The continued relevance of these columns reminds us that good journalists can make a difference."
—*Kirkus Reviews*

One More Time

ONE MORE TIME

THE UNIVERSITY OF CHICAGO PRESS· CHICAGO AND LONDON

THE BEST OF
Mike Royko
WITH A FOREWORD BY STUDS TERKEL

COMMENTARIES BY LOIS WILLE

The University of Chicago Press, Chicago 60637
The University of Chicago Press, Ltd., London
© 1999 by The University of Chicago
All rights reserved. Published 1999
Paperback edition 2000
08 07 06 05 04 03 02 01 00   3 4 5
ISBN: 0-226-73071-9 (cloth)
ISBN: 0-226-73072-7 (paperback)

Frontispiece: Mike in his office at the *Chicago Daily News*. Courtesy Chicago Sun-Times, Inc.

Photographs on pages 3 and 49 courtesy Chicago Sun-Times, Inc.
Photographs on pages 131 and 207 courtesy *Chicago Tribune*.

Columns dated September 26, 1963, through November 3, 1983, are reprinted by permission of Chicago Sun-Times, Inc. Columns dated January 12, 1984, through March 21, 1997, are reprinted by permission of the *Chicago Tribune*.

Library of Congress Cataloging-in-Publication Data

Royko, Mike, [date]
    One more time : the best of Mike Royko / commentaries by Lois Wille ; foreword by Studs Terkel.
        p.   cm.
    ISBN 0-226-73071-9 (alk. paper)
    I. Chicago (Ill.)—Social life and customs.   2. United States—Social life and customs—1971–   3. United States—Social life and customs—1945–1970.   4. Royko, Mike, 1932–
I. Wille, Lois.   II. Title.
F548.52.R684   1999
977.3'11043—dc21   98-46699
                                                                                            CIP

∞ The paper used in this publication meets the minimum requirements of the American National Standard for Information Sciences—Permanence of Paper for Printed Library Materials, ANSI Z39.48-1992.

When I was a kid, the worst of all days was the last day of summer vacation, and we were in the schoolyard playing softball, and the sun was down and it was getting dark. But I didn't want it to get dark. I didn't want the game to end. It was too good, too much fun. I wanted it to stay light forever, so we could go on playing forever, so the game would go on and on.

That's how I feel now. C'mon, c'mon. Let's play one more inning. One more time at bat. One more pitch. Just one? Stick around, guys. We can't break up this team. It's too much fun.

But the sun always went down. And now it's almost dark again.

—*Mike Royko, on the death of the* Chicago Daily News, *March 3, 1978*

CONTENTS

ACKNOWLEDGMENTS

The idea for this book was Mike's. Thinking he might not survive brain surgery, he asked me to put together a final collection of his columns. *One More Time* is the result of that conversation, and it would not have been possible without the efforts of a group of Mike's friends and his son, David Royko. These friends who meant so much to Mike and gave so freely of their time are Lois Wille, Wayne Wille, Wade Nelson, Ellen Warren, Rick Soll, Pam Zekman, Jim Warren, Morgan Powell, Hanke Gratteau, Janan Hanna, and Clarence Petersen.

We first met at my house in August 1997 and divided up every column from the thirty-four years of Mike's career. Their task was to read each column and pick the best of the nearly 8,000 columns Mike wrote. More columns were purposefully selected than we could use. So, once everyone's selections were gathered, it fell to Hanke Gratteau to narrow them to a usable number and then to Lois and Wayne Wille for further refining. Considering the gems Mike regularly wrote, selecting the best was not an easy job. My thanks to all of you for your labor of love.

Thanks also to the University of Chicago Press for their enthusiasm for this project and especially our editor, John Tryneski, always gracious and always ready with valuable suggestions.

My thanks to Mike's friend Sam Sianis, who was like a brother, for lending us a photograph of him and Mike in Billy Goat's Tavern. And thanks also to the guy Mike would choose to walk down to the O.K. Corral with him, John Sciackitano, for the title of this book.

My gratitude to Nigel Wade and Larry Green at the *Chicago Sun-Times* and Joe Leonard at the *Chicago Tribune* for allowing us to reprint these columns and photographs. And I am grateful to Phil Krone for all the things he did that made such a difference.

And a special thank you to Lois and Wayne Wille. Lois so beautifully captured Mike's life and the times in the introductory pieces to each decade. And Wayne had the arduous task of transferring all 110 columns to computer disks. Their expertise and support meant so much to me.

—*Judy Royko*
September 1998

FOREWORD

"I love thee, infamous city," Baudelaire sang of Paris. Five gets you ten that Mike Royko, serenading his home town, never, ever used that verb. It just wasn't his style. Yet you know he shared the French poet's passion.

It was his fellow townsman, Nelson Algren, who said it for Mike. "Once you've come to be part of this particular patch, you'll never love another. Like loving a woman with a broken nose, you may well find lovelier lovelies. But never a lovely so real."

It was "the real" of Chicago—and metaphorically of our society—that Royko searched out. His was the rapture of Parsifal seeking the Grail. He had become the chronicler of the human comedy. This was not his intent, hell, no. He was merely pursuing his trade: a newspaperman. His findings appeared, on page three, five days a week for thirty-four years. He had vintage years with the *Chicago Daily News,* and when the paper folded he kept at it, fervor and wit undiminished, with the *Sun-Times* and the unlikely *Tribune.*

His move to the World's Greatest Newspaper (as the *Tribune* described itself) came about when the *Sun-Times* was bought by Rupert Murdoch. He explained it in wholly understandable Roykoese: "No self-respecting fish would ever want to be wrapped in his paper."

On occasion, I'd saunter into his office, unannounced. He'd look heavenward with one of those why-hast-thou-forsaken-me looks and growl, "Oh, God." His voice was one octave lower than Chaliapin's. His glasses slipped down toward the tip of his nose. He was listening. Some nobody was at the other end of the phone. Sometimes it was a cry for help. He was no Miss Lonelyhearts, but there it was. Sometimes it was an astonishing tip. Sometimes it was just a funny Chicago story. The human comedy had him on the hip. Again, the growl, "Oh, God."

Most often, it was from somebody up against it. A nobody who reflected pretty much everybody, who, at one time or another, had been shafted by Mr. Big. Not to mention the inevitable call from some fat stuff with clout, whose venality Royko had exposed to a harsh light. (While we're on the subject of clout, a singularly Chicago term, you'll find in this book a hilarious contretemps between Royko and the editor of a modish New York magazine who has annoyed Mike more than somewhat in her misuse of the word. As you may gather, Royko was not too wild about the Big Apple and its trendsetters.)

Mike's pieces seemed to flow so naturally, to read so free and easy. You'd think it was a snap, his daily chore. The laughter it evoked, or the indignation, or the catch in the throat, you must understand, did not come about by happenstance. He worked like a dog, obstinately gnawing away at the bone of truth. So it was with nailing that right word, that telling phrase. After all, they were as much the tools of his trade as the gimlet eye was to the jeweler. His obsession with detail was positively Dickensian.

As a matter of course, he discomfited the powerful, whether they were in public or corporate office. He was, in this matter, indiscriminate. He figured that, more often than not, they were the same boys. On occasion, the demon that possessed him, that sprung forth a natural eloquence, was deflected and he may have winged the sparrow rather than the vulture. But those occasions are worth only a forgettery in our remembrance of things past.

During Royko's vintage years, when Richard the First held court in the palatinate called Chicago, he wrote what is *in*arguably an urban classic, *Boss*. Jimmy Breslin, no small potatoes himself, the only big-city minstrel in the same class with Royko, called it "the best book ever written about a city of this country."

The word got around and in time Mike Royko became the most widely read daily newspaper columnist in the country. Some years ago, a celebrated young journalist, who had coauthored a bestseller, passed through town on a book promotion tour. As we sat in Riccardo's, Chicago's favorite watering hole for newspaper people, he told me of a suggestion made to him by his equally celebrated editor. "Why don't you try doing here, in Washington, what Royko does in Chicago?" My companion went on, "I tried it for three weeks and came near to a nervous breakdown. I gave up, of course." A long pause. "How does he do it? Day after day, year after year, how the hell does he do it?" He had me there. I didn't know.

I know now. He was possessed by a demon. How else to explain the tavern keeper's kid, in a world he never made, a world compressed into one, cockeyed wonder of a city; of "haves" kicking the bejeepers out of the "have-nots"; of Jane Addams and Al Capone; of Florence Scala, a neighborhood heroine, and Richard J. Daley—and of Slats Grobnik, for God's sake. Royko was the right one in the right city at the right time: to tell us in small tales what this big, crazy world in the last half of the twentieth century was all about. And the devil made him do it.

The columns that make up *The Best of Mike Royko* were chosen with loving care by his devoted colleagues. There are scores more, but these will do. There's Mike's sense of the burlesque in his portraits of Slats, the tavern clod; and yet, there is one of Grobnik's remembrance of a time past, a time of innocence, when a spark was there of something that might have been, a lasting ache. The low comedy is there in Mike's high old time with our town's upper crust and their devotion to Thanksgiving haggis (sheep's guts), as he contrasts this delicacy with his tribe's celebrated gourmet dish, czernina (duck's blood soup).

There's the unveiling of Picasso's gift to Chicago. What appears to be a put-down of the work, "a big, homely metal thing," becomes something else. It may have "a long stupid face" but "it has eyes that are pitiless, cold, mean." Royko's eye is something else. He says that, accidentally or not, Picasso captured the spirit of Chicago as the speakers said it would. "Its eyes are like the eyes of every slum owner who made a buck off the small and weak. And of every building inspector who took a wad from a slum owner to make it all possible." "Any bigtime real estate operator will be able to look into the face of the Picasso and see the spirit that makes the city's rebuilding possible and profitable." You get the idea. It is Royko's bite at its sharpest. The last line says it all: "Picasso has never been here, they say. You'd think he's been riding the L all his life." Mike always felt that our city's motto, *Urbs in Horto* (City in a Garden) needed updating: *Ubi Est Mea* (Where's Mine?).

Yet, the heart of all his work lies in his deeply moving tales of our city's heroes and heroines, of the bungalows, the two-flats, and the projects. What Sandburg and Algren celebrated in their poems and stories, Mike did as a newspaperman.

I cannot bring this overture to a close without a reference to my favorite Mike Royko column. It appeared October 25, 1972. He wrote it the day Jackie Robinson died. It is his recollection of a Sunday, May 18, 1947, the day Jackie first appeared in Wrigley Field. Hundreds of stories and scores of books have celebrated Jackie's trials and triumphs. Mike's piece was not about Jackie. It was about Jackie's people, who were in the stands that day. "In

1947 few blacks were seen in the Loop, much less up on the white North Side at a Cubs game. This day they came by the thousands, pouring off the northbound Ls. . . . They didn't wear baseball-game clothes. They had on church clothes and funeral clothes—suits, white shirts, ties, gleaming shoes, and straw hats. I've never seen so many straw hats. As big as it was, the crowd was orderly. Almost unnaturally so. . . . The whites tried to look as if nothing unusual was happening, while the blacks tried to look casual and dignified. So everybody looked slightly ill at ease. . . . Robinson came up in the first inning. . . . They applauded, long, rolling applause. A tall, middle-aged black man stood next to me, a smile of almost painful joy on his face, beating his palms together so hard they must have hurt."

Well, you'll find the column in this book. The last lines will kill you. It's about that white tavern keeper's kid, that middle-aged black man, and the bargain they struck. Read it and weep.

So, we read Royko one more time.

I guess Baudelaire did speak for Mike, after all: "I love thee, infamous city."

—*Studs Terkel*

PART ONE

THE SIXTIES

It is highly unlikely that any readers of the *Chicago Daily News* of September 6, 1963, put down the paper and cried, "Hey, a star is born!" How could they have guessed that the entertaining but modest little essay on the woes of a tavern owner, published deep inside the paper next to a commentary on attitudes toward mental illness, would evolve into one of the most dazzling features in American journalism? That its mix of the tough and the tender, the profound and the hilarious, would rollick on without letup for three and a half decades?

The young man who was introduced that day as the paper's new columnist probably had no inkling of what was to come, either. Mike Royko, said the *Daily News* in a brief note to its readers, was a native Chicagoan who "reports in the great tradition of Chicago newspapering. He thinks, talks and writes in Chicagoese. . . . He is 31, has a wife named Carol and two young sons." And he must have thought that getting his own column in one of the most respected newspapers in the country was a fitting punch line to a brazen stunt he had pulled eight years earlier.

In 1955, Air Force Sergeant Mike Royko requested a transfer back home to Chicago's O'Hare Field because his mother was terminally ill. The O'Hare base had no need for a radio operator—Mike's specialty—so he was ordered to report for duty as a military policeman. Appalled at that prospect, he hunted around for something else he could do and learned that the base newspaper needed an editor. "So I told the personnel officer I was a former reporter for the *Chicago Daily News*. I just flat-out lied," Mike confessed nearly forty years later to interviewer Chris Robling on WBEZ-FM, Chicago's public radio station. "I guess after three years in the service they didn't check résumés." He got the job, spent a three-day pass in the city's public library reading books on newspaper reporting and design, and soon was producing some of the liveliest reading in the city. By the time he was discharged, he was having so much fun that he scrapped plans to return to college and become a lawyer. Instead he worked his way up from a neighborhood newspaper to the City News Bureau—a service run by Chicago's daily newspapers—to covering county government for the *Chicago Daily News*. This was hardly a prize assignment. Pre-Royko, the drab reports from the Cook County Building barely made it past the paper's early editions. Suddenly, the county beat was yielding one outrageous, enlightening story after another. The new reporter was using a technique unheard of in local political coverage at the time: He was relating exactly what public officials said and did.

Readers loved it. So did Mike's editors, who asked him to supplement his reports with a column every Saturday. His weekly forays into the eccentricities of county government made the paper's daily columnist seem so bland and inconsequential that the inevitable happened. Mike got his job, although initially he was confined to two or three columns a week. Now he could broaden his sights to include the Chicago City Council and its mighty boss, Mayor Richard J. Daley. He could attack thick-headed bureaucracy wherever he found it and give voice to its victims. Mike leavened the mixture with neighborhood characters, boyhood pals real and imaginary, his beloved Chicago Cubs—nuggets of an autobiography of a city kid.

The Royko column became the talk of the town, and by the start of 1964 it was expanded to five a week. Mike was as fearless as he was funny, readers thought. They didn't know that underneath the tough exterior ran a vein of insecurity. When President John F. Kennedy was assassinated, Mike did not write about it—he stayed out of the paper to make room for reports and commentaries from the *Daily News* national staff. In the spring of 1964, when his editors told their new star that he would be part of the *Daily News* delegation to the Republican National Convention in San Francisco, he refused to go. He told interviewer Chris Robling, "I said, 'I write about local stuff. I want the readers to get to know me. And the way they get to know me is by my writing about something that I know about and they know about. Suddenly you want me to go out and write about national stuff? I'm not qualified. Let me do what I can do. I can cover the aldermen, I can cover the mayor, I can do local stuff real good. If I get out there, I won't be sure of myself. Give me some time.' So I didn't do it."

It was the civil rights crusades of the 1960s that yanked Mike out of his familiar territory. Moved by the brutal treatment of Freedom Riders in Alabama, he traveled to Selma and Montgomery early in 1966, using the same techniques in his reports and columns that he had perfected in covering Chicago government:

Let people hang themselves with their own words. Nail every irony and hypocrisy, every vicious stupidity. That summer, the civil rights struggle shifted to Chicago. Mike's powerful coverage enraged many *Daily News* readers—a heavily white, suburban, conservative bunch. The paper's circulation chiefs complained that Mike was driving away subscribers, although afternoon newspapers around the country were already hemorrhaging, with or without courageous columnists. Other Royko columns gave his editors heartburn, too, yet they always appeared in the paper with insults intact. Among his favorite targets were polluting utility companies and steel companies and the civic big shots who ran them; the fat and stuffy *Chicago Tribune;* and the cozy alliance between corporate chiefs, most of them Republicans who lived in the suburbs, and the arrogant Daley machine that ran the city.

Barely three years into his column, Mike's impact was so strong that *Daily News* editor Roy Fisher decided to move him from the columnists' page inside the paper to the prominence of page three. Mike balked. He worried that his columns weren't significant enough for that spot, that he would finally be exposed as a guy who got into the business because of his flair for the con job. But Fisher prevailed. Mike fought his anxieties and wrote on without a hitch. By this time, the mail and telephone calls from people with tips and gripes and praise and weird anecdotes were so overwhelming that the *Daily News* provided Mike with an assistant, the first in a series of young reporters whose careers blossomed under his guidance and whose devotion helped sustain him years later.

He experimented with new styles, and several became his trademarks. There is the gleeful put-down of angry readers (you would think that they would learn to avoid dueling with him, but, thankfully, they never did). The stinging ridicule of New York City sophisticates (and, later, anything and anyone in California). The cold anger at injustice that jolted an otherwise humorous piece (see the concluding paragraphs of "Picasso and the Cultural Rebirth of Chicago"). And the debut of his celebrated alter ego, Slats Grobnik. Slats first appeared as an overgrown, tattooed schoolyard bully. Mike apparently had second thoughts about that image, because the next time we meet Slats he has shrunk to Mike's own scrawny boyhood proportions and become his best buddy, as in the lovely "He Can Dream, Can't He?" included here. That column is an example of another Royko specialty: the choice of a word, almost always a simple one, that perfectly set the tone of the entire piece—in this case, the repeated use of "hiss" and "trot."

Mike's timetable in writing his column was established early and rarely varied. Mainly, it was: Get to work in the morning, read the papers, the mail, and "the wires"—the news-agency material in those pre-computer days—listen to phone callers, roam the newsroom talking to colleagues, and in general fuss around until an idea hits. Then write, rewrite, polish, and turn it in for the next day's paper. This process could take anywhere from a few hours to ten or twelve or more, and he did this five days a week, sometimes six. Almost every column was conceived and finished in a day. One exception was his classic Christmas story, "Mary and Joe Chicago-Style." He started it in 1963, didn't like it, tinkered with it in 1964, still didn't like it, tried again in 1965 and 1966, and finally put it in the paper in 1967, still not satisfied that it worked. He was wrong. It drew such a remarkable response that it was read from pulpits, tacked onto bulletin boards, and published around the country in magazines, newsletters, books, and other newspapers. The *Daily News* received thousands of requests for copies.

By 1967, Mike had created so many memorable columns that a Chicago publisher, Henry Regnery Company, produced a collection, *Up Against It.* Mike dedicated it to Larry Fanning, the *Daily News* editor who had given him the column in 1963. In an introduction, the famous political cartoonist Bill Mauldin wrote, "[Mike] is trapped. Being driven by a talent that is even stronger than his social proclivities, he must write his stories, and do them beautifully, and each one is a stepping stone to the big time he dreads. That's how the American dream works. This book . . . will involve him in cocktail parties and TV panels. The more he glowers at gushy ladies the more thrilled they'll be. Mike is one of the few newspapermen in Chicago who hasn't been afraid to give Mayor Daley hell. Now he'll probably run into the Mayor socially and have to exchange small talk with him. . . . He has written about Chicago in a way that has never been matched. It will probably never be matched in the future, either, because by purchasing this book you have contributed to the enrichment and corruption of this fine boy."

Bill Mauldin was too pessimistic. Mike continued to write about Chicago in a way that has never been matched. But Mauldin was right about the stepping stones to the big time. They came, in tragic succession, the year after the book appeared—1968. The murder of Martin Luther King, Jr. The murder of Robert F. Kennedy. The growing agony of the war in Vietnam. The riots during the Democratic National Convention in Chicago. As Mike wrote about these tumultuous times his old Chicago boundaries fell away permanently. His columns became the leading attraction in the package of news reports and features the *Chicago Daily News* sold to other papers, giving him a national audience. A second collection of columns was published, *I May Be Wrong, But I Doubt It!* The first of dozens of national honors arrived: The Heywood Broun Award from the American Newspaper Guild for his commentaries on the Democratic convention. As the decade closed, Mike Royko accepted an offer from the editors of E. P. Dutton & Company in New York to write a biography of the only other person who epitomized Chicago as fully as he did: Mayor Richard J. Daley.

September 6, 1963
(This is the first column Mike wrote.)

Tavern Gets Taken for a Ride, and a Taxi Driver Mourns

It was a sad surprise to hop into a cab and find that the driver was a man we once knew as a neighborhood tavern keeper.

"What happened to your tavern?" we asked, as he skillfully gave a compact car the choice of dropping back or plunging into the Chicago River.

"They came in and renewed us. You know, the urban. So I got out of the business."

It has come to that. At last, after an endless army of enemies has tried, somebody has come along who can defeat the tavern keeper, a breed hardier than cactus.

But then, who can oppose the planner, the expert, the coordinator, with his big charts and graphs?

Somebody always tries when an architectural landmark, such as Hull House, is at stake. But they lose, too.

There is nobody to stand up for the neighborhood tavern keeper. Most of his friends can't stand up.

"You know, people forget all the good we've done," said the former tavern keeper.

"They think that all we ever did was get people drunk. Sure, but we did other good things, too.

"Take Little League Baseball. We were sort of like pioneers in that.

"I used to sponsor a whole softball team. They weren't kids, of course. Their fathers played.

"Every Sunday we'd have a game with a team from another neighborhood. We'd play for a half-barrel of beer. Then, after the game, they'd come over to my tavern and drink it.

"Ain't that better than sitting around all day moping or watching television? We got the people out into the fresh air.

"Today, what kind of places do people go to? Cocktail lounges. Places without any lights. They mess up their stomachs with fancy drinks. And it ain't the whisky that kills 'em, it's the other stuff they mix in—juice and stuff.

"I was thinking of opening up one, but the first thing that happens is those hoodlums from the Bossa Nova or whatever they call it—they move in as your partner.

"Another thing. People are moving out into the suburbs and that is making it tough on the neighborhood guy. And it is not as safe for the guy who wants a drink.

"Take one of my relatives. He moves to the suburbs. He ain't got a neighborhood tavern he can walk to. So one night he goes out for a drink. He has to take his car. On the way home he hits a tree and puts his head through the windshield. It messed up the top so bad he's got to wear one of those toupees.

"Now, if he would of stayed in his old neighborhood, he could of walked to a tavern. The worst that would of happened is that he might of walked into the tree.

"And if you go into one of these cocktail lounges and try to start a conversation, they think you're a creep. You got to sit quiet and drink. No singing, no jokes, no nothing.

"I was thinking of opening up another place. But where? I looked around that Old Town neighborhood, but I couldn't stand running one of those joints.

"You got to play long hair music on a record player. And people sit around playing chess. Then those goofy folk singers come in and play guitars. At least, if it was an accordion . . .

"And all they want to do is talk about philosophy and what meaning there is in their lives. What kind of talk is that in a tavern? I was in one of those joints and asked if anybody knew what was the score of the Cub game. Some babe in black pants laughed at me. Or maybe it was a guy in black pants.

"I took a fare over to one of those fancy projects a couple of days ago. You know, where the rich ones live, not the poor ones. There was a cocktail lounge right inside of it.

"And there were all these housewives, or whatever they were, sitting there drinking martinis. Right in the middle of the afternoon.

"They wouldn't a done that in my joint. I'd tip off the old man. That would be all."

March 15, 1966

Complete Apology for Overrating the Irish Thirst

The phone has been ringing most of the afternoon and evening. Angry Irishmen are on the other end.

They say that I have insulted them and they demand an immediate apology and a retraction.

Their outrage is the result of Monday's column in which I suggested that the Irish have a great capacity for beer and boasting.

Not to cop a plea—but I didn't mean it in a critical way. I have always admired people who can hold their drink and there is nothing wrong with harmless boasting, so long as it isn't dull.

But most of the callers did not see it that way. As one man put it:

"How would you like a punch in the head?"

Or as a male schoolteacher asked:

"Is that responsible journalism?"

My answer to both questions was a fast "no."

Another man related in detail his war record, his civic contributions, and his qualities as a family man and neighbor, and said he resented the implication that Irish boast.

With St. Patrick's Day almost here, it would not be prudent to walk the streets of this city with a sizable number of Irishmen mad at me.

Besides, it is now clear to me that it was an unfair thing to write.

So I will do as the many callers demanded: I will apologize. I will retract. I will admit my error.

First, the part about beer-drinking.

The Irish do not have a great capacity for beer. I'm sorry I suggested they did.

There. That should be a satisfactory retraction and apology. But just to be safe, I'll make it stronger.

The Irish, in fact, have a very limited capacity for beer.

Germans, for instance, can consume far more impressive quantities of the suds than the Irish and still be on their feet singing university songs.

(I realize that this may get the Germans angry at me, but I'll apologize to them later.)

Then there are the Poles. They are capable of far greater feats of beer-drinking when they put their minds to it. There are still Division Street bars that tap a full barrel every time another customer walks in.

Even the Italians might drink more beer than the Irish if they didn't prefer Chianti.

The Latvians, the Turks, the Croats, the Malaysians, the Zambians, the Franifs, the Muktow Indians on the eastern coast of Zorff—they can all pour down more beer than the Irish.

(When I apologize and retract, I can't stop.)

The apology and retraction would not be complete if I didn't explain how I was misled. It was due to a shoddy job of reporting.

Had I called a few taverns in Irish neighborhoods before I wrote yesterday's column I might have avoided all of this trouble.

As it is, I called one tavern owner after the complaints started coming in and asked him how much beer he sells on St. Patrick's Day. He said:

"I don't think I could even measure it."

I take this to mean that it is a microscopic amount, which proves even more conclusively my error.

And I should have recalled what was said by a Mooney, a Sully, a Danny, a Tommy, and a few others one night when the subject of drinking beer came up. They all denied that they had unusual capacities.

As Mooney put it: "I used to think I could put it away, but I'm nothing compared with Sully." Sully said: "Hah, you should see Danny. Even I can't keep up with him." Danny, in turn, protested: "Listen, there's nobody like Tommy. Not even me." As I recall, Tommy tried to say something but shyness or something rendered him speechless.

August 8, 1966

T-Shirted Punks Slay a Dragon

It was a big day for the punks. Coming from all over Chicago's Northwest Side, they gathered in Hanson Park, strutting and telling each other how tough they were going to be.

The uniform of the day was white undershirt and tight pants. Or unbuttoned sport shirt and tight pants. The punk, for some reason, likes to show off his hairless chest and bony rump.

Despite their great numbers, they were an unimpressive sight. They were the kind of well-fed, well-clothed kids usually seen sprawling in open convertibles or hanging around a pizza parlor or drive-in.

In the beginning they did what punks are good at. They stood on the sidewalk and swore and spat and shouted at the civil rights people who arrived in cars, pulling off Central Avenue into the Hanson Park parking area.

When a punk got off what he thought was a fine witticism, such as "Hey, you nigger-loving preacher, why ain't you in church?" he rushed about and told his friends what he had said and how the minister had flinched and how good he felt and what he would do later when he got his hands on a dirty so-and-so of a . . .

When a blond kid spewed a mouthful of spit into the interior of a car, his friends pummeled his back as though he had struck a grand-slam home run. And the punk looked proud yet humble.

The march began and the police set the rules: The civil rights people would march on one side of the street; the counter-demonstrators would stay on the other.

For the first block or two on Central Avenue, the punks were content to play their role—swearing and chanting, "Two, four, six, eight; we don't want to integrate."

But when the march turned on Fullerton Avenue, the punks got ambitious. Some rocks flew. A policeman was hit in the face. Bottles burst and cherry bombs exploded. The shouting got louder and the curses more vicious.

This is when it could have become a riot—during the first few blocks on Fullerton. The punks wanted to be rioters. They truly did. And there were enough of them, if you included their giggly girlfriends and several hundred empty-headed men and women.

But to riot takes a certain suicidal instinct that wasn't present this Sunday afternoon. A mob has to act like an enraged bull, charging over and over again, not noticing its own blood. Fortunately, the punks didn't have the stomach for it. They were like bad-tempered cocker spaniels, snapping and snarling, but running when kicked in the ribs.

One tossed a rock, then turned and ran back into a crowd of his companions. He didn't know a policeman was walking briskly behind him. When he turned, the policeman jabbed his nightstick into the youth's tummy. He grunted and whined. He was still whining when they pushed him into a paddy wagon.

When a large group tried to charge across the street, a policeman fired warning shots and the mob broke. One youth was almost crying from fright.

A husky man was inspired by the punks and he charged the marchers. The police warned him to stay back but he came on. Four or five clubs crashed against his head and he went down, bleeding heavily, while cherry bombs went off in a grotesque salute to his efforts.

The sight of his blood shocked the punks and they shouted, "Police brutality!"

When a bottle was tossed, a policeman went alone into a street-corner crowd. The bottle-thrower tried to twist away and the policeman flicked his billy. The youth pitched forward and his friends jumped back.

By the time they had walked a mile, it was raining hard and the urge for combat was gone. But they followed along, shouting and telling each other what they'd do in the next block, and the next.

A few took to the alleys and tried to loft rocks over the rooftops, but the police ran them out.

The crowd had shrunk to half its former size by the time the march turned down Parker, a street of bungalows. The residents came out on the porches, but few said anything. The shouting still came from the punks.

An old man made the most intelligent comment of the day when he stood on his porch and barked:

"Hey you, kid, get off my grass."

A punk turned and motioned to the other side of the street and whined: "What you yelling at me for? Why don't you yell at the niggers?"

The old man snapped:

"Because they ain't on my grass. You are."

When the march returned to Fullerton, where the earlier action had been, the punks were wet from the rain and tired from the hike.

Some tried for a last show of bravado, but it wasn't impressive. About fifty swaggered out of a side street and a tall police commander barked:

"OK, you want to get pinched? The first forty of you line up right here. I'll put you in the wagon, if that's what you want. C'mon. C'mon." They turned and shuffled away. They actually looked hurt.

Some men, overripe from their Sunday drinks, came out of the Neighborhood Inn and the Derby Lounge to shout drunken threats but policemen walked them back inside.

The marchers got back in their cars and sped out of the parking lot south on Central Avenue. This time nobody shouted or spat.

The remaining punks shuffled about rather aimlessly.

A police captain went over to a paddy wagon and opened the door. Inside were six kids, about fifteen or sixteen. They wore undershirts and a couple had Tyrolean hats.

"You learned your lesson?" asked the captain. He appeared ready to let them go.

One of them pouted and said: "Wha'd we do, huh? Wha'd we do?" His lips trembled.

The captain slammed the door and told the driver, "Take 'em to the station. Let their mommies and daddies come down for 'em."

The trouble is, mommy and daddy will probably be proud. They should be. They taught them.

August 16, 1967

Picasso and the Cultural Rebirth of Chicago

Mayor Daley walked to the white piece of ribbon and put his hand on it. He was about to give it a pull when the photographers yelled for him to wait. He stood there for a minute and gave them that familiar blend of scowl and smile.

It was good that he waited. This was a moment to think about, to savor what was about to happen. In just a moment, with a snap of the mayor's wrist, Chicago history would be changed. That's no small occurrence—the cultural rebirth of a big city.

Out there in the neighborhoods and the suburbs, things probably seemed just the same. People worried about the old things—would they move in and would we move out? Or would we move in and would they move out?

But downtown, the leaders of culture and influence were gathered for a historical event and it was reaching a climax with Mayor Daley standing there ready to pull a ribbon.

Thousands waited in and around the Civic Center plaza. They had listened to the speeches about the Picasso thing. They had heard how it was going to change Chicago's image.

They had heard three clergymen—a priest, a rabbi, and a Protestant minister—offer eloquent prayers. That's probably a record for a work by Picasso, a dedicated atheist.

And now the mayor was standing there, ready to pull the ribbon.

You could tell it was a big event by the seating. In the first row on the speakers platform was a lady poet. In the second row was Alderman Tom Keane. And in the third row was P. J. Cullerton, the assessor. When Keane and Cullerton sit behind a lady poet, things are changing.

The only alderman in the front row was Tom Rosenberg. And he was there only because it was a cultural event and he is chairman of the City Council's Culture Committee, which is in charge of preventing aldermen from spitting, swearing, and snoring during meetings.

The whole thing had been somber and serious. The Chicago Symphony Orchestra had played classical music. It hadn't played even one chorus of "For He's a Jolly Good Fellow."

Chief Judge John Boyle had said the Picasso would become more famous than the Art Institute's lions. Boyle has vision.

Someone from the National Council of Arts said it was paying tribute to Mayor Daley. This brought an interested gleam in the eyes of a few ward committeemen.

William Hartmann, the man who thought of the whole thing, told of Picasso's respect for Mayor Daley. Whenever Hartmann went to see Picasso, the artist asked:

"Is Mayor Daley still mayor of Chicago?"

When Hartmann said this, Mayor Daley bounced up and down in his chair, he laughed so hard. So did a few Republicans in the cheap seats, but they didn't laugh the same way.

After the ceremony, it came to that final moment—the mayor standing there holding the white ribbon.

Then he pulled.

There was a gasp as the light blue covering fell away in several

pieces. But it was caused by the basic American fascination for any mechanical feat that goes off as planned.

In an instant the Picasso stood there unveiled for all to see.

A few people applauded. But at best, it was a smattering of applause. Most of the throng was silent.

They had hoped, you see, that it would be what they had heard it would be.

A woman, maybe. A beautiful soaring woman. That is what many art experts and enthusiasts had promised. They had said that we should wait—that we should not believe what we saw in the pictures.

If it was a woman, then art experts should put away their books and spend more time in girlie joints.

The silence grew. Then people turned and looked at each other. Some shrugged. Some smiled. Some just stood there, frowning or blank-faced.

Most just turned and walked away. The weakest pinch-hitter on the Cubs receives more cheers.

They had wanted to be moved by it. They wouldn't have stood there if they didn't want to believe what they had been told—that it would be a fine thing.

But anyone who didn't have a closed mind—which means thinking that anything with the name Picasso connected must be wonderful—could see that it was nothing but a big, homely metal thing.

That is all there is to it. Some soaring lines, yes. Interesting design, I'm sure. But the fact is, it has a long stupid face and looks like some giant insect that is about to eat a smaller, weaker insect. It has eyes that are pitiless, cold, mean.

But why not? Everybody said it had the spirit of Chicago. And from thousands of miles away, accidentally or on purpose, Picasso captured it.

Up there in that ugly face is the spirit of Al Capone, the Summerdale scandal cops, the settlers who took the Indians but good.

Its eyes are like the eyes of every slum owner who made a buck off the small and weak. And of every building inspector who took a wad from a slum owner to make it all possible.

It has the look of the dope pusher and of the syndicate technician as he looks for just the right wire to splice the bomb to.

Any bigtime real estate operator will be able to look into the face of the Picasso and see the spirit that makes the city's rebuilding possible and profitable.

It has the look of the big corporate executive who comes face to face with the reality of how much water pollution his company is responsible for—and then thinks of the profit and loss and of his salary.

It is all there in that Picasso thing—the I Will spirit. The I will get you before you will get me spirit.

Picasso has never been here, they say. You'd think he's been riding the L all his life.

September 14, 1967

It Wasn't Our "Clout" She Stole, But a Counterfeit

Many people depend on *Vogue* magazine to tell them what to wear, what to talk about, and what—if anything—to think.

If *Vogue* tells them to wear bed pans trimmed in daisies in the Easter Parade, they will run to the nearest medical supply store to be fitted.

Somebody recently sent me a page from *Vogue* with an item circled. The page claims to contain the "in" things that people are talking about. *Vogue* writes:

"People are talking about . . . the rise of the word 'clout.' Among those with 'clout' are President Johnson, the Pope, and Ho Chi Minh of Hanoi." (*Vogue* does not want us to confuse him with the Ho Chi Minh of Burlington, Iowa.)

Even for a New York magazine run by a bunch of women, it is a surprisingly dumb thing to write. And they have a lot of nerve stealing an old Chicago word and distorting its meaning.

The dictionary definition of clout is, of course, a blow, a shot-in-the-head; to strike something.

But there is also the old Chicago meaning. *Vogue* apparently had that one in mind, but they are confused.

"Clout" means influence—usually political—with somebody who can do you some good.

A Chicago policeman might have enough "clout" with a ward boss to get a promotion to sergeant. The ward boss might have enough "clout" with the mayor to get his contractor-brother some profitable highway repair work. The mayor might have enough "clout" with the White House to get federal projects and funds for Chicago.

In simple English, a bailiff might say:

"Somebody beefed that I was kinky and I almost got viced, but I saw my Chinaman and he clouted for me at the hall."

As everybody knows, that means:

"A citizen complained that I did something dishonest and I was almost fired, but I contacted my political sponsor and he interceded in my behalf with my department head."

So naturally, President Johnson does not have "clout." He doesn't need it. But somebody else might have "clout" with him—such as Bobby Baker.

And if the pope has "clout" with anybody—the matter should be discussed by theologians, not by *Vogue* writers.

Trying to be helpful, I called *Vogue* in New York. After clearing through a couple of underlings, I was permitted to talk to Miss Arlene Talmy, an associate editor who is in charge of telling us what people are talking about.

I asked her what *Vogue* meant by the item on "clout."

She shrieked: "My God! Everybody knows what it means."

(I mentally bet myself that she was wearing a hat and boots while she worked and that she used to smoke with a cigarette holder, when it was fashionable.)

"Maybe everybody you know thinks that the President, the Pope and Ho Chi Minh (the one in Hanoi) have 'clout,' but I don't know what you mean by it. Clout with whom?"

"Oh, my God!" she shrieked again. (He has clout too?) "I told you, EV-er-eeee-body is using it EV-er-eeee-where. I mean, I've seen it in an English paper, in an Italian magazine, and, of course, here in New York. Reallllly, it's not that new."

But what does it mean?

She stopped shrieking. Her voice shifted to the patient tone one uses with a child, a ninny, or a hick newspaperman from Chicago.

"Let me explain it to you then, so you will understand."

"Please do."

"It means the ability and the means and the power to return a blow when somebody has attacked you."

"Does it?"

"Of course," she said. "EV-er-eee-body knows that."

"You are wrong."

She didn't say anything for a moment. Then she stuttered. Boy, it felt good to make a smart aleck broad like her stutter. I'll bet nobody has told her she was wrong since she left Iowa, or Nebraska, and went to New York to become a career woman and ruin her complexion.

Before she could start shrieking again, I told her what "clout" meant and that the word had been stolen from Chicago by New York and was being distorted.

"WELL! That may be what it means in Chicago—but that isn't what it means elsewhere."

She hung up before I could invite her to call me the next time she hears a new "in" word among the "in" people in the ladies room at *Vogue*.

October 27, 1967

Let's Update City's Image

Chicago needs a new city seal.

The old seal—with its themes of a garden-city, an Indian, an early settler, and a cherub—is out of date.

We need a seal that captures the modern spirit of Chicago.

Therefore, I am launching a city-wide contest for a new seal. It is open to all doodlers, sketchers, and serious and amateur artists.

Below you see an example of what I have in mind.

The clasped hands represent the true spirit of Chicago friendship—especially when the concrete is being poured.

Under the clasped hands, you see the happy city worker clearing the way for still another new improvement.

And the exploding car in the right-hand corner represents the festive spirit of Chicago.

Once we have a new city seal, we will need a new city motto. That I have provided.

The old one is *Urbs in Horto* (City in a Garden).

The invention of the concrete mixer has made the old motto meaningless.

The new motto—*Ubi Est Mea*—means "Where's Mine?"

The phrase "Where's Mine?" can be heard wherever improvements for the city are being planned.

It is the watchword of the new Chicago, the cry of the money brigade, the chant of the city of the big wallet.

The sketch in today's column is merely a rough suggestion, an idea, a guideline, for what your entries might contain.

Except for the city motto, all artists are encouraged to draw upon their imagination.

Some may choose to portray something that brings in the spirit of the new Lake Michigan—an oil slick, a dead alewife, a growling germ.

Others may wish to portray the spirit of urban renewal. Or the theme of the new Chicago's air.

The capacity of our different racial groups to live together in peace and good will might be an inspiration.

It is even possible that someone might want to include Mayor Daley, who discovered Chicago, in a city seal.

The rules for this contest are simple.

Entries should be drawn large enough to be reproduced. Make them about the size of an alderman's wallet—about eight inches across or bigger.

Use the suggested slogan—"Where's Mine?"

As entries are received, I will show them in this column.

Final judging will be done by a panel of distinguished Chicagoans, none of whom has ever been convicted of a heinous crime, held public office, appeared in a society page story, or served on one of the mayor's committees.

The winner and the runners-up will receive many wonderful prizes. The prize list has not been completed, but it includes:

- An all-expense-paid fishing trip in the south end of Lake Michigan.
- Dinner for four at the Red Star Inn, if it isn't gone by then.
- A free chest X-ray at the hospital of your choice.
- A course in remedial English—or basic English—for the Chicago public school student of your choice.
- A picture of your old neighborhood—if you can find it under the concrete.

December 19, 1967

Mary and Joe Chicago-Style

Mary and Joe were flat broke when they got off the bus in Chicago. They didn't know anybody and she was expecting a baby.

They went to a cheap hotel. But the clerk jerked his thumb at the door when they couldn't show a day's rent in advance.

They walked the streets until they saw a police station. The desk sergeant said they couldn't sleep in a cell, but he told them how to get to the Cook County Department of Public Aid.

A man there said they couldn't get regular assistance because they hadn't been Illinois residents long enough. But he gave them the address of the emergency welfare office on the West Side.

It was a two-mile walk up Madison Street to 19 S. Damen. Someone gave them a card with a number on it and they sat down on a bench, stared at the peeling green paint and waited for their number to be called.

Two hours later, a caseworker motioned them forward, took out blank forms, and asked questions: Any relatives? Any means of getting money? Any assets?

Joe said he owned a donkey. The caseworker told him not to get smart or he'd be thrown out. Joe said he was sorry.

The caseworker finished the forms and said they were entitled to emergency CTA bus fare to Cook County Hospital because of Mary's condition. And he told Joe to go to an Urban Progress Center for occupational guidance.

Joe thanked him and they took a bus to the hospital. A guard told them to wait on a bench. They waited two hours, then Mary got pains and they took her away. Someone told Joe to come back tomorrow.

He went outside and asked a stranger on the street for directions to an Urban Progress Center. The stranger hit Joe on the head and took his overcoat. Joe was still lying there when a paddy wagon came along so they pinched him for being drunk on the street.

Mary had a baby boy during the night. She didn't know it, but three foreign-looking men in strange, colorful robes came to the hospital asking about her and the baby. A guard took them for hippies and called the police. They found odd spices on the men, so the narcotics detail took them downtown for further questioning.

The next day Mary awoke in a crowded ward. She asked for

Joe. Instead, a representative of the Planned Parenthood Committee came by to give her a lecture on birth control.

Next, a social worker came for her case history. She asked Mary who the father was. Mary answered and the social worker ran for the nurse. The nurse questioned her and Mary answered. The nurse stared at her and ran for the doctor. The doctor wrote "Post partum delusion" on her chart.

An ambulance took Mary to the Cook County Mental Health Clinic the next morning. A psychiatrist asked her questions and pursed his lips at the answers.

A hearing was held and a magistrate committed her to Chicago State Mental Hospital on Irving Park Road.

Joe got out of the county jail a couple of days later and went to the county hospital for Mary. They told him she was at Chicago State and the baby had been placed in a foster home by the Illinois Department of Children and Family Services.

When Joe got to Chicago State, a doctor told him what Mary had said about the baby's birth. Joe said Mary was telling the truth. They put Joe in a ward at the other end of the hospital.

Meanwhile, the three strangely dressed foreign-looking men were released after the narcotics detail could find no laws prohibiting the possession of myrrh and frankincense. They returned to the hospital and were taken for civil rights demonstrators. They were held in the county jail on $100,000 bond.

By luck, Joe and Mary met on the hospital grounds. They decided to tell the doctors what they wanted to hear. The next day they were declared sane and were released.

When they applied for custody of Mary's baby, however, they were told it was necessary for them to first establish a proper residence, earn a proper income, and create a suitable environment.

They applied at the Urban Progress Center for training under the Manpower Development Program. Joe said he was good at working with wood. He was assigned to a computer data processing class. Mary said she'd gladly do domestic work. She was assigned to a course in key-punch operating. Both got $20-a-week stipends.

Several months later they finished the training. Joe got a job at a gas station and Mary went to work as a waitress.

They saved their money and hired a lawyer. Another custody hearing was held, and several days later the baby was ordered returned to them.

Reunited finally, they got back to their two-room flat and met the landlord on the steps. He told them Urban Renewal had ordered the building torn down. The City Relocation Bureau would get them another place.

They packed, dressed the baby, and hurried to the Greyhound Bus station.

Joe asked the ticket man when the next bus was leaving.

"Where to?" the ticket man asked.

"Anywhere," Joe said, "as long as it is right now."

He gave Joe three tickets and in five minutes they were on a bus heading for Southern Illinois—the area known as "Little Egypt."

Just as the bus pulled out, the three strangely dressed men ran into the station. But they were too late. It was gone.

So they started hiking down U.S. 66. But at last report they were pinched on suspicion of being foreigners in illegal possession of gold.

March 19, 1968

Ghetto Burial for a GI Hero

Some anti-busing ladies from the Northwest Side came downtown to picket us, which is OK. I believe in peaceful demonstration.

Some of the ladies had signs that asked why we aren't telling the truth. I thought we were, or were at least doing our best. They apparently think otherwise.

But if it is truth they want, here's a true story for them to think about.

Phillip Craig Skinner was young and black. But if white people can be believed, he was the kind of Negro, that rare kind, they wouldn't mind having live next door.

He never got in trouble. He went through Parker High School, studied, played football, was on the swimming team, and graduated with good grades.

His generation is the generation of change, black power, black pride, militancy. But Phillip didn't get deeply involved in any organized movements.

When he finished high school, he enrolled in a Negro college in Missouri. He was getting good grades, but he left to join the United States Marine Corps.

Phillip went to Vietnam and was promoted to lance corporal.

He wrote home often, to his father, a Chicago policeman and World War II vet, and his mother, who is divorced and remarried.

In his letters to his father, he wrote about his ambition to finish his military service and join his father as a policeman.

"When I get back from Vietnam, I'll go through police training," he wrote, "then we can be partners, Dad."

He didn't make it. While carrying a rocket launcher up a hill during fierce combat, he was shot in the head. He wasn't yet old enough to vote.

But he came close to becoming that clean, well-educated, law-abiding, public-spirited, polite, responsible, cultured, refined, lawn-tending Negro the white ladies say they wouldn't mind having live next door to them—because they really don't believe he exists.

There is a little more to the story of Phillip. Being dead didn't change his skin color.

His mother tells it:

"After the Marine major left our living room, I asked my husband to call a funeral chapel to arrange for my son's burial.

"The man on duty said we could come to the chapel on appointment and furthermore that he was not sure the government provided good caskets for Vietnam victims. He felt certain that we would want to 'look over' his line.

"I called the chapel the next day to arrange for an appointment. Suddenly the impact of our ghetto address seemed to have struck home.

"There was some discussion over the phone as to why I had chosen that chapel, things to the effect that they had left this area when it had changed. Actually, they aren't very far from where we live and it is a nice funeral home.

"My husband visited the chapel. He was not led into the business office but was asked to wait in a dark corner of one of the parlors.

"The man scribbled some figures on a scratch pad and handed them to my husband, all the while explaining that 'While we are willing to handle this body, you understand, there are many excellent Negro undertakers on the South Side.' He went on about the chapels that 'would be near and convenient for the persons attending the wake.'

"By that time we were getting that feeling that Negroes acquire through a lifetime of such experiences—that of carrying a chip on their shoulder.

"So we did not inconvenience the white chapel by asking them to handle the body of a young man who gave the most there is to give.

"But I'll never understand what he gave it for. For that undertaker? Did he and other black boys give their lives in the hope that a few dozen black children could walk into a school without being spectacles? What did he give his life for?"

If anyone has a good answer to the question, I'll be glad to pass it on to Phillip's mother.

April 2, 1968

LBJ Deserved a Better Fate

There were those who screamed with a vicious joy when President Johnson, in that slow, sad way of his, said he is not running again.

There were others who reacted with sullen cynicism, asking what his angle is.

The white racists said, "good." The black racists said, "good." The superhawks said good and the doves said good. And most of all, the young said good. The young, who are so sure they have the answer in Bobby with the flowing hair.

They were all so busy being jubilant in this strong man's terrible moment that many didn't listen to the serious thing he told them.

The president of the United States told the people of the United States they are so divided against themselves he dares not take part in a political campaign for fear that it could get even worse.

But they answered, many of them with one last jeer of contempt and hatred.

It figured. Unrestrained hatred has become the dominant emotion in this splintered country. Races hate, age groups hate, political extremes hate. And when they aren't hating each other, they have been turning it on LBJ. He, more than anyone else, has felt it.

The white racists, those profoundly ignorant broads who toss eggs at school buses, blamed him for the very existence of the Negro. To them he was a "nigger lover."

The black separatists could find no insult too vile to be used on him. To them he is a white racist. That he launched some of the most ambitious civil rights legislation in the nation's history means nothing in a time when black scholars say Abe Lincoln was the worst kind of bigot.

The superhawks complained that he wasn't killing the Viet Cong fast enough.

The doves portrayed him as engaging in war almost for the fun of it.

And the young, that very special group, was offended by him in so many, many ways.

For one thing, he was old. They might have forgiven him that if he had at least acted young. But he acted like a harassed, tremendously busy, impatient man with an enormous responsibility. Just like their old man.

He offended them by failing to pander to them, by not fawning over them and telling them that they were the wise ones, that they had the answers, that they could guide us. He didn't tell them that because he was the man charged with running the country, not them.

He isn't at all like Sen. Robert Kennedy. Bobby tells it like it is. He tells them how wonderfully wise and profound they are. A forty-two-year-old father of ten wears a kid's haircut and stands there saying he is part of their generation, and they cheer him for telling it like it is.

LBJ offended others by engaging in an "unjust" war. Their collective conscience rebelled against the "unjust" war. So they portrayed him as the eager murderer of babies. Just how many of these conscience-tormented young men are more tormented by the thought of being rousted out of bed at 5 A.M. by a drill sergeant than by the thought of a burned village, we'll never know.

And he offended many by his lack of style and wit, his sore-footed-hound-dog oratory.

So the abuse he took from all was remarkable. Presidents, like all politicians, have to take abuse. It is within the rules of the game to criticize them, to spoof them, to assail them.

But there may not have been anything in our history to compare with what has been tossed at President Johnson in the last four years.

A play that says he arranged the murder of John F. Kennedy has been a hit with the intellectuals, and those who think they are.

A somewhat popular publication of satire called *The Realist* printed something so obscene about him that I can't find a way to even hint at it.

High government officials were hooted down when they tried to represent the administration point of view on campuses, those temples of free speech.

Every smart punk grabbed a sign and accused him of being in a class with Hitler or mass-murderer Richard Speck. The nation's nuts vowed to come to Chicago during the Democratic National Convention and turn it into anything from an outdoor orgy to a historic riot as their contribution to the democratic process.

He needed more personal protection than any President in history. That can't feel very good. But it was necessary. We have people who burn cities and many others who go to movies and howl with glee at the violent scenes.

If you live in a big city, you see the hate that threatens it. He lived in the whole country and looked at it all. And he couldn't see a way to unite it.

Maybe he wasn't the best president we might have had.

But we sure as hell aren't the best people a president has ever had.

April 9, 1968

Millions in His Firing Squad

FBI agents are looking for the man who pulled the trigger and surely they will find him.

But it doesn't matter if they do or they don't. They can't catch everybody, and Martin Luther King was executed by a firing squad that numbered in the millions.

They took part, from all over the country, pouring words of hate into the ear of the assassin.

The man with the gun did what he was told. Millions of bigots, subtle and obvious, put it in his hand and assured him he was doing the right thing.

It would be easy to point at the Southern redneck and say he did it. But what of the Northern disk-jockey-turned-commentator with his slippery words of hate every morning?

What about the Northern mayor who steps all over every poverty program advancement, thinking only of political expediency, until riots fester, whites react with more hate, and the gap between races grows bigger?

Toss in the congressman with the stupid arguments against busing. And the pathetic women who turn out with eggs in their hands to throw at children.

Let us not forget the law-and-order-type politicians who are in favor of arresting all the Negro prostitutes in the vice districts.

When you ask them to vote for laws that would eliminate some of the causes of prostitution, they babble like the boobs they are.

Throw in a Steve Telow or two—the Eastern and Southern European immigrant or his kid who seems to be convinced that in forty or fifty years, they built this country. There was nothing here until he arrived, you see, so that gives him the right to pitch rocks when Martin Luther King walks down the street in his neighborhood.

They all took their place in King's firing squad.

And behind them were the subtle ones, those who never say anything bad but just nod when the bigot throws out his strong opinions.

He is actually the worst, the nodder is, because sometimes he believes differently but he says nothing. He doesn't want to cause trouble. For Pete's sake, don't cause trouble!

So when his brother-in-law or his card-playing buddy from across the alley spews out the racial filth, he nods.

Give some credit to the most subtle of the subtle. That distinction belongs to the FBI, now looking for King's killer.

That agency took part in a mudslinging campaign against him that to this day demands an investigation.

The bullet that hit King came from all directions. Every two-bit politician or incompetent editorial writer found in him, not themselves, the cause of our racial problems.

It was almost ludicrous. The man came on the American scene preaching nonviolence from the first day he sat at the wrong end of a bus. He preached it in the North and was hit with rocks. He talked it the day he was murdered.

Hypocrites all over this country would kneel every Sunday morning and mouth messages to Jesus Christ. Then they would come out and tell each other, after reading the papers, that somebody should string up King, who was living Christianity like few Americans ever have.

Maybe it was the simplicity of his goal that confused people. Or the way he dramatized it.

He wanted only that black Americans have their constitutional rights, that they get an equal shot at this country's benefits, the same thing we give to the last guy who jumped off the boat.

So we killed him. Just as we killed Abraham Lincoln and John F. Kennedy. No other country kills so many of its best people.

A week ago Sunday night the president said he was quitting after this term. He said this country is so filled with hate it might help if he got out. Four days later we killed a Nobel Peace Prize winner.

We have pointed a gun at our own head and we are squeezing the trigger. And nobody we elect is going to help us. It is our head and our finger.

April 11, 1968

Are You Really a Cubs Fan?

The bookies say the Cubs are contenders for the pennant, so it must be true. And now the city is crawling with Cub fans.

But are they really Cub fans? Were they around, were they loyal, when everything the Cubs did was disgusting? Were they out there cheering when the only thing to cheer about was when the ball came off the screen and hit the batboy in the head?

There is one way to find out: If you are suspicious of someone, make him take the Cub quiz. It is guaranteed to weed out impostors.

Don't expect to answer many questions correctly even if you are a loyal, old-time fan. It is hard. I made up the test and even I can't get them all right.

Here it is: Five correct answers qualifies you as a true-blue Cub fan and permits you to paste this column to the front of your face.

QUESTIONS
1. What position did Max Stang play?
2. The fans in the left-field bleachers used to throw packages of something at the Immortal Hank Sauer. What did they throw? Keep your answer clean.
3. Name at least one Cub pitcher of the 1950s who wore a golden earring.
4. The Cubs had a thirty-eight-year-old rookie in the 1950s. What was his name?
5. Which current Cub swears the most?
6. What did the immortal Wayne K. Otto hit?
7. Which of these three players pitched a one-hitter in the 1945 World Series: Eddie (Curly) Cronin, Greg Czag, or the immortal Dicky Gongola?
8. Name two radio or TV figures who were once Cub batboys.
9. The Cubs once had an outfield that was so slow they were known as the Quicksand Kids. Two of them were Hank Sauer and Ralph Kiner. What pathetic wreck played between them in center field?

10. Which of these two players always had sore feet: Heinz Becker or the immortal Dominic Dallessandro?

11. The Cubs once had a first baseman who really couldn't hit. Nobody could hit the way he couldn't. His name was Kevin Connor or something like that. He was so bad I still try to blot his name out of my mind. Anyway, he became a TV star. What is his name now? (A tip: It is not Kup.)

12. The immortal Lennie Merullo couldn't field or hit, and he wasn't fast. What was he known for?

13. Quick. When a ball goes over the left-field wall, what street does it land on?

14. Cub games are broadcast on radio station WGN. What station used to broadcast them?

15. The Cubs had a pitcher who was born in Ozanna, Poland. What's his name?

ANSWERS

1. None. He was Gravel Gertie, the immortal vendor.

2. Chewing tobacco, whenever he hit a home run or did some other heroic thing.

3. The immortal Fernando Pedro Rodriguez. He was undefeated as a pitcher in 1956. He also failed to win a game.

4. The immortal Fernando Pedro Rodriguez. You know, the guy with the golden earring.

5. It is a tossup between Ron Santo and Leo Durocher. Expert observers say Durocher swears more when he is angry; Santo, when he is happy. (This column is educational.)

6. Nothing. But Hack Wilson once hit him. He was a sports-writer, so he probably deserved it.

7. None. They were all my relatives and enjoy seeing their names in the paper.

8. The immortal Vince Garrity and the immortal Walter Jacob-son. Garrity said he enjoyed being a batboy, except when the ball came off the screen and hit him in the head. Jacobson says he didn't like the job because players amused themselves by throwing their underwear at him. Now that he is a newscaster nobody throws underwear at him, but they should.

9. Frank Baumholz. He played in the mid-1950s, but as late as 1965 or something he was seen lying in the grass in center field, catching his breath.

10. Becker had sore feet. Dallessandro had tiny feet. It used to take him twenty jumps to get out of the dugout.

11. Chuck Connors or something. I still can't remember, because he was such a terrible hitter.
12. He was best known for not being able to field, hit, or run fast.
13. Waveland Avenue. But to hear Jack Brickhouse yell, you'd think it landed in his eye.
14. WIND used to broadcast Cub games. It's the station that used to broadcast the immortal Howard Miller.
15. Moe Drabowsky. Not only was he born in Ozanna, but he is still considered the best pitcher Ozanna, Poland, ever produced. The best hitter from Ozanna was the immortal Ziggy Grobnik, Slats' father. He once hit his wife twelve times without a miss. But that's another game.

June 6, 1968

(Mike wrote this column a few hours after he learned that Sen. Robert F. Kennedy had been shot in California. Kennedy died the next day.)

How about Gun as Our Symbol?

Maybe it's time to change the words to our song, to bring it up to date and capture the national spirit:

> *Oh, say can you see by the pawn shop's dim light*
> *What a swell .38 with its pearl handle gleaming.*
> *In a gun catalog is a telescope sight;*
> *I'll send for it quick, while the sirens are screaming.*
> *And the TV's white glare, the shots ripping in air*
> *Give proof through the night that our guns are still there.*
> *Oh, don't you ever try to take my guns away from me*
> *Because the right to shoot at you is what I mean by liberty.*

And why not? We should glorify the gun. It is our national symbol. Who owns an eagle? How many of us have ever seen an eagle? But guns—we have 100,000,000 of them in private circulation. Maybe there are as many bibles around as guns, but their impact doesn't show.

This country has so many guns because guns are very useful. I know this to be the truth because the gun lovers and their lobbyists, such as the National Rifle Association, tell us so.

They tell us that guns are good for fighting crime.

If you have a gun in your house, you can shoot a burglar.

Of course, the burglar can buy a gun, too, so maybe he will shoot you.

Or, he might break into your home when you aren't there and steal your gun. Then he can use it to shoot a storekeeper and a cop. But they might arrest him so the net result would be one storekeeper and one cop shot, and a burglar in jail.

The gun is so effective as a crime-fighting device that the United States, with more privately owned guns than any other country, has the highest crime rate in the world.

What I've never understood, though, is why people can legally own rifles, shotguns, or pistols, but can't own other fine anti-crime weapons.

Why can't I own a machine gun? I'm not much of a shot with a pistol, but I'm sure I could wing a burglar with a machine gun.

In fact, I'd like to buy a surplus tank from the Army—fully activated, of course.

I want a tank because the gun people say we might have to fight off foreign invaders some day. Apparently our Army, Navy, Air Force, Marines, and nuclear stockpile aren't up to the job.

If that's so, I'd feel more comfortable in a tank with my cannon blazing.

While waiting for the invasion, I could put it to home use. There isn't much difference between a tank and the legal guns. You aren't any more dead when struck by a tank shell than a shotgun blast.

Grenades should be legal, too. A fellow could knock out an entire burglary gang with one grenade. Yet, a grenade isn't any more lethal than a cheap mail-order rifle. You can't kill a president at two hundred yards with a grenade, even if you have a strong arm.

Gun-lovers instruct us that our right to build private arsenals is guaranteed by the Second Amendment to the Constitution.

That's the one gun-lovers always quote this way: "The right of the people to keep and bear arms shall not be infringed."

Actually, it doesn't say just that. The entire sentence is: "A well-regulated militia, being necessary to the security of a free state, the right of the people to keep and bear arms shall not be infringed."

So gun-lovers interpret this to mean that in order to have a well-regulated militia, anybody should be able to own guns. Not having graduated from West Point, I don't know if that is entirely true. It does seem like a strange way to build a militia.

But if they look at it that way, they should do something to help the dope fiend.

We all know that morphine can be a useful pain reliever. Yet you can't buy it in the drug store.

It seems reasonable that if guns should be sold to almost anybody in order to build a state militia, morphine should be sold to almost anybody to help those in pain.

And what about that part of the Declaration of Independence that proclaims our right to "the pursuit of happiness." Many people find their happiness in marijuana or LSD, but the cops pursue them while they pursue their happiness.

Tradition is a big factor in gun ownership. Americans used guns to shoot Indians, the British, wild turkeys and buffalo, Mexicans, and each other.

It's no longer necessary for us to shoot Indians, the British, wild turkeys and buffalo, Mexicans, and each other, but we still own the guns. Tradition.

I believe in tradition.

An even older tradition than gun ownership is the right to keep pigs, chickens, goats, and cattle in your backyard.

But they won't let me. So I consider the Health Department to be un-American.

Everybody should be able to keep pigs, chickens, goats, and cattle in their backyards. Or in their high-rise apartments. Or in their office lobbies.

That way, if the Communists ever take over all the farms and meat-packing houses and try to starve us to death (they won't dare shoot it out because of our guns), we will be well stocked with our own food supply.

I'd write more about our precious right to bear arms but I've got to go to a meeting of a committee to replace the torch in the Statue of Liberty's hand with a .22 pistol.

So if you want to fight for your right to own guns, cut this column out and send it to your congressman or your senator.

Quick, while they are still alive.

July 8, 1968

He Can Dream, Can't He?

It was early last Thursday morning and I heard a strange sound. It was Slats Grobnik's voice. He was in front of the house yelling: "Yo, ho, ho . . . can you come out?"

He was on the sidewalk and he had a big brown paper bag in his arms. He pointed at it with one finger.

We met in the gangway a few minutes later.

He opened the bag. "Lookit," he hissed.

"Wow," I hissed.

There were Zebras by the package, and cherry bombs, torpedoes, and skyrockets, more Zebras, pinwheels, and other great stuff.

"Wherejagettum," I hissed.

"Gynatruck cameroun' sellnum," he hissed.

"Boy," I hissed.

"Let's go," he hissed, and we trotted quietly out of the gangway and into the alley.

He found an empty soup can.

Then he took a thick, stubby cherry bomb out of the bag and placed it on the ground. He put the can over it so just the wick stuck out.

He lit a punk with a match, then touched the punk to the cherry bomb wick. And jumped back.

The sound bounced off the garages and the houses. It rattled windows and shook porches. Mortar trickled from between bricks. Cats fled.

The can leaped at the sky, climbing higher than the garages, above the power lines, beyond the rooftops, almost disappearing in the clouds.

Then it fell slowly, clattering on the pavement.

Slats picked it up. The unopened end was puffed out, the inside scorched by the force of the explosion.

"Lookit," he hissed.

"Boy," I hissed.

"Let's try it with a coffee can," he hissed. We blew up the coffee can. Then we shot two juice cans at the same time.

Somebody came out on a back porch and shook his fist.

We tossed a Zebra firecracker into his yard, then turned and trotted quietly up the alley and into the street.

As we trotted, we tossed torpedoes against the brick walls of buildings, leaving a wave of explosions behind us.

"Torpedoes are just as loud as cherry bombs," I shouted.

"No they're not," Slats shouted.

"Well, they're as loud as Zebras," I shouted.

"Yeah," he shouted, banging one against the candy store wall.

"Don't waste 'em," Slats yelled, lighting one whole package of Zebras and tossing it on Mr. Yoboff's porch.

"I won't," I yelled, dropping one whole package of Zebras into Mr. Lynch's mailbox.

"They got to last all day," Slats bellowed, laying out a row of torpedoes on the streetcar tracks.

"I know," I bellowed, aiming a barrage of rockets at the school windows.

We trotted down the street, as the streetcar set off a chain of explosions and Lynch's mailbox sailed into the yard and Mr. Yoboff's porch trembled and three of six school windows suffered direct hits.

"This is more fun than I've had in years," Slats howled.

"Me, too," I howled.

Everybody was outside, shaking their fists.

We trotted faster. At the end of the street, on the corner, all the guys were waiting. They all had big brown paper bags.

We trotted faster. But we didn't get any closer. All the guys started fading away, disappearing. Slats started disappearing.

It was last Thursday morning and I was awakened by a strange sound. It was the alarm clock. I listened for the "yo ho ho, can you come out?" Nothing.

Ahhh, nuts.

July 31, 1968

The Accordion vs. the Guitar

The accordion is said to be slipping out of sight as a popular instrument.

Since 1950, when 130,000 were sold, it has dropped to a recent one-year sale of 35,000.

Guitars, meanwhile, are being sold by the millions.

There was a time when, in my neighborhood alone, there must have been 35,000 accordions. The only guitar player was a hillbilly who always strummed sad songs because hard times had forced him to leave his native Wilson Avenue and live with people who used garlic.

There were a lot of reasons why the accordion was popular among the working and drinking classes.

It made a lot of noise for just one instrument. There was no future as a tavern or wedding virtuoso if you took up the flute or harp. You needed a big instrument that would drown out the sound of stomping feet, breaking glasses, and falling bodies.

Also, the accordion looked something like the only other mu-

sical instrument people in the neighborhood were familiar with—
the juke box. It gleamed and had as many colors as new kitchen
linoleum.

Nobody saw sense in spending money on something like a violin, which was small, made of wood, and would break if you hit
someone with it.

Some people, mostly girls, played the piano. But it never caught
on big because you couldn't take it to a picnic.

One of the better accordion players I knew was Slats Grobnik.

Like others, he studied at Walter's Academy of Music, which
was next to the Exterminating Store on Milwaukee Avenue.

Walter was the dean of the academy and was also famous for
his Saturday night concerts at the Jump Rite Inn. He knew more
dirty lyrics to "I Got a Girl Friend Her Name is Mary Polka" than
any accordionist I ever heard.

Slats didn't want to play the accordion. He preferred the violin
because it was small and he was lazy. But his mother said: "You
can't play the violin. People will think we're Jewish."

"Besides," she said, "if you learn the accordion you can earn
money playing on weekends at the taverns. And that will give you
a chance to get to know your father."

This was not a minor investment, the accordion lessons. In the
beginning, Walter loaned an accordion free and charged only for
the lesson. But as soon as a kid remembered to take his finger out
of his nose and press a key, Walter told the parents that the boy
was a genius and should own his own instrument.

If a youth had talent, and was too dumb to conceal it, he would
probably get an accordion with his initials on the front. Then he
was trapped, because it was hard to resell with initials.

As soon as his repertoire included one polka and a Hit Parade
fox-trot he was dragged into the parlor and forced to perform for
his aunts, uncles, and snickering cousins.

Next it would be a picnic and the chance to show you could
play with mosquitoes in your ears and somebody spilling beer on
the keys.

Then on stage at the neighborhood movie house's Saturday Talent Show. It was a thrill to stand there with all your friends in the
front rows yelling that you stink.

For the very best, the big-time was going on Morris B. Sachs'
Radio Amateur Hour and playing "Lady of Spain I Adore You."

The biggest competition for first place was always an Irish
tenor who sang the Lord's Prayer, and a girl tap dancer.

It wasn't hard to beat the girl tap dancer because when you heard one tap on the radio, you heard them all. But first prize always seemed to go to the Irish tenor who sang the Lord's Prayer. It was no surprise to our neighborhood when Morris B. Sachs went into politics.

It is to be expected that the accordion has given way to the guitar. That's the result of the nation's wealth and buying power shifting from the adult to the child.

With his own money, today's teenager can buy the instrument of his choice. If he has no money, he can still persuade his parents to give him a guitar by threatening to have a nervous breakdown or father a child.

The teenager selects the guitar because he is, basically, a slothful creature, easily offended by physical exertion. The accordion is a large instrument that requires a certain amount of heaving and sweating if it is to be played noisily.

The guitar, however, is a light instrument, easily carried by a teenage girl, or even a teenage boy. And you get a tremendous noise out of it, especially when it is combined with a youth who sings at the top of his adenoids about how his heart is broken because he and his love want to get married but nobody will buy them a car.

And that, in simple sociological terms, is why we have millions of little John Lennons making our music.

There is no reason to regret this, though. If the accordion had remained popular, the country would be overrun today by a horde of teenage Lawrence Welks. And half the parents would be in hock paying for bubble machines.

August 28, 1968

Cops Threaten Law and Order

Thomas E. Foran, the U.S. Attorney for northern Illinois, says Chicago police have shown "wonderful discipline" in their handling of the Lincoln Park demonstrators during the Democratic Party's National Convention.

Foran is either stupid or a liar.

Or maybe he's been wandering around in the wrong park.

Chicago's police, for his information, have been beating innocent people with, to coin a phrase, reckless abandon.

I have always been under the impression—and maybe Foran can enlighten me—that when three or four policemen beat someone bloody, it should be for something serious enough to require an arrest.

They didn't arrest John Linstead, a *Daily News* reporter, after they split his scalp, clotted the blood in his leg, and left him lying in the street.

The club-swingers were so modest they didn't wear name tags or badges. Their modesty is much like that of the thief who wears a mask.

In general, the biggest threat to law and order in the last week has been the Chicago Police Department.

They have made the streets on the Near North Side unsafe for law-abiding citizens.

I've lived in this city all of my life. I've never been robbed, mugged, or seriously threatened. I've walked in Negro ghettos and tough white neighborhoods—even the mayor's racist neighborhood.

The only time I've run to save my hide was Monday night. A group of Chicago police were after me. My crime was watching when they beat somebody who didn't seem to deserve it.

When Foran talks about "wonderful discipline," he sounds like a boob. He's not. It's just that he, like anyone else on the public payroll in Chicago, is a flunky for the mayor. Therefore, we shall give him all the attention a flunky deserves and not refer to him again. He can go somewhere and babble all he wants about his favorite brand of unreality.

But our mayor, the architect of the grand plan for head-bashing, is wandering around loose and making predictable statements.

The great dumpling says newspapermen ought to move faster when cops come at them. That way they won't be banged about.

How in the hell, the mayor might demonstrate, can you move fast when there are six people slugging you from one direction and a parked car is blocking your retreat from another?

If the mayor will put that trick on film, I'll sell tickets and guarantee a full theater.

He can't, of course, because it's just another case of Daley talking nonsense with all the solemnity of history.

He likes to do that. When he dedicated a street for the Rev. Dr. Martin Luther King Jr., he yakked about what big buddies he and Dr. King were, forgetting that somewhere in the records were all the things he had said that indicated Dr. King was, for him, an unwelcome jerk.

When he put up those low-income prefabs a few days before the convention mainly for the benefit of the national TV audience, he talked as if he had done something else lately about Negro housing, which he hadn't.

He's been conning people so easily, I'm sorry to say about my fellow Chicagoans, that he thought he could keep it up this week.

But sorry, mayor. When your trained musclemen slapped around the nation's press, I was listening. They think you are nothing but a less articulate version of Gov. George Wallace.

That's not much, after thirteen years in office.

November 14, 1968

Haggis? Then Try Czernina!

In a few weeks Chicago's most prominent Scotsmen will hold a formal dinner and make a big fuss out of eating something called haggis.

No offense meant, but haggis is just a disgusting version of hash. It's made from the chopped heart, liver, and other innards of a sheep, mixed with oatmeal and spices, stuffed in the sheep's stomach, and cooked.

The Scotsmen, who gather by the hundreds, act as though they like it. At least that's what the society reporters say.

But I suspect that enjoying it isn't really their object. They are trying to impress us with what iron-gutted guys they are, delighting in shocking non-haggis eaters.

Many people do that with different foods—snails, raw oysters, chocolate-covered ants.

I had an uncle who always showed off by eating mounds of horseradish and hot banana peppers. He said you weren't a man if you couldn't down them without watery eyes. I remember the surprised look on his face the day the bottom of his stomach fell off.

But most people don't make a big show the way haggis eaters do. I don't mind their eating haggis. Anybody who enjoys it should eat it, if he can catch a sheep. But they should be modest about it and not throw it into our faces every year.

Because, frankly, it is not a big deal.

And neither is snail-eating, oyster-swallowing, and the rest of it.

If that is all they can handle, they are minor league.

If I may brag, I happen to be a lifelong czernina eater.

And I'll put czernina up against haggis any day. I'll even form a team of czernina eaters and we'll be glad to eat haggis—if the haggis eaters eat czernina.

It's just soup. Variations of it can be found in most Slavic countries.

Czernina eaters don't get together and rent a hall and call up the society reporters and send out news releases the way haggis eaters do.

We just sit down and have a bowl or two and let it go at that.

It's not hard to make, either.

You start with a broth. Then you add prunes and raisins.

But the main ingredient is blood.

For a nice sized pot, you use about a pint, I guess.

It's not human blood, of course. The blood of a duck is used. Most poultry stores will drain one for you, if you bring your own jar.

The blood adds color and the distinctive flavor.

It also adds the excitement of seeing some new in-law's face when, after he's had three bowls, you tell him what's in it.

I know an Irishman who married a Ukrainian girl and he was crazy about her mother's cooking. When he later learned the truth about czernina, though, the shock was severe. He even went to his priest to ask if he had done something wrong. The priest told him that as long as the blood was from a duck, and not from a Protestant, it was OK. But for a long time, he sat up late at night wondering if he was going to turn into a bat.

The worst experience I remember was suffered by Ruby Peak, a little bald widow who lived above the war surplus store. Mrs. Peak was from Arkansas and ran a rooming house on Madison Street until Mr. Peak passed away.

One day Mrs. Peak was sitting in Mrs. Novak's kitchen while Mrs. Novak ran out to the store to get some prunes and raisins.

Mrs. Peak felt like a snort, which is the way she usually felt, so she looked in the refrigerator.

Mrs. Novak was just coming up the stairs when she heard a terrible scream and the sound of breaking glass. She rushed in, thinking a fiend had set upon Mrs. Peak.

The old lady was sprawled in a chair, waving her arms and gagging. A dark stain ran from her chin down the front of her dress. On the floor was a broken jar and a big dark puddle.

Mrs. Peak pointed at it and said:

"I thought the filthy stuff was wine."

She never did believe Mrs. Novak's story about making soup that night, saying that in all her days on Madison Street, that's one thing she never heard of anyone drinking.

And from then on, she warned everybody at the corner tavern not to let their kids play near Mrs. Novak's house.

November 22, 1968

Haggis Eaters Strike Back

Letters, calls, complaints, and great thoughts from readers.

CHESTER KWIATT, Springfield—When you wrote about czernina soup, you brought back some real nostalgia in my life.

Always I have said my mom's cooking was the best of any Polish food I have ever had, bar none: potato drop noodles, potato pancakes, pierogi, sausage soup, and czernina.

Whenever I occasionally bring up the subject of czernina and tell my listeners how it is made with the blood of a duck, they scream with horror and don't believe me.

Yes, mother even raised her own ducks.

I can still see her, after all these years, with the live duck held between her knees, holding its head with one hand, and with a sharp knife in the other hand slashing and sawing away at the duck's throat, then pointing it at a porcelain pitcher, straining to get every drop of the precious blood.

Boy, we all sure did lick our soup bowls clean.

COMMENT: You sure make it sound yummy.

ALLAN W. MOLLISON, Robinson, Ill.—Shame on you for besmirching the Royal Haggis. If you only taste a bit of it you would think it manna from Heaven.

And if you could watch a few braw laddies "piping in the Haggis" you really would see something.

COMMENT: If you could watch Mr. Kwiatt's braw mom piping out the duck, you really would see something.

D. R., Chicago—If you had ever eaten haggis, you would make a big fuss over it, too. We Scots don't eat it to impress people, we eat it because it tastes good. If we wanted to impress people with what we can eat, we could do a much better job than eating your rotten czernina. And I am a former champion haggis eater—a half-pound eaten in 2 minutes and 56 seconds.

COMMENT: I can see that you aren't trying to impress anyone.

MRS. CATHERINE POWERS—You challenge we haggis eaters to try czernina, whatever that may be?

Well, you have left out the most important reason we eat haggis. Have you ever heard of Robert Burns? We Scots celebrate the anniversary of his birth.

We love it and we don't think of what is in it and what it is made from.

Besides, how much we eat once a year is about a teaspoonful.

COMMENT: You better tell that to old big mouth D. R., the champion, before he grabs your teaspoonful.

ARNOLD HARTLEY, N.Y.—I read your column on what makes the measure of a man—haggis or czernina.

It is neither. The measure of a man is sanguinaccio and neither Scot with his haggis, nor Slav with his czernina, can stand up to the Italian with this.

Sanguinaccio is made in the following manner:

Slaughter a pig and save the blood drained from its throat. Bring to a boil. Add baking chocolate, sugar, candied fruit, triple sec, vanilla extract. Let it solidify.

The result is sanguinaccio—candy for a gourmet. A great Neapolitan invention, like Sophia Loren. It takes a MAN to appreciate one or the other.

COMMENT: Sounds like it might taste good if you didn't add all that sweet stuff to it.

MRS. BETTY MCLUER, La Grange—Your column on czernina really got to me. I'm also mad about it.

The only difficulty is that I haven't had any in years. Out here in the suburbs the store would think I'm Mrs. Dracula if I asked for some fresh duck blood.

COMMENT: Not if you don't say it is for soup. Just tell them you have a pet duck that is anemic.

CHARLOTTE LAWRENCE, Morton Grove—The sisterhood of our synagogue is planning a cookbook. We are hoping to include a section of favorite recipes from well-known personalities such as yourself.

Won't you please take a few minutes to sit down and type a favorite recipe of yours?

COMMENT: Yes, and here are the ingredients. You take this scared duck, see, and you clamp it between your knees. . . .

July 17, 1969

He Rockets into the Past

The color TV flickered in the corner of the Bethany Nursing Home recreation room. A silver spaceship shone on the screen.

A very old man sat and stared. The TV voice said the rocket would leave for the moon in thirty minutes.

"I would never have dreamed of such a thing when I was a boy. It was so different then."

When he, George Parkinson, was a boy, things were different. The year he was born, 1875, Ulysses S. Grant was in the White House. Mark Twain was writing *Tom Sawyer.* General Custer would soon ride to his death. There were thirty-seven states in the Union. Alexander Graham Bell made a telephone.

The TV voice said that former President Johnson was at Cape Kennedy watching.

"Johnson," the old man said, falling silent for a moment. "I was born in Springfield, you know, and my mother was a friend of Mary Todd Lincoln. She always felt that Abe didn't treat Mary Todd as well as he should have. My mother knew Abe, too. Not well, of course. She knew Mary Todd much better."

The spaceship was on the screen and the TV voice was talking about thrust, speed, power. The old man leaned forward, but that hurt, so he sighed and sat back.

"I was about five when my father took the family west in a covered wagon. My mother, four brothers, and I. We settled in Wichita. It was a frontier town then, mud streets, cowboys. It was just on the fringes of civilization."

Barely on the fringes. Just beyond, Billy the Kid was still shooting people. Jesse James was alive and in hiding. The Apaches and Sioux were fighting us furiously. Texans drove their longhorn steers to Kansas.

The old man pulled his eyes from the spaceship and let his mind drift back.

"I didn't see any of the famous badmen myself, but they were there. Five of them rode into a town nearby and left their horses in front of the bank. A lawyer across the street could see that they were robbing it. He took his rifle and shot all five of them as they came out. I don't remember who they were. Maybe the Daltons or somebody like that. They left their bodies in the street all day, as a warning."

The countdown reached ten minutes, and the TV voice was dwelling on the magnitude of the scientific achievement.

"There was not much talk of science when I was a boy," the old man said. "People were most concerned about their health and their cattle's health."

Science. The year Mr. Parkinson was born, Louis Pasteur was on the brink of his discovery. He was twenty-two when Roentgen discovered the X-ray, and twenty-five when the Curies isolated radium. Now he was looking at a spaceship on a color television set, in an air-conditioned room, sitting in a plastic chair.

The vapors poured from the bottom of the ship. It would be soon. The TV voice talked of the enormous speed of the thing.

The old man shook his head in disbelief. "I find it hard to comprehend such things. You know, I became a preacher right after I finished high school, and I went to Oklahoma territory and rode a pony on a four-church circuit. It took so long to get around.

"Why, when my wife and I hitched up the horses to visit a ranch, a ten-mile trip would take us all day."

When Mr. Parkinson was riding his circuit, a man named Francis Train set a world speed record. He circled the globe in 67 days, 13 hours. The astronauts would do it in an hour and a half.

The TV voice mentioned the hundreds of thousands of people at Cape Kennedy, and the enormous traffic jam.

"So many cars," the old man said. "I didn't see a car until I was a grown man. It was when I came east to study at Harvard's divinity school. I went back west, of course. I was a minister for many years, many years."

The early car came into production when he was twenty-six. A couple of years later he read about someone named Orville Wright flying a thing with wings for a few brief moments.

They were counting tense seconds now. The old man clenched his brown-flecked hands tighter and leaned his chin on them.

Then it came. The colors blazed. The giant thing screamed and strained. The old man sucked in his breath.

It heaved and then jumped toward the sky, and the voice said: "We have a liftoff."

"The moon," Mr. Parkinson said, a hint of delight in his voice. "The moon."

December 16, 1969

A Jumbo Gripe on Airplanes

A publicity man for an airline phoned and asked if I wanted to take a ride high above Chicago in a new jumbo jet.

I asked him why he thought I would want to go riding around in a jumbo jet. He said the airline wanted to show some of us how nice jumbo jets are.

"We will have stewardesses serving refreshments," he said.

With five taverns within walking distance of my desk, I asked him why he thought I would want to go five miles straight up to get a drink.

He started telling me how smooth a ride you get in the jumbo jet.

I've never understood what that is supposed to mean. For a smooth ride, you can't beat jumping off the top of the Hancock Building, but I'm not going to do that, either. So I told him flat out:

"I don't ride on airplanes."

He was silent. If you tell a clergyman that you don't go to church, he can take it. But airline people get all tense and sweaty when you say you don't fly.

Then he chuckled suavely. Airline men all chuckle suavely, which is why I prefer railroad workers, who occasionally cackle, or hee-haw, but never chuckle suavely.

"Maybe it's time you did," he said between suave chuckles.

"I wouldn't walk into an airplane if it was riveted to the Earth," I told him.

"Never?" he said, now sounding genuinely amazed.

For 5,000 years, people never flew. Some very civilized men never got more than a foot or two off the ground. Beethoven, Buddha, Plato, Shakespeare, Don Juan, King Tut, and Lenny da Vinci all did their things without once having a stewardess plump their pillows. They got where they were going. But today, if you say you don't fly, you're considered strange.

"Never," I told him. He quickly said good-bye and hung up, probably fearing that I would utter further heresies.

And it is the truth. The closest I get to airplanes is when they fly so low over the house that the stewardess could hand me a drink, if my fists weren't clenched.

A long time ago, I rode in airplanes. But that was before I figured out what was really happening.

It occurred to me that I was in a metal container that was 5 miles above the Earth, moving at 600 miles an hour, 10 miles a minute, a mile every 6 seconds.

I asked myself: "What the hell am I doing in a metal container, 5 miles above the Earth, moving at 600 miles an hour?"

I closed my eyes and pictured myself in a thin suit of armor running 600 miles an hour smack into a brick wall. The thought upset me.

Then I thought of myself in an aluminum box, being dropped off a cliff 5 miles above a sidewalk. That sickened me.

When I staggered off that plane, I vowed I'd never again go 600 miles an hour in a metal container. And I haven't.

I haven't missed a thing. Some men enjoy having a stewardess plump up their pillow, or put a meal on their lap, or fetch them a drink. I've always been able to plump up my own pillow, make a sandwich, and get my own drink. If I want a woman to whom I have not been introduced to fetch me drinks or plump my pillow, I'll go to a joint in Cicero.

Since I discovered that I could live without airplanes, I have become convinced they are worthless devices. They may even be the worst thing ever invented, besides cars.

If there were no airplanes, we wouldn't be worrying about Russia and China. In their long histories, they never built a decent navy, and that would be the only way they could use the Bomb on us—they'd have to float it across, drag it up the side of a mountain, and roll it off a cliff.

If airplanes hadn't been invented, rockets and missiles wouldn't have followed. Wernher von Braun would have been just as happy and fulfilled as foreman of a clock factory.

And there would be no plans to build an airport in Lake Michigan, because if airplanes hadn't been invented, anybody who talked about an airport in the lake would be put away.

Even with airplanes, that's not a bad idea.

PART TWO

THE SEVENTIES

Mike Royko refused to ask the *Chicago Daily News* for a leave of absence to work on his biography of Mayor Richard J. Daley. He felt that being out of the paper for a prolonged period wouldn't be fair to his employers. Besides, the other three Chicago dailies were scrambling to find their own "Mike Roykos"; each time a new candidate debuted, Mike was compelled to up the ante with ever more scintillating columns. He was too fierce a competitor to step back for a few months or so. All of his research, including dozens of interviews, and the organizing and writing of the book were crammed into his already prodigious work schedule. Weekends, which he had always tried to reserve for his wife, Carol, and their boys, David and Robert, were sacrificed.

When *Boss* was published in 1971, it was a sensation. Critics praised it on two fronts: its penetrating analysis of America's last great political machine and its entertaining portrait of a brawling ethnic conglomerate. "The best book ever written about a city of this country," wrote Jimmy Breslin, Mike's New York City counterpart. Mike and Carol went to New York, where he reluctantly made the rounds of television interview shows and book parties, grumbling that he was a writer, not a performing seal. *Boss* became a national bestseller and a fixture on political science reading lists. It even was transformed into a musical. On the book's dedication page, Mike wrote: "For Dave and Rob and all the Sundays missed."

The year after *Boss* appeared, Mike won the Pulitzer Prize for commentary, only the third person to receive this new addition to the Pulitzer roster of journalism awards. He was now widely regarded as the best newspaper columnist in the country, turning down flattering job offers (from the *Washington Post* and his old punching bag, the *Chicago Tribune,* among others) as well as countless requests for speeches and other public appearances. It was a heady time, one he could not have imagined in his early newspaper years, when he sold tombstones to supplement his paltry salary. He and Carol moved out of their rented flat and bought a house on Chicago's Northwest Side. They bought a second place, a lovely little hideaway on the shore of a small Wisconsin lake. They sailed to Europe aboard the S.S. *France* (Mike was afraid to fly) with Dave and Rob and saw London, Paris, Rome, and Munich.

He threw gigantic parties for his readers. The first, a penny-pitching contest in a driveway-parking area adjacent to the newspaper plant, had to be closed off early in the day because the turnout was so huge. His dog contest—no purebreds allowed—drew thousands of contestants and their humans to the Chicago Park District's Soldier Field, home of the Chicago Bears. Awards were given in such categories as the laziest dog (the winner had to be carried to the podium), the most disobedient, and the one who looked most like Mike. Unfortunately, this First Annual Mike Royko Dog Contest was also the last; the park district staff complained that cleaning up afterward was too burdensome.

The column grew in confidence and scope. He wrote more frequently about the war in Vietnam, the most compelling issue of the day, than about Chicago politics. Often, as in "Viet Verdict: Mostly Guilty," it was with a twist so fresh, clear, and logical that all other commentaries on the subject seemed pedantic and excessively wordy. "Let's Look at Immunity," written the day President Richard Nixon announced he would resign, exemplifies the Royko genius for spotting irony and hypocrisy. His ideas were often picked up and reworked later by well-known syndicated columnists, without, of course, his special flair.

His most memorable column during this period may have been "A Faceless Man's Plea," an account of appalling indifference on the part of the Veterans Administration. The day after it appeared President Nixon opened his press conference by announcing that he had ordered the VA to take immediate corrective action. Mike's brand of humor—wacky and audacious as ever but perhaps more adroitly crafted than in his early years—still played a major role in his repertoire (see "How to Cure a Hangover" and "So, Let's All Pick a Quote").

He worked at perfecting punchy twists at the end of his columns. "I sweat out the closer more than I do the lead," he told Chris Robling in the 1993 interview. "I don't worry about the lead. Just get it started somehow, get people into it, and tell the story. My approach has always been to keep it fairly simple, not to use words that send people to the dictionary. Whatever word pops into my mind, if it does the job, that's it."

Softball, played Chicago-style with a 16-inch whopper, was a hobby as well as a column topic. Mike organized, managed, and pitched for a *Daily News* team, all with the same intensity that he poured into his column. His proudest moment came in 1976 when he broke his leg in a slide to first and played on to get another hit and finish the game (he did, however, switch to catcher from pitcher in the closing innings). He didn't seek treatment until the next day, when a horrified physician sent him directly to a hospital.

Mike's newspaper, unfortunately, was not thriving along with its famous columnist. The *Daily News* had long been considered the best-written paper in the city, with more honors and awards than all the others put together. But that wasn't enough to counter the impact of evening television newscasts, jammed rush-hour expressways to the suburbs, busier family schedules, and other lifestyle changes that were pummeling afternoon newspapers and their distribution systems. Among the victims was *Chicago Today,* the afternoon paper owned by the *Chicago Tribune;* it died on September 13, 1974. That left the *Daily News* alone in the afternoon, but its circulation continued to fall, and it searched desperately for a cure. Front pages veered from the sedate to the silly. Editors and managing editors came and went. Mike told his newsroom pals that working for the *News* was like growing up in a broken home. Worried coworkers streamed in and out of his office cubicle, a sunny corner overlooking the Chicago River, to exchange rumors about the paper's future or seek career guidance or gripe about the latest foolish headline and the way their stories were chopped up. Mike became the office therapist. Sometimes it seemed as if he couldn't start work until the day shift went home. But his colleagues were like another family to him, and he didn't want to brush them off.

Late in 1976, the newspaper's publisher, Marshall Field V, made one final attempt to salvage it. He asked James F. Hoge, the talented, aggressive young editor of the *Chicago Sun-Times*—also owned by Field Enterprises—to take on the same job at the *Daily News.* Hoge moved quickly with a variety of changes, including giving Mike Royko the title of associate editor and formalizing his role as consultant-in-chief. Hoge's administration had barely taken hold on December 20, 1976, when it was rocked by a news bulletin: Mayor Daley, seventy-six years old and eighteen months into his sixth four-year term, had collapsed and died that afternoon in his physician's office. The column Mike wrote that evening,

"Daley Embodied Chicago," surprised some with its benevolent shadings. But, as was apparent in *Boss,* Mike understood and in a sense admired the driven, competitive, fiercely loyal side of this man who, like Mike himself, had pushed his way to the top of his field.

The quality of the *Daily News* improved under Jim Hoge, but its circulation did not. On March 4, 1978, after 102 years and fifteen Pulitzer Prizes, the paper died. Most of the staff was dismissed. About eighty were asked to join the *Sun-Times,* which would have to lay off some of its own people to make room for them. Mike Royko, of course, was one of those invited to make the switch to the *Sun-Times,* which shared the riverfront building with the *News.*

At first he said yes. Then he said no. "If the *Daily News* hadn't hired me, I probably would be out of journalism," he told interviewer Chris Robling. "That's where I grew up, really. I knew everybody at the paper. I ran the softball team. I knew the copy clerks, I knew the editors. . . . I was the guy people would come to with their complaints." Like most *Daily News* people, he considered the *Sun-Times* the enemy, an inferior paper that happened to be more successful only because it was published in the morning instead of the afternoon. Many *Sun-Times* people, understandably, were resentful that so many colleagues were being laid off to make room for the *Daily News* folks.

Jim Hoge was persuasive. He asked Mike to give it six months and then quit if he still felt like it. Mike agreed. "It worked out better than I thought," he told Chris Robling. In fact, he soon concluded that by combining the two news organizations, "we were able to produce one of the best newspaper staffs in the country, best I've ever been on."

Mike settled in to page two at the *Sun-Times* and re-created his softball team. The paper's readership, largely from the city, seemed even more attuned to the Royko style than the suburban-oriented *Daily News.* Thousands of Mike's *Daily News* fans shifted to the *Sun-Times.* With its outstanding investigative reporting, sophisticated writing and editing, and progressive editorial policy, it developed into strong competition for the *Chicago Tribune.* That paper was changing for the better, too, shedding the right-wing ideology that had permeated its news reports and improving its stodgy writing and design.

But Mike Royko's newfound comfort at the *Sun-Times* was cut short with a tragedy that nearly destroyed him. Carol, his sweetheart since she was six years old, died suddenly of a brain aneurysm in September 1979. She was forty-four years old. For the first time since his early teens, he was unable to work. He took a few weeks off, and then a few more. He apologized to readers in a short message, reprinted here, that exposed the depths of his wounds. Finally he did come back, with another column destined to be cherished and reprinted for decades. It was a heartbreaking example of why Mike had forged a unique bond with readers, unmatched by any other columnist in the country: This man who so disliked public appearances and interviews and valued his privacy could, when he chose, open his soul through his writing.

January 16, 1970

The Kids Tell It Like It Is

Trying to commemorate the birthday of the late Dr. Martin Luther King raised some special problems.

The birthdays of most famous men are usually observed in Chicago by the mayor leading the plumbers' union in a parade down State Street.

But the mayor and the merchants turn pale at the thought of Dr. King's admirers gathering on State Street.

So that leaves the other traditional observance—the classroom discussion, with children being told about the famous man.

In most cases, this is easy.

We are taught that Columbus discovered America, that Washington was the father of our country, that Lincoln preserved the Union.

There is nothing as easy to teach as a success story. And, professionally, most of our national heroes were successes.

Dr. King's birthday complicates things. A teacher might wind up with these results:

"All right, class, you all had a chance to study the life of Dr. Martin Luther King. Now I will ask you questions and you will all answer. Ready?"

(Chorus) "Ready!"

All right, class. Who was Dr. King?

"A famous black man."

And what is he most famous for, class?

"He tried to get equality for other black people."
And did he succeed?
"No!"
And what else is he famous for, class?
"He won the Nobel Peace Prize."
And is there peace?
"No!"
Excellent, class. Now, how did Dr. King try to accomplish these goals?
"Through nonviolent demonstrations."
And what happened?
"Some of the nonviolent demonstrators got killed."
Very good, class. And did Dr. King ever come to Chicago?
"Yes!"
Why did he come here?
"To get better housing for black people."
And how did he do this?
"By holding peaceful marches."
And what happened on the marches?
"He was hit in the head with a rock."
Did he try any other tactics in Chicago, class?
"Yes! The conference table."
Who was at the conference table?
"All the leaders."
And what happened, class?
"They promised better housing for black people."
And did that happen, class?
"No!"
Very good, class. Now, did Dr. King ever go to Memphis, Tennessee?
"Yes!"
Tell me why he went there, class.
"To help garbagemen get better pay."
Excellent. And what happened in Memphis?
"He got killed."
Correct. Now, just a few more questions, class. What were his most famous words?
"I have a dream."
Very good, children, and did his dream come true?
"No!"
Correct. Well time is up. Class dismissed. You did very well.
"Yeah, well my daddy still says he was a troublemaker."

July 20, 1970

A *Shovelful of Bad Thinking*

Richard J. Daley had been mayor only two days when he stood on a vast stretch of empty city land, holding a silver-painted shovel in his hand.

"This is my first official act as mayor of Chicago," he told the hundreds of people who stood there with him. "Let's do more and more of these fine things for the people of the city."

Then he thrust the shovel into the ground and turned the first clods of dirt, while the cheers of the people rolled across the emptiness.

It seemed like a fine thing for the people, as he put it, at the time of the ceremonial groundbreaking, April 22, 1955.

The old slum buildings that once covered the land had been bulldozed and the city would put up high-rise public housing projects and fill them with poor families.

Some people warned against it, saying that cramming thousands of poor families into twenty-story buildings was dangerous. Some day, they warned, the high-rises would be far more evil than the rickety slums they replaced.

But the high-rises were the most practical "land use," which was another way of saying that going up was the best way to put the most blacks into the smallest space. That way, they wouldn't be spilling out of their black part of town.

So last Friday, two policemen lay dead near the spot on which the mayor had stood fifteen years earlier, so full of optimism that the Cabrini-Green project and others like it were the answer to the black housing problem.

Where he had broken the ground, other policemen were hugging the ground while gunfire whined down at them from the beehive buildings. Others crouched or leaned across their squad cars, scanning the windows of the high-rises through the telescopes on their rifles.

For some, it wasn't a new experience. The sound of sniper fire has become as familiar in Cabrini-Green as the roar of the jets in the suburbs.

There have been times when bullets, and hand-thrown objects, rained down from the apartments for days on end. During a riot, a fireman described being between the skyscraper slums as something like "standing in a waterfall of bottles."

It's even more dangerous inside than outside, where there is at least space to run. Riding the elevators in the buildings may be the most dangerous form of transportation in this city. "I'd rather drive without brakes on the Dan Ryan expressway," said a black man who lived there until he could find a flat in a conventional slum. Police have been trapped in stalled elevators and fire-bombed from above. Tenants have been murdered, raped, and robbed in them.

But the tenants ride them, because that's the only way, besides the stairs, to get "home." Anyway, the stairs aren't much safer, and it's not easy to climb 5, 10, or 15 flights every day.

Besides the people who live in the project, the police are the only real experts on Cabrini-Green, because they are the only outsiders who go in there regularly. The minds that conceived the place, built it, and filled it now turn to the police to tend it.

And so the police have become the only link in the nightmare world of noise, heat, crowding, violence, poverty, and ignorance.

They are expected, somehow, to keep under control something that is inevitably as explosive as a nuclear reaction.

That's why the two uniformed men were walking there, in the open, a couple of blue targets on a baseball field, strolling where thousands of eyes could see them from the high buildings.

Neither of them—Sergeant James Severin and Patrolman Anthony Rizzato—were even policemen when the ground was broken for the project. Neither of them had anything to do with creating the project.

More important, neither could do anything about it.

They couldn't offer jobs or training to black youths, because they didn't represent the big all-white trade unions. They couldn't offer a way out of the project, because they were not part of the real estate power structure that controls the city's housing patterns for its own profits.

All they could do is gutsily walk around, try to make friends, and persuade people that a white man in a uniform is not necessarily an enemy or an oppressor. By now, everyone has read that both men volunteered for it because they had social consciences. My best friend grew up with Severin and said that even in grammar school "he was the kind of kid who wanted to help people. He thought being a cop was the way to do it."

But they didn't belong there. It was a nice idea, but, as Rizzato's brother, also a policeman, said: "Look what it got him." The brother is right. In this stage of the urban war we are in, it's asking too much for a policeman to play good-will ambassador for society, at least in any situation where he doesn't have an even chance.

They could be two of the most decent policemen in the city, as they apparently were, and they would still be nothing but a couple of white heads on blue uniforms to the emotionally brutalized young men of the high ghettos, just as the nicest black kid in the city couldn't dare walk through Cicero or Bogan without expecting violence.

We've come too far in the wrong direction to expect the Officer Friendly approach to work in places like Cabrini-Green, the Taylor Homes, or any of the other towering ghettos that are more heavily populated than many suburbs. When they were built, out of ignorance and political cunning, we took a giant's step in the wrong direction.

Unless the people who have the power to make changes are willing to walk there, and hold out something besides their hands, men like Severin and Rizzato shouldn't be expected to.

Maybe nobody should walk there, or live there. Maybe just once, this bigness-crazy city should recognize that something is too big and that something smaller would be better, and should tear those damn places down.

The man who breaks ground for that kind of project will be looking beyond the end of his shovel.

October 22, 1970

Let's All Drink to Billy Goat

Billy Goat's Tavern closed at 2 this morning, but as usual the old man with the white beard, the bad leg, and the cane didn't want to go home.

It wasn't until after 3 that William (Billy Goat) Sianis, the city's greatest tavern keeper, would stop talking and allow his nephew, Sam, to help him into his car and drive a few blocks to the St. Clair Hotel, where he lived.

Then he went to his room, fell over, and died.

It was typical of Billy Goat that he would die during the only five hours of the day when his place wasn't open for business. That's how good a businessman he was.

And it was also typical that he would hang around his own place for more than an hour after it closed. That's how much he loved the tavern business.

"Why don't you go sit in the park like a decent old man?" I'd sometimes ask him.

"Why should I go to a park," he'd cackle, "when I can sit in my tavern. Nobody can roll me in my own tavern."

"Why don't you retire, you greedy old Greek?" I would ask him.

"I got too many relatives to support," he would say. And that was true. Like any good Greek immigrant, Billy Goat brought a small army of relatives to this country. Most of them worked for him at one time or another. You could tell which bartenders and sandwich counter men were related to him by their accents.

His place was just off Rush Street, in that dark slice of the city that runs below Michigan Avenue, then turns under Wacker Drive.

It was near the cocktail lounges, bistros, and hotel bars. But it was a tavern, pure and simple and honest. It is the closest thing to a neighborhood tavern that the Rush Street area has. Its stock in trade is the stein of beer and the shot. Some of its bartenders get furious when people ask for things like stingers and pink ladies.

He ran his tavern by his stern rules: cash, no fighting, and printers from the newspapers weren't supposed to sit on the stools if they had ink on their pants.

Sometimes his rules were strange, as in the case of the miniskirts. He disapproved of them.

"I can't get used to women sitting there with that much showing," he would say. "I keep expecting the vice detectives to come in and arrest me for running a house."

And so one day he declared that in his place men at the bar could not look at the legs of women sitting at the tables. He would sit like an eagle, watching the young men and if one of them turned on the stool, Billy would limp over and sternly tell him to face the other way.

"Are you nuts?" one grown man blustered. "You can't tell me I can't look at a girl's legs."

"In my place," Billy intoned, "I can tell you anything I want. Go around the corner, if you want to look at legs. But remember, they'll charge you twice as much for beer."

Billy became famous for his stunts with his pet goat, which he kept when his place was located across from the Chicago Stadium.

He liked to smuggle it into places where one normally wouldn't expect to see a goat, such as a World Series game or a hospital room. He was a sly old man who knew the value of publicity and got more of it than any of the places that hire expensive public relations men.

That was the only criticism I ever had of Billy Goat—that he kept a goat instead of a mean watchdog, which I always contended was a traditional part of a tavern business.

"I'll tell you why I don't have a dog," Billy said one night, after somebody burglarized his place. "I had a dog once. But he bit a customer and I had to pay all the medical bills. But that wasn't bad enough. The customer was the kind of bum who drank nothing but martinis, and so naturally the dog got sick and I had to pay his medical bills, too. That's why I prefer goats. Besides, if things get real tough, you can get milk from a goat. You can even make a good stew from a goat. What can you do with an old dog?"

I could never pierce his logic. What can you do with an old dog? About all you can do is have a drink to his memory when he is gone, which I intend to do at 7 A.M. when Billy Goat opens. It won't be business as usual, because he won't be there, laughing triumphantly over such great events as the election of Spiro Agnew, to whom he claimed a relationship, or the marriage of Aristotle Onassis. ("She's not good enough for him," Billy always said.)

The whole city should take a few minutes off and go in a tavern and have a drink to the memory of Billy Goat, a fine old dog.

August 20, 1971

Mighty Teddy Still the Champ

These are the days when the sports pages read like the Dow Jones report.

This professional athlete is retiring at twenty-nine because the owner of his team won't give him a tax-free million-dollar loan. That one is playing out his option. And that one is saying nothing because his business agent is doing the talking.

What exciting stuff. There is nothing that thrills me as much as the question of whether some twenty-eight-year-old muscle-head will earn $100,000 a year or $150,000.

To clear my brain of such things, I took a ride a few nights ago out to Kelly Park, 42nd and California.

About 2,500 people were there, most of them from the bungalows that surround the dusty softball diamond.

Some were squeezed into the tiny grandstand, but most of them were standing along the foul lines.

They were betting like crazy.

"I got fifty," said a fat man in a blue work shirt.

"On who?" asked a fat man in a tight golf shirt.

"Onasobies," the first man said.

Translated, that means: On the Sobies.

The Sobies were one of the two teams playing for the championship of the city's park teams. They represented the South Side.

The Sobies are named in honor of Sobie's Tap, in Cicero, which is named in honor of Ron Sobieszczyk, once a basketball player at DePaul University.

For years, the Sobies have been one of the great 16-inch softball teams in Chicago, although they are now sponsored by Dick's Place, in Lyons, and Co-ordinated Industry, and not by Ron Sobieszczyk.

Most of the Sobies players have fine gravy-stained names, such as Teddy Serma, Hank Zitnik, Bill Bereckis, Jimmy Mikuta, and John Horacek.

And Frank Szczech, which is pronounced the way it is spelled.

The Sobies were playing the Rogues, who represented the North Side, and are sponsored by Northern Home Furnishings. I guess they couldn't get a tavern to buy their uniforms.

Most of the Rogues have names stained with garlic and tomato sauce—Mike Mareno, Bobby Garippo, Ray Cordabello, and Vito Maggarise.

That's the wonderful thing about 16-inch softball. It's the only way that on one side of the field you can have Garippo, Cordabello, and Maggarise, and on the other side you have Zitnik, Bereckis, and Horacek, and they have heavy bats in their hands, and they aren't charging across Ashland, Grand, or Milwaukee Avenue, shouting "Wop" and "Polack" and beating each other's heads in.

In writing about Chicago softball, it is almost mandatory that one mention the potbellies, the balding heads, and funny aspects of the game.

That's when you write about picnic games—not the Sobies, the Rogues, and several others that are the class of several thousand teams.

"These guys," said Jack Ratkovic, who runs Kelly Park, "could play the Cubs or Sox in 16-inch softball, and kick hell out of them. I'd bet my house on it. I'd even bet your house on it."

Ho. Ho. Beat the Sox or Cubs?

When they start playing, you know what Ratkovic is talking about.

There are 200,000 softball players, of all ages, in the Chicago area.

About 40 of them are good enough to play for the Sobies or the Rogues. I wouldn't bet my house on them against the Cubs, but I'd bet some of the furniture.

Any resemblance between the way they play softball and the way most of us weekend, picnic, charley-horsed, limping, sweating, grunting, and panting part-time athletes play it is an insult to them.

They throw the ball faster than we hit it. The teams make one, maybe two errors a game. And most of them have been playing longer, and more often, than the major league players.

The youngest player on the Rogues is about twenty-five. The oldest is about thirty-eight.

The Sobies kids are about twenty-four. Most are in their thirties.

And then there is the miracle man—Teddy (The Champ) Serma.

Teddy Serma. There ought to be a statue of him in every empty lot in the city, every school yard, every patch of land on which you can lay out a softball diamond.

Before the game, I interrupted his smooth, relaxed warm-up. He was gliding in the outfield, pulling in deep flies.

How old are you, Teddy?

"I'm thirty-nine."

One of his teammates, a lad of thirty-seven, said:

"Ha! He says he's thirty-nine. His Social Security is printed in Roman numerals, that's how old he is."

From the neck down, Teddy Serma could be nineteen. Big shoulders on his wiry 5' 7" frame.

But there is little hair on his head, and his face has deep lines. Most people guess him from forty to forty-five.

But he plays center field where, on the top teams, you have to run like a rabbit. And he bats leadoff, a spot reserved for somebody who can fly.

How often do you play, Teddy?

"I still play a lot. Maybe sixteen or seventeen times a week. See, I play on more than one team.

"I can play that many because on Saturdays and Sundays, I'll play about four games a day in different parks, different leagues.

"In a season? Oh, I play about 250 games. I been doing that for about twenty years now."

The game began and Serma trotted out to center field. As usual, he ran like a young Willie Mays. He hit the ball hard. In the third inning, he piled into the second baseman to break up a double play and the second baseman lay still for a minute before coming to.

A moment didn't pass when Serma wasn't letting go with a patented pepper talk, a rising, ringing cry that goes: "C'ma, C'ma, C'MA, C'MAAA!"

When it ended, his team had lost, 13 to 7. But at the last out, Teddy's eyes were gleaming and he was yelling: "OK, we get 'em next time. C'ma, C'maa, C'MAA, C'MAAA!"

And one of the champion Rogues walked by him and said, with great respect: "Teddy, you will always be the greatest, pal."

Teddy works for the American Can Company and, as far as I know, he doesn't have an agent, has never played out his option, and wouldn't know a tax shelter from a subway station.

But if you ever get a chance to see him play, do it. You'll wonder what makes some of these guys you see on TV worth so much money.

October 25, 1971

The Old Man and the Farm

The old farmhouse stood along a winding dirt back road. It was the last house before the road disappeared into the heavy Wisconsin forest.

Except for a light in the house, the farm might have been deserted. Stacks of wood, boards, logs, railroad ties, and crates were everywhere in the yard. The machinery and tools were old and appeared unused.

But a light was in the window, and on a fence post was nailed a hand-lettered cardboard sign offering "Fresh honey."

The only animals in the yard were a friendly dog that trotted to the car, and a cat that sat atop a pile of lumber and stared.

A minute passed, then the door of a shed opened and an old man came out. He was short, almost dwarf-life, and built so squarely he seemed to have no neck. His overalls were the color of tree bark and a shapeless old work cap was pulled over his brow.

He walked heavily, with his arms hanging at his sides like a football lineman. "You want honey?" he asked in a thick Slavic accent. "Come in house."

The steps led to an enclosed porch in which more wood was stacked, and into the kitchen.

An old black wood-burning kitchen stove stood in the corner of the room. The oak table could have been as old as the house.

An old woman sat dozing in a wheelchair in the living room.

"He wants honey," the old man said. The old woman nodded.

The man pulled a chair from the table and said, "Sit." Then he opened a cabinet. The shelves were filled with jars of all sizes and shapes, old coffee jars, jam jars, all filled with honey.

"How many you want? Two?" He brought out two quarts.

How much? I asked.

He shrugged. "Two dollar."

He took the two bills, laid them in the center of the table and sat down. "Where you come from?" he asked. "Chicago, huh? Is work in Chicago? Is peoples got work? Good."

He looked at the dollar bills, smiled and said: "You have drink with me, huh?"

From under the sink he brought out a bottle of vodka, and carefully poured two shots.

He downed his drink, put the bottle back, and sat down again.

"Chicago, huh?" he said, pronouncing it shee-kah-goh. "Long time ago, I go Chicago. No more now. Too far go. I'm too old go Chicago."

How old are you? I asked.

"I'm eighty-six now. Too old to work farm, too. Now I take care of bees, sell honey."

The farm, how long did you work the farm?

He thought for a moment. "I came here in 1912. I buy eighty acres, all woods, big rocks. I cut down trees by myself. Cut up wood, chop up wood, take in wagon and sell to brewery. I clear all eighty acres, me and wife. Nobody around here then."

You came to northern Wisconsin from Europe?

He shook his head. "No. I come from old country in 1900. No work in old country. My father, he work fifteen hours a day for ninety cents. Nothing to eat, no work.

"In 1900 I leave old country and go to Pennsylvania. Work in coal mines. Twelve years I work in coal mines. I save money, and in 1912 I come here and buy eighty acres for $800."

And there he stayed for almost sixty years. Now, he said, all of the original eighty acres, except the house and yard, have been sold for a modest sum. Small farms in northern Wisconsin aren't selling for much. Few people want to work as hard as one must to make a living from it. His sons have grown and gone to cities to find jobs.

A cold drizzle was starting to ride in on a north wind. He put some more wood into the black stove and moved the coffeepot over the heat.

Then he walked slowly back to the car and held out his hand. I've never seen a hand quite like it. The fingers were so stubby, they all looked like thumbs. The hand was dark and callused from the wrist to the cracked nails.

"You got regular work in Chicago?" he asked. "You got steady job? Good. That's good. What you do?"

I told him I worked for a paper.

He nodded. "Good. Every day you work, huh? Regular work. Good. Is that hard work on newspaper? Hard work?"

I told him that I used to think it was. But not anymore.

February 1, 1972

The Day Slats Fell for a Girl

Valentine's Day was never one of Slats Grobnik's favorite events. He was just a toddler when he saw a card with a drawing of a heart, pierced by an arrow, but his reaction was: "Good shot."

He preferred Halloween, when he could spring from dark gangways or drop from a tree and unnerve pedestrians. He did this the rest of the year, too, but on Halloween fewer people complained to his parents.

Valentine's Day meant nothing to Slats because he didn't think much of girls. As he put it: "When you hit 'em, they cry. They must be queer."

Year after year, he was the only kid in school who didn't bring valentine cards to class. He brought envelopes, but they contained notes saying things like: "This is your final warning. Give me a nickel or I'll bend your bicycle spokes."

Naturally, he was the only boy who didn't receive any valentines. Once, a teacher mistakenly felt sorry for him and gave him a card. He promptly reported her to the principal, saying: "Next, she'll be molesting me."

His mother used to tease him about his indifference to girls. She said: "Why do you think your father comes home at night?"

Slats thought about that, and said: "Because the tavern closes?"

Later, his mother worried about his attitude, so she consulted his Aunt Wanda Grobnik, who was famous for her seances and readings of coffee grounds. Aunt Wanda looked at Slats' palms for a long time. Then she carefully felt his skull. And she concluded: "He's dirty. Maybe a bath would help."

His father tried talking to him. He thought Slats might appreciate girls if he explained the facts of life.

Slats listened carefully. Then he went to his mother and said: "Get yourself a gun, Ma. If he tries that stuff, no jury in the world would convict you."

But it finally happened. A new girl moved into the neighborhood. On her first day at school, Slats punched her on the arm, as he did with all newcomers. He waited for her to cry. Instead, she threw a rock at his head.

Slats found her irresistible. He had never met a girl like her before, and the change in him was remarkable.

He began washing his neck every day, his ears every second day. He changed stockings every morning, switching them with his brother, Fats Grobnik.

He even poured great quantities of Brilliantine on his hair, although he still wouldn't comb it.

The girl wasn't impressed. So Slats tried to dazzle her with some of the athletic feats that had made him famous.

"Watch," he said, and with a loud hissing sound, he would spit through his teeth halfway across the street, a neighborhood record.

But she still threw rocks at his head.

So he tried a different approach. He stared at her, the way he had seen Charles Boyer stare at a woman in a movie. With one eye drooping.

He would sit in school staring that way for hours. The girl didn't notice. But the teacher did, and she gave him better grades because, in the past, both eyelids had drooped.

The staring routine finally caused trouble when the girl noticed him and screamed. But that's because it was almost midnight, and he was sitting in a tree outside her window.

This was when he worked up enough courage to actually talk to her. He decided to do it by phone. But when he called her, and she answered, he was so confused that he just stood there, breathing heavily into the phone.

He was still standing there, breathing heavily into the phone, when the police traced the call and got to the phone booth. They let him go after he promised not to do it again. "It already cost me one nickel," he said. "I'm no playboy."

In desperation, he decided to give her a handmade valentine. When the day came, he asked his mother what it should say, and she suggested he write something romantic.

He nodded and began writing. It came to almost six pages. He put it in an envelope, went to school, and left it on the girl's desk.

The girl read it, then showed it to the teacher, who took it to the principal, who called in a juvenile officer.

"That's the way my father explained it to me," Slats said, so they let him go.

It was the last time Slats tried being romantic. From then on, he threw rocks at the girl's head, and stopped changing his stockings. His Aunt Wanda nodded and predicted that he would marry young.

April 14, 1972

He's Convinced Archie's Real

Does Archie Bunker live? Indeed, he does. If you doubt it, just ask Professor Willard Williamson, of Harper Community College. He's been doing some firsthand research.

Not long ago, Professor Williamson decided to buy a house in Hanover Park, a suburb northwest of Chicago. He found something he liked for $37,000 in a subdivision called Greenbrook.

On a Thursday, he looked at the house and talked it over with his wife.

On Friday, he and the owner of the house agreed to the price.

On Saturday, the phone rang in Professor Williamson's present home. He picked it up and this conversation took place:

Williamson: "Hello."

Woman caller: "Why are you moving to Hanover Park?"

Williamson: "What?"

Woman: "Why are you moving to Hanover Park?"

Williamson: "Who is this?"

Woman: "I live in the block where you're moving, and we don't want you here."

Williamson: "Why?"

Woman: "Don't you know why?"

Williamson: "I can't imagine why."

Woman: "Think about it." And she hung up.

So Professor Williamson thought about it.

Since he is white, it couldn't be his race the woman objected to.

And since his wife is white, they couldn't be objecting to her race.

And since his infant daughter, Julie, is white, it couldn't be Julie.

That left only Joy, his eleven-month-old adopted daughter. And Joy is black.

Williamson phoned the man who was selling the house, Randy Larson, to tell him about the phone call.

But Larson already knew, because he had run into even more problems.

Word had spread through the block that the house was being sold to a family with a . . . eek . . . black baby. And several of the neighbors were in an uproar.

They had confronted Larson in front of his ranch house when he got home and told them he had sold them out, left them holding the bag, betrayed them.

Their real estate values (about $35,000 to $45,000 a house) would topple, and their good life would sour, all because of that . . . eek . . . black baby.

Larson went in the house and closed the door to their wailings. He was somewhat surprised by their reactions, since they aren't the belly-scratching Bunker types.

A little later, Larson heard something and looked out the window.

His neighbors were back, on his lawn, and the man from across the street was setting fire to a wooden cross, the favorite symbol of the Ku Klux Klan.

Larson dashed outside and angrily carried the charred cross across the street and dumped it on his neighbor's lawn.

The neighbor called Larson this and that, and in a moment they were having a push-pull wrestling match.

Then everybody went home mad.

The next day—a Sunday—Professsor Williamson drove over to talk to Larson about the furor.

"Just after we got there," he says, "about ten people from five households showed up and came in.

"They said their main concern was that Joy would lower their real estate values.

"One guy said a family with an adopted black child already lives a few blocks away. He said: 'This will double our black population.'

"They said things like: 'How would you like to look out of your window and see something like THAT?' And: 'We don't want THAT kind of person in our neighborhood.'

"At least one of the women—and she did most of the talking— is a schoolteacher. And I'm told that another one of the women is too.

"At first I tried to tell them that their economic arguments were silly.

"But after a while, I just tuned them out. I decided I was sitting in a zoo and talking to them wouldn't do any good.

"When my wife and I got in the car, my first reaction was to cancel the whole thing. We didn't want to live in a neighborhood of mental and moral midgets.

"But before we got home, we realized we had to go through with it. As a teacher [of philosophy], I tell students to stand up for their principles. If we backed down, that would be worse than any harassment we would get.

"And since then, we've had calls from other people in that area who say they are sympathetic and are on our side."

So before long, Professor Williamson is going to be moving into that house, which is in the 5800 block of Farmington Court, in Hanover Park.

And those people will have to look out of their picture windows and see . . . eek . . . a black child.

It wouldn't surprise me if real estate values do go down. If word gets out that there are that many yahoos in one block, who would want to move in?

October 25, 1972
(Mike wrote this column the day Jackie Robinson died.)

Jackie's Debut a Unique Day

All that Saturday, the wise men of the neighborhood, who sat in chairs on the sidewalk outside the tavern, had talked about what it would do to baseball.

I hung around and listened because baseball was about the most important thing in the world, and if anything was going to ruin it, I was worried.

Most of the things they said, I didn't understand, although it all sounded terrible. But could one man bring such ruin?

They said he could and would. And the next day he was going to be in Wrigley Field for the first time, on the same diamond as Hack, Nicholson, Cavarretta, Schmitz, Pafko, and all my other idols.

I had to see Jackie Robinson, the man who was going to some-how wreck everything. So the next day, another kid and I started walking to the ballpark early.

We always walked to save the streetcar fare. It was five or six miles, but I felt about baseball the way Abe Lincoln felt about education.

Usually, we could get there just at noon, find a seat in the grandstand, and watch some batting practice. But not that Sunday, May 18, 1947.

By noon, Wrigley Field was almost filled. The crowd outside spilled off the sidewalk and into the streets. Scalpers were asking top dollar for box seats and getting it.

I had never seen anything like it. Not just the size, although it was a new record, more than 47,000. But this was twenty-five years ago, and in 1947 few blacks were seen in the Loop, much less up on the white North Side at a Cub game.

That day, they came by the thousands, pouring off the northbound Ls and out of their cars.

They didn't wear baseball-game clothes. They had on church clothes and funeral clothes—suits, white shirts, ties, gleaming shoes, and straw hats. I've never seen so many straw hats.

As big as it was, the crowd was orderly. Almost unnaturally so. People didn't jostle each other.

The whites tried to look as if nothing unusual was happening, while the blacks tried to look casual and dignified. So everybody looked slightly ill at ease.

For most, it was probably the first time they had been that close to each other in such great numbers.

We managed to get in, scramble up a ramp, and find a place to stand behind the last row of grandstand seats. Then they shut the gates. No place remained to stand.

Robinson came up in the first inning. I remember the sound. It wasn't the shrill, teenage cry you now hear, or an excited gut roar. They applauded, long, rolling applause. A tall, middle-aged black man stood next to me, a smile of almost painful joy on his face, beating his palms together so hard they must have hurt.

When Robinson stepped into the batter's box, it was as if someone had flicked a switch. The place went silent.

He swung at the first pitch and they erupted as if he had knocked it over the wall. But it was only a high foul that dropped into the box seats. I remember thinking it was strange that a foul could make that many people happy. When he struck out, the low moan was genuine.

I've forgotten most of the details of the game, other than that the Dodgers won and Robinson didn't get a hit or do anything special, although he was cheered on every swing and every routine play.

But two things happened I'll never forget. Robinson played first, and early in the game a Cub star hit a grounder and it was a close play.

Just before the Cub reached first, he swerved to his left. And as he got to the bag, he seemed to slam his foot down hard at Robinson's foot.

It was obvious to everyone that he was trying to run into him or spike him. Robinson took the throw and got clear at the last instant.

I was shocked. That Cub, a hometown boy, was my biggest hero. It was not only an unheroic stunt, but it seemed a rude thing to do in front of people who would cheer for a foul ball. I didn't understand why he had done it. It wasn't at all big league.

I didn't know that while the white fans were relatively polite, the Cubs and most other teams kept up a steady stream of racial abuse from the dugout. I thought that all they did down there was talk about how good Wheaties are.

Late in the game, Robinson was up again, and he hit another foul ball. This time it came into the stands low and fast, in our direction. Somebody in the seats grabbed for it, but it caromed off his hand and kept coming. There was a flurry of arms as the ball kept bouncing, and suddenly it was between me and my pal. We both grabbed. I had a baseball.

The two of us stood there examining it and chortling. A genuine major-league baseball that had actually been gripped and thrown by a Cub pitcher, hit by a Dodger batter. What a possession.

Then I heard the voice say: "Would you consider selling that?"

It was the black man who had applauded so fiercely.

I mumbled something. I didn't want to sell it.

"I'll give you ten dollars for it," he said.

Ten dollars. I couldn't believe it. I didn't know what ten dollars could buy because I'd never had that much money. But I knew that a lot of men in the neighborhood considered sixty dollars a week to be good pay.

I handed it to him, and he paid me with ten $1 bills.

When I left the ball park, with that much money in my pocket, I was sure that Jackie Robinson wasn't bad for the game.

Since then, I've regretted a few times that I didn't keep the ball. Or that I hadn't given it to him free. I didn't know, then, how hard he probably had to work for that ten dollars.

But Tuesday I was glad I had sold it to him. And if that man is still around, and has that baseball, I'm sure he thinks it was worth every cent.

November 1, 1972

Viet Verdict: Mostly Guilty

During the mid-'60s, both Jacqueline Susann and Bernard Fall wrote books.

Miss Susann's books were lurid trash. They received scathing reviews. But *The Valley of the Dolls* sold about 10 million copies. Her next book sold about 5 million.

Mr. Fall's books were brilliant studies of Vietnam and the war. They received excellent reviews. At last count, one had sold 55,000 copies. It was, by far, Mr. Fall's biggest seller.

That may be something to think about the next time there is an argument about how we got into this long, costly mess of a war.

Instead of pointing the finger of blame at this politician, or that general, or those think-tank policy makers, the finger should return to where it was during the many years of death and debate— up our collective nose. Then it might be pointing in roughly the right direction.

During all those years, we weren't kept in darkness. We were lied to and much was kept secret. But we don't have a government-controlled press. And Big Brother hasn't taken over the tube yet.

To the contrary, more information flowed out of this war than probably any in history. Despite its great unpopularity, the press— in the form of papers, magazines, books, and electronics—did possibly the finest job of covering and explaining a war as has ever been done.

But most people were too busy. After one sets aside a certain number of leisure hours for pro football, baseball, the Wide World of Sports, and the late movie, who has time for Bernard Fall? Especially when "The Valley of the Dolls" is only half read.

It was much less demanding to embrace some empty-headed slogan—"We got to stop the Commies somewhere, right?" "The president knows facts we don't know, right?"—and to let it go at that.

Those who felt otherwise, and bothered to look beyond the government's official line, received a strange reward for good citizenship. For his display of statesmanship, Sen. William Fulbright became one of the most maligned men in American life. Wayne Morse, one of two senators to vote against the Gulf of Tonkin Resolution, couldn't get re-elected. Dr. Benjamin Spock, who was one of the country's most respected men as long as he stuck to diaper rash, became a trouble-making, treasonable jerk when he concerned himself with napalm rash.

Those who preferred Fall to Susann and marched in the streets were labeled Commies, faggots, cowards, hippies, and bums. Those who stuck flags in their lapels and stood on the curb and jeered were patriots.

Even now, as the war ends, the Spocks and Morses and Fulbrights are still considered troublemakers by the majority—even though the events and the outcome show they were right all along.

But the popularity of the sloganeering fools—the John Waynes, the Bob Hopes, and Howard Millers—remains intact. They were easy to understand. And THEY didn't march in the streets. THEY didn't question our leaders. THEY didn't make the job of the hard-working policeman more difficult by congregating in the Civic Center Plaza.

When the Pentagon Papers were revealed, the greatest public indignation was not over the realization of how badly we had been lied to. The anger was over the audacity of somebody "stealing" secret documents and somebody else printing them. You would think Daniel Ellsberg had run off with somebody's hubcaps.

It's interesting that during all those years, the one person who could rock the national boat and not be hated was Ralph Nader. That's because he didn't ask about the blood that was being shed in Vietnam. He questioned whether the color TV sets on which we saw it being shed were worth the money we paid.

He treated us as "consumers" and demanded that we get our money's worth, and we liked that. But those who treated us as citizens, with all the responsibilities that involves, were told to shut up and stop causing trouble. It's more comfortable being consumers, and patting our bellies, than being citizens and having to flex our brains.

We take such pride in the phrase, "the richest and most-powerful nation in the history of the world." It's a thought that makes the skin tingle while standing up for the National Anthem at a football game.

You would think that so rich and powerful a nation also would be the most interested and the most involved nation.

But we're not. Millions of people never looked beyond the length of Abbie Hoffman's hair when thinking about the war. More people asked "why are they in Lincoln Park" than why we were in Vietnam.

In a courtroom, ignorance of the law is no excuse. In the court of conscience, which is where we stand with our 40,000 dead and countless maimed, ignorance is no better an excuse.

November 8, 1973

Bellying Up to Success

A recent magazine survey shows that the average American male worries more about the size of his belly than any other part of his body.

That probably surprises people who think that the sexual revolution would have provoked concern about other physical attributes, but the magazine, *Psychology Today,* says it isn't so.

The survey shows that the stay-young-and-lean syndrome has changed the attitude toward a potbelly, which was once considered a fine thing for a man to have.

If the survey had been taken thirty-five years ago, they would have found pride, if anything, in a bulging middle. Of course, such a survey could not have been taken then. Any pollster who asked men to describe how they felt about parts of their own bodies would have been knocked down and beaten.

The potbelly was viewed as a mark of success. Every alderman had one. An alderman who didn't look well fed would have been suspected of honesty, and therefore of stupidity.

It was the sign of maturity. A young man wasn't grown until he could belly up to the bar. And how could you belly up to a bar without a belly?

The finest athletes had them, especially bowlers, softball players, perch fishermen, and furniture movers.

So did all the civic leaders, such as the desk sergeant, the bookie, and the tavern owner.

The greatest stomach in our neighborhood belong to Slats Grobnik's uncle, Beer Belly Frank Grobnik.

He claimed his stomach was the secret of his legendary strength and agility. He could lift a jukebox in his arms and dance with it, which he did every Saturday night in the tavern.

"I'd like to see some greasy tango dancer try it," he'd boast, as he clumped around the saloon.

He was proud of this talent, so he was offended and started a brawl when he tried to go dancing at the Aragon Ballroom and they wouldn't let him in unless he checked his jukebox at the door.

Like most men of great bellies, Frank used it to communicate emotions. When he finished a hearty meal of beer and hard-boiled eggs, he would thump it with his broad hand.

Everybody knew Frank had just eaten by the deep sound that rolled through the neighborhood.

He scratched it when he was tired, and rubbed it when he was hungry. And when he was angry, he would thrust it forward and use it as a weapon. Those who felt the wrath of his belly said it was like being struck by a fat truck.

It was always Slats' dream to have a belly like his Uncle Frank's. But nature didn't intend it. He was so skinny you could actually see through him in a bright light. At the beach, he once drank too much strawberry pop and looked like a tall thermometer.

Nature decided that Slats' physical distinction would be his remarkably long, hooked nose.

When Slats was born, his father took one look and said to the nurse: "What do we feed it—birdseed?"

His Aunt Wanda, who had knowledge of the occult, asked Mrs. Grobnik: "Think back. Before Slats was born, did anything frighten you or give you a bad shock?"

"Yes," said Mrs. Grobnik, "my husband did."

As Slats grew up, he became sensitive about his nose. Any time another kid so much as sneezed, Slats thought he was being made fun of and would start swinging. Goofy Archie, who had hay fever, spent his summers sneezing and ducking.

Because of Slats' sensitivity, people tried to persuade him that a prominent nose was a mark of distinction.

"Abraham Lincoln had a long nose," his mother told him.

Slats nodded sadly. "Yeah, that's probably why they plugged him."

The candy store man told him: "What you got, kid, is a Roman nose."

Slats thought about that, then threw a rock through the candy store window. "Nobody can call me a Dago," he said.

A teacher, trying to be progressive and kind, finally thought she had the solution.

She asked Slats to play the part of Cyrano in a school play.

"Cyrano's nose was rather long," she told Slats, "but he was very brave and honorable and smart."

"Sounds like me, all right," said Slats, giving the teacher a punch.

The teacher's idea didn't work.

Slats read the script until he reached the part where Cyrano hides under the beautiful Roxanne's balcony and whispers sweet love words for a handsome, but inarticulate, young man to repeat to her.

That's when Slats flung the script down and walked out, saying: "I ain't playing the part of no pimp."

November 23, 1973

Hearty "Hallo" from Greece

For days, terrible rumors had been sweeping Billy Goat's Tavern.

They all concerned the recent trip to Greece by Sam Sianis, the owner. He went to Greece, where he was born, to marry a girl named Irene.

But he got there just as the student uprising began and troops, tanks, and martial law moved in.

So everybody in the tavern was saying Sianis was in a Greek prison, or Sianis was trapped at the airport, or Sianis was captured by the students, or that he had fled to the mountains.

One customer summed up everybody's grief when he lifted his face from the bar and wailed:

"He said that when he came back he'd have a big party. Jeez, those damn students. What a tragedy."

The basis for the rumors was one phone call Sianis made to the tavern after he landed in Athens.

Unfortunately, the connection was bad and the call was taken by one of Sianis' relatives, all of whom work in the tavern-grill.

Nobody knows what Sianis said because Sianis' relatives speak limited English. The ones behind the grill can say only: "Wan doobla-cheese weet onion." Those who tend bar can say: "Wan stein bee!"

The relative who took the call could report only: "I no no wha' hap, bus eeesh nah goo!"

I was distressed by the rumors because I'm partly responsible for Sianis being in Greece in the first place. I have been playing matchmaker.

When the famed Billy Goat Sianis died, the bar was inherited by Sam, his nephew, whom Billy Goat had brought here as a boy from a small village in Greece.

Billy Goat's funeral was hardly over when many young ladies, and some who weren't too young, began coming to the tavern and making goo-goo eyes at nephew Sam.

Some were sincere in their overtures, since Sam, at thirty-seven, is a fine figure of a man. He is only 5′ 7″, but he has a nineteen-inch neck and can lift a bar stool by one rung with his teeth.

Others, however, were attracted by the fact that Sianis' place sells more Schlitz than just about any joint in town, which means he is a man of considerable means.

I feared that one of these women would turn his head with her wiles, and an unfortunate marriage would occur.

So I urged him to go back to his native Greece and find a nice girl who knows nothing of checking accounts, charge accounts, Bonwit Teller, property laws, Gloria Steinem, tennis clubs, and property laws.

My motives were partly selfish. Billy Goat's is my favorite tavern, and a tavern is only as happy as its owner, and a tavern owner cannot be happy with a wife who expects him home before 3 A.M.

"Remember Zorba!" I kept telling him. "No henpecked man, he."

So after several vacations in Greece, Sianis returned this summer with a picture of the beautiful Irene and an announcement that he would return in November to marry her.

"She's good woman," he said. "She don't say much."

And that was why he happened to be there this week in the midst of unrest, troops, tanks, and martial law.

Finally the tension became so great that the bartenders were drinking more than the customers, which can happen when they become nervous, and when the owner is out of the country.

That is why I put through a transatlantic phone call, hoping to get some information. One of his relatives gave me a relative's number in Athens. The number was "seesha fy seesha, fy seesha fy fo!"

The call went through. Several voices said: "Huh?" Then Sianis himself came on.

"Wash new?" he said.

I told him that the customers feared for his safety and about the rumors.

He said things had, indeed, looked bad for a while.

"When I get off airplane, I look for Irene, but she's not there. I figure that maybe I'm making a mistake if she can't even meet me.

"Then I get in cab and I go two blocks and then the soldiers jump out and surround me.

"I say: 'Wash wrong?' They say: 'We gotta war.' I say: 'Who's gonna win?' They say: 'We gonna win.' I say: 'I'm on your side.'

"Then they tell me that nobody is supposed to be out this late. Ees Marshall's law. I ask them Marshall who? In Chicago, my place stay open until 2 A.M., so it wasn't too late.

"They tell me that I better get off the street until the war is over. So I been off the street all week."

Did this mean that he is being kept from Irene, and that the wedding is off, and the Chicago free party, too?

"Nah," said Sianis. "Irene is right here with me. We gonna get married next week. Here, I put her on the phone. Irene, say hallo."

She came on the phone and said: "Hallo!"

I said: "Hello. Are you looking forward to the wedding?"

She said: "Hallo!"

I said: "Do you think you will like Chicago?"

She said: "Hallo!"

Sianis came back on and said: "Her English ain't too good yet."

The tavern will remain a happy place.

December 10, 1973

A Faceless Man's Plea

Leroy Bailey had just turned twenty-one. He was one of seven kids from a broken family in Connecticut. He had been in the infantry in Vietnam for only one month.

Then the rocket tore through the roof of his tent while he was sleeping and exploded in his face.

He was alive when the medics pulled him out. But he was blind. And his face was gone. It's the simplest way to describe it: He no longer had a face.

That was in the spring of 1968. He went to an Army hospital, was discharged and shipped to Hines Veterans Administration Hospital, west of Chicago.

After three years and much surgery, they told him there was little more they could do for him. He still had no face.

Now Bailey spends most of his life in the basement of his

brother's home in suburban La Grange. The brother moved here from the East to be near him while he was hospitalized.

He knits wool hats, which a friend sells for him. He listens to the radio or to a tape player.

Because of his terrible wound, most of the goals and pleasures of men his age will always be denied him.

But there is one thing he would like to be able to do someday. It isn't much, because most of us take it for granted.

He would like to eat solid foods.

Since 1968, he has eaten nothing but liquids. He uses a large syringe to squirt liquid foods down his throat.

Last year, through some friends of his brother, Bailey met a doctor who specializes in facial surgery.

The doctor, Charles Janda, of Oak Brook, said he believed he could reconstruct Bailey's face so that he could eat solid foods.

But it would require a series of at least six separate operations, possibly more.

Bailey eagerly agreed, and the first operation was performed at Chicago's Mercy Hospital.

Then Dr. Janda and the hospital sent their bills to the Veterans Administration.

They did this because Bailey and his brother were under the impression that the VA would pay for any treatment he needed that wasn't available in the VA.

The VA refuses to pay the bills. The reason was explained in a remarkable letter sent to Bailey by a VA official:

> Dear Mr. Bailey:
>
> Reference is made to the enclosed invoice for services given to you for selective plastic surgery done on Sept. 22, 1972.
>
> It is regretted that payment on the above cannot be approved since the treatment was for a condition other than that of your service-connected disability.
>
> Outpatient treatment and/or medication may only be authorized for the treatment of a disability which has been adjudicated by the Veterans Administration as incurred in or aggravated by military service.
>
> Any expense involved for this condition must be a personal transaction between you and the doctor.

It is astonishing, I know, but the VA actually told him that he was being treated for something "other than that of your service-connected disability."

Until he was hit by a rocket, Bailey had teeth. Now he has none. He had eyes. Now he has none. He had a nose. Now he has none. People could look at him. Now most of them turn away.

Bailey believes that the VA thinks he wants the surgery just to look better, that it is "cosmetic" surgery.

Even if that were so, then why the hell not? If we can afford $5,000,000 to make Richard Nixon's San Clemente property prettier, we can do whatever is humanly possible for this man's face.

But Bailey insists it isn't his appearance that concerns him. He knows it will never be normal.

He explains his feelings in an appeal he filed months ago with the VA:

> The only thing I am asking for is the ability to chew and swallow my food.
>
> This was the purpose for the whole series of painful and unsuccessful operations I underwent in Hines Hospital between the day of my injury in May, 1968, and my eventual discharge from the hospital in 1971.
>
> At the time, I was told the very depressing news that nothing further could be done.
>
> I will never be able to accept this decision. . . .

In some bureaucrat's file cabinet is Bailey's appeal. It has been there for many months.

Every day that it sits there, Bailey takes his syringe and squirts liquid nourishment down his throat.

If his appeal is turned down, he will spend the rest of his life doing that. Not even once will he be able to sit down and eat at the dinner table with his brother's family, before going back down to the basement to knit hats.

December 11, 1973

The VA Does a Fast Reversal

A year after giving the brush-off to blind, faceless Leroy Bailey, the Veterans Administration has reversed itself in almost a matter of minutes. Monday, after I wrote about Bailey's case, the VA bureaucrats suddenly found new energy, compassion, and ability to make a decision.

The VA says it now has decided to pay the medical bills Bailey incurred in trying to get his face rebuilt enough to eat solid foods.

It was an interesting study of a governmental bureaucracy in action.

Late in the morning, we were called by Don Monico, a VA public relations man.

He couldn't answer questions, but he said we should talk to Vern Rogers, a bigger VA public relations man.

Mr. Rogers, in turn, said that he was not speaking for himself. He was speaking for Alton Pruitt, director of the West Side VA Hospital.

(In a bureaucracy, it is usually done like this, if possible. That way, nobody is actually speaking, since Mr. Rogers is not speaking for himself, and Mr. Pruitt isn't really speaking.)

Anyway, Rogers-speaking-for-Pruitt said the whole matter was being referred immediately to some mucky-muck board in Washington.

"It will go to Washington for an administrative review. And whether or not payment will be made will have to be determined by a board of medical examiners."

This, of course, was laughable. Why was a big review needed to make the decision to let Bailey chew food?

Rogers-speaking-for-Pruitt wasn't sure about that.

But a moment later he said that Mr. Pruitt would actually come on the phone and speak for himself. Which he did.

"I was just on the line to Washington," Mr. Pruitt said. "The VA is going to go ahead and pay. We also are going to ask him to come in so we can make a complete assessment of his needs."

Just like that. It shows how efficient a government agency can be—a year late—if its inefficiency is suddenly splashed across a newspaper.

But that still doesn't explain why the VA originally wrote Bailey that his facial surgery "was for a condition other than that of your service-connected disability."

I tried to get an answer.

That letter had come from Jack Pierce, chief of the medical administration service at the West Side VA.

But it wasn't signed by Mr. Pierce. It was signed by a J. Funches "FOR" Mr. Pierce.

Mr. Pierce wasn't available to discuss it. So we contacted Josephine Funches, who signs letters for Mr. Pierce.

She didn't remember too much about the case. "I think I may have read an article about him in the paper," she said.

But you wrote a letter to him.

"I may have signed a letter, but that letter was just sent out over my signature, that's all."

Do you follow this procedure? Mrs. Funches signed the letter for Mr. Pierce. But she says the letter was somebody else's creation.

So we tried the public relations man again, Rogers-who-speaks-for-Pruitt.

"That [the letter] was an error on the part of the Veterans Administration," said Mr. Rogers.

Any idiot can see that. The question is, who made the error?

"A clerk made the mistake," said Rogers.

There's your bureaucracy. If what Mr. Rogers says is true, a clerk decided that Bailey's terrible injury wasn't the result of the war. And he typed Mr. Pierce's name. And Mrs. Funches signed the letter for Mr. Pierce.

If that is the way they do things, there must be a lot more Leroy Baileys out there.

May 31, 1974

How This City Really *"Works"*

To the well-paid suburban executive who commutes to Chicago's Loop, looks at the skyline, lunches in a private club, and says: "This city works" . . .

And to the suave high-rise dweller, who has a view of the lake, jogs in the park, dines in the better French restaurants, and says: "This city works" . . .

To the portly politicians, who sit atop it all, doling out their street lights, making garbage pickup a royal gift, getting their cut off the top, and bragging that "This city works" . . .

To all of you, I introduce John Karpowicz, seventy-eight, former milk truck driver, tavern keeper, and landlord.

You will like Mr. Karpowicz immediately. He is a lean, dignified man whose suit is always well pressed. He has the slightly formal politeness of the European-born.

And he smiles a lot. After awhile, though, you realize his smile is one of bewilderment, not humor. He still can't believe these things have happened to him.

What happened to him is this:

Seventeen years ago, Mr. Karpowicz was a man of means.

Through hard work and thrift, he had accumulated almost $40,000 in blue-chip stocks.

It hadn't been easy. Since 1913, when he came here from Poland, he had driven a truck, run a small neighborhood tavern on Cermak Road, and moved up to a liquor store on Division Street.

In 1957, he decided the most prudent use of his money was in real estate. It would be a hedge against inflation, and something for his old age.

Had he been shrewd, he would have looked toward the outlying neighborhoods, or the suburbs.

Instead, he went where he felt comfortable. The old neighborhood. He settled on a solid building at Division and Spaulding, a few blocks from Humboldt Park. He cashed in most of his stock and put a big down payment on a $56,000 building at 3258 W. Division Street. It had eight flats and a grocery store.

Mr. Karpowicz moved into the building. That is a good sign for tenants. When the landlord lives right there, the building usually will be well maintained.

And it was. He made expensive improvements. The tenants paid their reasonable rents on time. And every month he made his mortgage payment, until the building was his, free and clear.

Then the ethnic makeup of the neighborhood began changing, which is the history of Division Street.

In early Chicago days, there were the Germans and Scandinavians. Then the East European Jews. And the Poles and Ukrainians. As they made it, they moved out, and other newcomers moved in.

Mr. Karpowicz saw the Biltmore Theatre become the San Juan. The old Polish grocery stores closed and reopened with different spices. And the native language of his tenants changed.

One day in 1972, he walked out of his building and saw some young men spraying paint on the side of the building, making a Latin Kings slogan.

"They were such big letters," he recalls, holding his hands far apart. "I asked them not to do it. They said: 'Give us money.' I told them I had no money to give them.

"They looked at my building and laughed. They said: 'Such a big building and you don't have money?'

"Two days later, the gun was shot through my window. It was a shotgun. There were bullet holes in the walls.

"I went to the police and asked them for protection. The captain told me there was nothing he could do. He said those people were to get special privilege. He said he was told this by somebody downtown.

"I slept one more night in my own building. I packed and moved out.

"But they came back. They fired a shot through Mrs. Nelson's apartment. And another night they fired a gun into Mrs. Treadway's apartment.

"The tenants moved out. How can you live where people come and shoot at you?

"I talked to the police but they did nothing.

"Then the tenants who came were the kind who would not pay rent. They lived there, but they would not pay.

"And the vandalism began. I had converted from coal to gas heat. Somebody came and wrecked my heating system. They wrecked my plumbing and my electrical wiring. They wrecked everything.

"The city sent the inspectors. They couldn't protect me, but they sent inspectors to tell me my building had violations. I went to the compliance board and told them about the shooting. They laughed.

"The tenants moved out, and somebody came and set a fire. There are fires everywhere in that neighborhood. The building was boarded up. My whole life's work was in that building. It was a good building when I bought it. It was boarded up."

A few weeks ago, Mr. Karpowicz was told to go to court. The legal papers said he was being sued by the City of Chicago for $1,000. That was the cost of ripping down his building. It had become a menace to the public.

The papers came from Richard Curry, the city's chief attorney and a relative of the mayor. The papers were witnessed by Matt Danaher, the court clerk and a onetime protégé of the mayor. They are both big men in City Hall. They say the city works.

This week, Mr. Karpowicz went to court. He told the judge he has only his Social Security checks and a few hundred dollars a year from his remaining stocks. He said he couldn't afford to pay for the demolition of his building.

The judge didn't believe him. He told Mr. Karpowicz to come back in June with his income tax returns for the last three years to prove he has been wiped out.

Well, I've seen his tax returns. His income wouldn't pay Alderman Tom Keane's lunch tabs, or the mayor's sons' tailoring bills.

Mr. Karpowicz isn't going to pay for this final indignity. If somebody wants to flatten his building, they'll have to pay for it.

"I will go to jail first," he said, lightly slapping a table with his liver-spotted hand. "If this is the law and order we have, let the law and order demolish my building.

"What have I done to lose everything? I worked, I paid my taxes. What did I get? Did they protect me? They could shoot at me, they could burn me out. How can this happen?"

And how do you answer the questions of Mr. Karpowicz, citizen, taxpayer, property owner?

He's not alone. As if by design, neighborhood after neighborhood, from Woodlawn to Humboldt Park, has gone through the same thing. Waves of arson, and not one arsonist has been pinched.

Is it paranoid to wonder why such people are ignored when they need help, then, when desperate, are hounded by City Hall until they abandon their property as worthless, and it suddenly no longer belongs to them? Is it unduly suspicious to think about the big real estate men, later coming in and acquiring huge neighborhood tracts of this abandoned land for development?

"If I sell my last few shares of stock," says Mr. Karpowicz, "then I will have lost everything. Where will I go? How will I live? Do I get my food from the garbage cans?"

That's the real city that works.

August 9, 1974

Let's Look at Immunity

The last issue to be decided before President Nixon finally slinks into the sunset is whether he should be granted immunity from further prosecution.

Many people favor the tough, unforgiving approach and think the book should be thrown at him. No man is above the law, and all those myths.

Others believe that being driven from office and deprived of a hot-shot position in history is sufficient punishment.

You can get some very persuasive arguments for both positions, which makes it difficult to make up one's mind.

For example, the best hard-nosed position can be stated this way:

The price is a criminal penalty for disobeying the laws of the United States. Certainly, I have sympathy for any individual who has made a mistake. We all make mistakes. But also, it is a rule of life, we all have to pay for our mistakes. . . . Anyone should pay for violating the laws.

Those are the words of Richard M. Nixon.

Naturally, he wasn't talking about his own immunity from prosecution. He was talking about amnesty for draft resisters in Canada and our federal prisons.

But I'm sure Mr. Nixon would agree there is little difference between their amnesty and his immunity. In this case, the words mean essentially the same thing.

Both he and the draft resisters would like to avoid being punished for breaking laws of the United States. The draft resisters believe what they did was right. Mr. Nixon also believes—or believed at the time—that the things he did were right.

But since he was so flatly against amnesty for them, it is difficult to understand how he could now favor amnesty for himself.

He has often said that amnesty would be an "insult" to those who fought in Vietnam.

But wouldn't amnesty for Mr. Nixon be an "insult" to Jeb Magruder, Charles Colson, John Ehrlichman, and all of those who so bravely lied to save Mr. Nixon's hide and got only prison sentences for their efforts?

Somebody once suggested that amnesty be granted draft resisters if they agreed to serve for three years in something like the Peace Corps.

Mr. Nixon put on his best sneer while answering that one. He said:

Those who deserted must pay their price. And the price is not a junket in the Peace Corps or something like that.

If Mr. Nixon believes that, he also must believe those who violate an oath of office, and break the nation's laws in the process, must also "pay their price."

And if their price shouldn't be "a junket," then his price should not be a substantial pension for himself and his wife, and comfortable retirement at San Clemente, Key Biscayne, and Bebe Rebozo's yacht. "Or something like that."

Amnesty means forgiveness, Mr. Nixon liked to say. *We cannot provide forgiveness for those who deserted their country.*

Immunity would mean forgiveness, too. And should we provide forgiveness for those who lie to their country, and break the laws of their country?

I could go on and on, using Mr. Nixon's own harsh and inflexible words against him. That's always easy to do with a hypocrite.

But just as I think Mr. Nixon is mistaken about draft resisters, I think those who want him punished to the fullest are mistaken.

For purely practical reasons, the faster the Nixon era is sneezed out of the public's head, the better off the country will be. And hauling him through the courts, and maybe into a prison, will accomplish just the opposite.

The only compelling argument I've heard for his prosecution— or a demand that he admit guilt before immunity be granted— is that it will convince the Nixon loyalists that he wasn't being framed, as they persist in believing.

But I doubt that even his public confessions would change the mind of people so knuckleheaded that today they cling to their faith in his innocence.

My personal reason for not wanting Mr. Nixon prosecuted is that he really didn't betray the nation's trust all that badly.

The country knew what it was getting when it made him president. He was elected by the darker side of the American conscience. His job was to put the brakes on the changes of the 1960s—the growing belief in individual liberties, the push forward by minority groups. He campaigned by appealing to prejudice and suspicion. What he and his followers meant by law and order was "shut up."

So whose trust did he betray? Not that of those who thought he was the answer. He was, indeed, their answer.

They gave him their mandate. And all the things he did—the abuses of power to suppress others—were logical extensions of that mandate.

He did his job. Let him quit and go.

December 27, 1974

How to Cure Hangover: First Try Moaning

This is the time of year all sorts of advice is written about hangovers.

The articles usually touch on three key points: What a hangover is, how to avoid one, and how to cure it.

Defining a hangover is simple. It is nature's way of telling you that you got drunk.

I've never understood why nature goes to the bother, since millions of wives pass on the information.

Except for abstinence or moderation, there is no way to completely avoid a hangover.

But there are certain rules that, if followed, will ease the discomfort.

First, stick with the same drink you started with. By that I mean that if you started the evening drinking champagne, beer, and frozen daiquiris, stick with champagne, beer, and frozen daiquiris the rest of the evening.

Drink quickly. If you can do most of your drinking within the first hour of the party and quickly pass out, you will have regained consciousness and be well on your way to recovery while others are still gadding about. By the time the Rose Bowl game comes on, your eyeballs will have come out from behind your nose.

Be careful what you eat, especially well into the night. Especially avoid eating napkins, paper plates, and pizza boards.

If you follow these rules, you'll still have a hangover. So the question is, how to get through it with a minimum of agony.

It should be remembered that part of a hangover's discomfort is psychological.

When you awaken, you will be filled with a deep sense of shame, guilt, disgust, embarrassment, humiliation, and self-loathing.

This is perfectly normal, understandable, and deserved.

To ease these feelings, try to think only of the pleasant or amusing things that you did before blacking out. Let your mind dwell on how you walked into the party and said hello to everyone, handed your host your coat, shook hands, and admired the stereo system.

Blot from your mind all memories of what you later did to your host's rug, what you said to that lady with the prominent cleavage that made her scream, whether you or her husband threw the first punch. Don't dredge up those vague recollections of being asleep in your host's bathtub while everybody pleaded with you to unlock the bathroom door.

These thoughts will just depress you. Besides, your wife will explain it in detail as the day goes on. And the week, too.

If anything, you should laugh it off. It's easy. Using your thumb and forefinger, pry your tongue loose from the roof of your mouth, try to stop panting for a moment and say: Ha, ha. Again: Ha, ha. Now pull the blanket over your head and go back to sleep.

The other part of a hangover is physical. It is usually marked by throbbing pain in the head, behind the eyes, in the back of the neck, and in the stomach. You might also have pain in the arms, legs, elbows, chin and elsewhere, depending upon how much leaping, careening, flailing, and falling you did.

Moaning helps. It doesn't ease the pain, but it lets you know that someone cares, even if it is only you. Moaning also lets you know that you are still alive.

But don't let your wife hear you moan. You should at least have the satisfaction of not letting her have the satisfaction of knowing you are in agony.

If she should overhear you moaning, tell her you are just humming a love song the lady with the prominent cleavage sang in your ear while you danced.

Some people say that moaning gives greater benefits if you moan while sitting on the edge of your bathtub while letting your head hang down between your ankles. Others claim that it is best to go into the living room, slouch in a chair, and moan while holding one hand over your brow and the other over your stomach.

In any case, once you have moaned awhile, you can try medication.

Aspirin will help relieve your headache. But it might increase the pain in your stomach.

If so, Maalox will help relieve the pain in your stomach. But it will make your mouth dry.

Water will relieve the dryness in your mouth. But it will make you feel bloated.

So it is best to take the aspirin and the Maalox and just hold your tongue under the kitchen faucet. Or rest it in the freezer compartment of your refrigerator.

If you don't like to take pills, then the headache can be eased by going outside and plunging your head into a snowbank. Be sure it isn't a snow-covered hedge.

If you eat, make it something bland, such as a bowl of gruel. I don't know what gruel is, but it sounds very bland. If you don't know what gruel is either, then just make something that you think it might be.

Most experts recommend a minimum of physical activity, such as blinking your eyes during the bowl games and moving your lips just enough to say to your wife: "Later, we'll discuss it later."

On the other hand, you might consider leaping out of bed the moment you open your eyes, flinging the windows open to let the cold air in, and jogging rapidly in place while violently flapping your arms and breathing deeply and heavily.

This will make you forget your hangover because it will bring on a massive coronary.

September 3, 1975

A Hard Look at Mooching

Gov. George Wallace
Montgomery, Alabama

Dear Gov:
Although I'm not running for anything, I have been bitten by the bug that is going around and I feel the urge to throw myself at your feet and admit the error of my liberal ways.

I was moved to this by the way Nelson Rockefeller recently slobbered over you while confessing that he was now wiser, and therefore tougher, about welfare moochers and the bumblers in Washington.

I've always said that what's good enough for a Rockefeller is good enough for a Royko, although I had yachts and fine wine in mind.

But these are hard-nosed and hard-eyed times, and since you are the symbol of these tough qualities, I want to get on your good side. As I've often told my Jewish friends, if a few of them had just stood up and cheered in those Munich beer halls, Hitler might have felt more kindly toward them.

Anyway, I want you to know that I also am tough when it comes to people getting something for nothing, especially when it is our tax money being thrown around by those Washington bureaucrats.

In fact, Gov, I'm going to share some shocking facts with you, stuff you haven't even mentioned.

Did you know there are eleven states that get about $14 billion more in federal funds than the people of those states pay in federal income tax?

That's right, Gov. In the year 1972, Washington gave those states about $52 billion in one form or another—welfare, farm subsidies, school aid, defense spending, and all that other wild green confetti that the pointy-heads toss around so freely.

Yet, those states paid only $38 billion in income tax.

OK, Gov, guess which states. Just name one to start.

I'll bet you said New York, right? We all know how New York blows our money.

Wrong, Gov. The eleven states are those that formed the Confederacy. Yep. Or is it Yup? For all your talk about those who mooch, you and your most devoted Deep South followers are just about the biggest moochers of federal money in the land.

You do a lot of yelling about the evils of the free lunch, but you are first in line.

And where does this money come from? Let's take Illinois, Michigan, Pennsylvania, New Jersey, and Ohio. These states send about $15 billion more to Washington than they get back. They're picking up your tab, Gov. Aren't you embarrassed?

Even New York—and I know how you like to hee-haw about the mess it is in—even New York comes a lot closer to paying its own way. It gets back only a tiny fraction more than it pays out.

In fact, New York could even be in the plus side if it was as clever as you are about welfare. I mean the other kind that goes to poor families, not your kind.

Gov, did you know that Washington picks up only 50 percent of New York's welfare bill? That's about what most states with big-city welfare rolls get from Washington.

Ah, but you shrewdy, you manage to work things out so that Washington pays 77 percent of Alabama's welfare bill. Over in Mississippi, it is almost 80 percent. Throughout the South it usually runs more than 70 percent. Those pointy-heads don't treat you too badly.

And did you know, Gov, that those New York City people pay about 25 percent of their own welfare costs? Why, that's a bigger share than the entire state of Alabama kicks in for its own needy. I'm shocked, Gov, that those effete New Yorkers are more willing to pay their own way than you good ol' boys.

Do you realize the situation we have here, Gov? We have Aid to Dependent States running wild! Yes sir, you sit down there making rough speeches, while we have to earn money to send to Washington so they can pass it on to you.

But I'll be honest, Gov. My bleeding heart liberalism won't quit. I really can't begrudge you the help you are getting from the rest of us.

I realize that in the South you don't have the kind of industry we do, the corporate wealth, the much higher family incomes.

So I don't mind that you get such a bloated share of the money we send to Washington. I figure that a country is like a family—if you are having hard times, and we've got something extra in the pantry, why, shucks, take what you need.

But I don't understand why you make such a big deal out of people who are on a more personal form of welfare because they have had hard times. I'm referring to the big-city blacks, Gov, since that's who you are always referring to, although you no longer like to come right out and say it.

Remember, Gov, the reason so many of them are on welfare up here is because of people like you down there. What kind of jobs do you think they can get with the kind of education you provided by blocking the schoolhouse door?

Anyway, the next time I pay my income tax, I'm attaching a note that says "Paid under protest." Not because you are a moocher, Gov, but because you're such a hypocrite.

Sincerely,
A DISGRUNTLED TAXPAYER

October 8, 1975

Poverty Aid, Chicago-Style

During the summer that just ended, City Hall spent millions of dollars giving summer jobs to city kids from poor families.

The money came from Washington. And so did the rules.

The youths had to be between fifteen and twenty-one. They had to live in Chicago. Their families had to be of low income. A family of four, for instance, couldn't earn more than $5,050 a year.

That's poor. But in Chicago, there's no shortage of poverty. So while thousands were hired, thousands were turned away.

Among the lucky youths who had summer jobs, I have discovered, were these two:

- A Harvard College student, age twenty, whose father is one of the city's most powerful and successful lawyers. The youth lives in Oak Brook, a wealthy and secluded western suburb, when he isn't attending one of the nation's most expensive colleges. (His tuition is higher than the maximum family income for the families of kids hired in the summer program.) Because he took a course in first aid at Harvard, where he is studying law, he had a summer job at the Chicago Fire Department's Sea Rescue Unit, located in Jackson Park, on the shores of Lake Michigan.
- The son of a man who is president of a Loop bank, vice chairman of another bank, and part-owner of a chain of motels. The

father is said to be a millionaire several times over, and has powerful connections in the Daley Machine. The family lives in a large house in Winnetka. The boy, a high school student, was hired as a swimming pool attendant. But he spent the summer doing odd jobs around the same Sea Rescue Unit in Jackson Park.

(I have omitted names, not because I'm worried by the influence of the fathers—I'm not—but because I see no point in embarrassing their kids.)

The fathers of both boys deny that their political clout had anything to do with getting the jobs. They said their sons got the jobs on their own, by applying like everyone else.

The banker, in fact, said he was "terrified" because his son had to ride the L to and from the city's South Side.

(He had nothing to worry about, according to a fireman I talked to. The fireman said the boy was picked up downtown each morning by a fire lieutenant, and was driven back to the Loop after work.)

Just how the sons of such rich men could qualify for the jobs isn't clear. The Mayor's Department of Manpower, which is supposed to handle these things, said it didn't know where the employment records were. The Model Cities Program, which also has a hand in funneling the federal money to various city agencies, also said it wasn't sure. (This is the same outfit, run by the mysterious Erwin France, that recently tried to move its headquarters into a luxurious Loop office building.)

However, the Mayor's Department of Manpower said that the fire department is supposed to maintain records on the people it hires for the summer program.

So we asked the fire department why the sons of rich men were hired.

And this led to a weird conversation with Fire Commissioner Robert Quinn, the mayor's old buddy, who is sort of the Casey Stengel of City Hall conversationalists.

Can you explain why these two young men were hired, commissioner?

"What's wrong with hiring them?"

Well, the federal funds are supposed to be used to hire kids from poor families.

"I don't know these two young men. But I'll tell you this: They're a credit to themselves; they're a credit to the organization;

they're a credit to youth! I say this to you, and I don't know them. Rich or poor, we're for everybody. You know, it isn't always the poor who need help."

One of them was hired to be a swimming pool attendant. Why was he doing odd jobs around a firehouse?

"Because he was working in both places, I think."

Firemen have to live in the city or you say you will fire them. But both these young men live in a suburb. Is this fair?

"Firemen are firemen—that's why. But the summer help is going to have to live in the city, too."

In the future?

"Absolutely. We're calling them in right now!"

Did you have anything to do with hiring them, because of their fathers?

"We have thousands of employees. I don't know the names of everybody. Everybody's just a number to me. If it comes up before me, I approve it."

Did they get their jobs through clout?

"Clout? What the hell is clout? I don't care for it, as long as they're able to produce. Sometimes it's not just poor kids who need help. What I see is a lot of kids who need help. Don't you think those rich kids need help?"

Maybe. But a poor kid from the West Side needs it more than a rich kid from Harvard.

"Well, what about Patty Hearst? There's a fine girl. She's rich and she was raised well, and look at her. No, in this city we try to help everybody—rich or poor, there's no influence. I don't work that way."

Hear that, Tania? If you beat the rap, come on out to Chicago. Just tell 'em that Bob Quinn sent you.

January 7, 1976

Daley Always a Quota Man

Let me say right in the beginning that I think U.S. District Judge Prentice Marshall is well meaning, but wrong.

Any arbitrary quota system for hiring and promoting cops probably is going to mean that some better-qualified person will be passed over.

But so what? That's the way things have always been done

around here anyway. The only difference is that now a federal judge has the clout, instead of some cigar-chomping ward heeler.

Listen to Mayor Daley howl about how evil a quota system is. The man has lived by quota systems—but they were always his.

First, there is the Irish quota system. Do I really have to explain it? Are there those who really believe that nobody else has been smart enough, or qualified enough, to be the police chief, the fire chief, the head of streets and sanitation, the head of the building department, the head of the zoning board, the head of the park district, and on and on?

Is it mere coincidence that the chief judge of the Circuit Court, a very powerful job, is Irish? And the judges below him in the powerful jobs running the various legal divisions are almost all Irish? The city is crawling with lawyers. Are the rest of them just too dumb to do these jobs?

The three most important elective offices by far in Cook County are those of County Board president (George Dunne), county assessor (Tom Tully), and state's attorney (Eddie Egan is Daley's candidate). They wear green on parade day.

That's how one Daley quota system works—if at all possible, give the job or office to an Irishman. And if you really have to give it to somebody else, put an Irishman in as the No. 2 man, so he can keep an eye on things.

Then there is the family quota system—for Daley's clan and those of other Machine powers. They pass down jobs and elective offices from generation to generation the way working people do their three-flats. There's a job somewhere, even if it is sleeping under a desk, for the mopiest in-law. And if he is smart enough to get his shoes laced on the correct feet, he will probably wind up as a supervisor.

Ah, but the mayor has an answer for those who questioned the fairness of a quota system that gives his own kids, Alderman Tom Keane's kid, and other Machine kids fat jobs and fat profits.

"They can kiss my ass," said the man who doesn't like quotas.

Then comes the biggest quota system of them all—the patronage system.

It is open to everyone—as long as you have a political sponsor and promise, from this day forward, to love, honor, cherish, and kiss the big mistletoe.

You hustle the vote and buy the tickets to the golf outing. If you are told to put in the fix in your city job, or court job, or inspector job, you put in the fix.

When they tell you to kick in a certain percentage of your earnings to the ward organization, you kick it in. You can be dumb, lazy, incompetent, dishonest, and sneaky, but as long as you deliver your precinct and don't rock the boat, you are qualified to be on the payroll.

You can even get caught. You might be fired, but when the heat's off, they'll put you on another payroll. I knew a cop who was such a crook, his own friends said: "He will steal a hot stove, and go back inside for the smoke." He got caught and was fired. A few years later he turned up as a big shot in the forest preserve rangers. He was, of course, a Tom Keane precinct captain.

Cops? Ask them and they'll tell you what talents you need to become a district commander. You need a talent for having political clout.

When political cartoonist Bill Mauldin was publicly mauled, a district commander was so close he could have been splashed with the blood. But he didn't see a thing. He knows how to be a district commander.

I know a fireman who has been on the job for almost twenty-five years. He has more brains in his big toe than Commissioner Quinn has in his entire skull. If he had clout, he'd be sitting at a desk downtown. But he has no clout, so he is still running into smoky hallways. The one time he got a favor—a transfer to a firehouse near his home—he had to drop $250 into a ward boss's lap.

That, too, is part of the quota system—keeping the moneybag filled.

So if the mayor thinks that he is getting an unfair deal, fine. There's something fair about that.

I suggest he try a softer approach. He might ask the judge if he has any mistletoe he'd like kissed.

May 5, 1976

Mr. Sinatra Sends a Letter

A short man with a thick neck just walked in and handed me an envelope and said: "Dis is fum Mr. Sinatra."

Sure enough, it was—a letter from Ol' Blue Eyes himself, telling me off good for my column about how he has a twenty-four-hour police guard outside his hotel suite while he's in Chicago.

Here's what he says:

"Let me start this note by saying, I don't know you and you don't know me. I believe if you knew me:

"First, you would find immediately that I do not have an army of flunkies.

"Secondly, neither myself, nor my secretary, nor my security man put in the request for police protection. It is something that's far from necessary.

"It's quite obvious that your source of information stinks, but that never surprises me about people who write in newspapers for a living. They rarely get their facts straight. If the police decided that they wanted to be generous with me, I appreciate it. If you have any beefs with the Chicago police force, why not take it out on them instead of me, or is that too big a job for you?

"And thirdly, who in the hell gives you the right to decide how disliked I am if you know nothing about me?

"The only honest thing I read in your piece is the fact that you admitted you are disliked, and by the way you write I can understand it. Quite frankly, I don't understand why people don't spit in your eye three or four times a day.

"Regarding my 'tough reputation,' you and no one else can prove that allegation. You and millions of other gullible Americans read that kind of crap written by the same female gossip columnists that you are so gallantly trying to protect: the garbage dealers I call hookers, and there's no doubt that is exactly what they are, which makes you a pimp, because you are using people to make money, just as they are.

"Lastly, certainly not the least, if you are a gambling man:

"(a) You prove, without a doubt, that I have ever punched an elderly drunk or elderly anybody, you can pick up $100,000.

"(b) I will allow you to pull my 'hairpiece.' If it moves, I will give you another $100,000; if it does not, I punch you in the mouth.

"How about it?

"(signed) Frank Sinatra.

"cc: The Honorable Richard J. Daley

"Police Supt. James Rochford

"Mr. Marshall Field, Publisher

"Mr. Charles Fegert, Vice President

"This material has been copyrighted and may not be reproduced unless used in its entirety and sets forth the following copyright notice: © Frank Sinatra, 1976."

Before I respond, I have to admit that receiving a signed, hand-delivered, copyrighted letter from Frank Sinatra was a thrill. Even if he did call me a pimp.

Way back, when we were both young, Sinatra was one of my heroes because (a) he was real skinny, (b) he had a big Adam's apple, (c) he had greasy hair, and (d) all the girls loved him. Me, too, except for (d).

For thirty years, I've considered him the master of pop singers. Why, in 1953, I played his great record of "Birth of the Blues" so often that a Korean house boy learned every word. And he probably taught the song to his children. So if Sinatra has a fan club in the Korean village of Yong Dong Po, it's because of me.

I mention this only to show how deeply it pained me to be critical of him. The pain may have been brought on by the French fries at lunch, but I prefer to think it was sentiment.

Anyway, here is my point-by-point response to his point-by-point response to my column:

- If you say you have no flunkies, I take your word and apologize. I even apologize to the flunky who delivered the letter.
- You say you didn't ask for the police guard. I'll buy that. But I didn't say you asked. I quoted the police public relations man, who said you did. I now suspect that what actually happened is that some politician sent the cop over to impress you. This point could have been easily cleared up before I wrote the column, but every time we called your suite, your secretary got snippy and hung up. I thought you didn't like smart-aleck broads.
- I didn't say you were disliked; the police PR man said it to justify the guard. I like you, Frank, honest. When you wore big bow ties, I wore big bow ties. When you wore big lapels and baggy pants, I wore big lapels and baggy pants. When you dated Ava Gardner, I dated Ava Grobnik. We're a lot alike.
- The reason people don't spit in my eye three or four times a day is that I duck fast.
- After rereading your massive file of news clippings, I agree that you have never punched any "elderly drunks." Most of the drunks you punched were younger.
- If you can prove, without a doubt, that I have ever been a pimp, I will give you $11.69. In cash. You're not the only high roller in town.
- I don't want to pull your hair. People would think we're a couple of weirdos.

However, for the sake of a sporting proposition, I'll do it. But only if I can make new terms for the bet.

If your hair doesn't move you can punch me in the mouth. (I figure that fans who can't get tickets for your show will pay 50 cents to touch my swollen lip.)

But if it does move, never mind the 100 Gs—you give me one of your old bow ties and an original recording of "Birth of the Blues." I still say it was your best song.

June 22, 1976

So, Let's All Pick a Quote

Like many orators, Mayor Daley likes to occasionally reach back into history or the Bible for quotations that help him make a point.

For instance, there was the time when the mayor was cautioning his listeners to avoid making wild accusations. The mayor put it this way:

"Like a guy said a long time ago: 'He who hasn't sinned, pick up the first stone.' "

The mayor further displayed his knowledge of biblical history on another occasion when he said:

"Even the Lord had skeptical members of his party." (Daley has yet to reveal which party claimed the Lord as a member.)

And most Daley watchers recall the time he declared:

"They betrayed Him. They crucified Him. They even criticized Him."

Last week, Daley again added to our knowledge when he turned to American history for a famous quotation.

He was making a speech at a dinner of Young Democrats, and he was predicting the Democratic convention would be held without rancor and disunity, which the mayor knows quite a bit about.

Daley told the audience:

"We'll have unity. There's no reason for disruption, as has been the case at the last two conventions. There's no reason for putting anyone out.

"We can repeat the words of Washington, as he said to his soldiers while crossing the Delaware:

" 'Let's all get in the boat!' "

Although the mayor is usually accurate in such matters, a number of amateur historians think he might have been mistaken in attributing this quotation to George Washington.

One of them said the only thing Washington is recalled to have said that night is: "It's sure cold."

The mayor might have been thinking of what Christopher Columbus said when his ship reached the shores of America for the first time. Columbus said to his men:

"Let's all get off the boat!"

Or is it possible the mayor was thinking about the words of Noah, who said:

"Let's all get in the Ark."

Then again, it might have been Admiral Farragut he had in mind. As every schoolkid knows, it was Farragut who, as he directed his ship through torpedo-filled Mobile Bay, declared:

"Let's not sink this boat."

Another Daley watcher suggested the mayor confused Washington with Teddy Roosevelt. It was Teddy who rallied his men forward at the Battle of San Juan Hill with the famous cry:

"Let's all get up this hill!"

Gen. Douglas MacArthur said something similar when the Japanese army forced him to leave the Philippines in 1942. That was when MacArthur declared:

"Let's all come back here some time."

Or could it be that Daley, a biblical scholar of note, had Moses in mind?

When the Egyptians pursued him, and the Red Sea parted, Moses said to his followers:

"Let's get out of here."

On the other hand, the mayor might have been thinking of something he read in *Moby Dick* when Captain Ahab, upon sighting the Great White Whale, says to his men:

"Let's all get that fish."

And we find a similar theme in *Julius Caesar,* with the treacherous Cassius unveiling his plot to kill Caesar by saying:

"Let's all stab the emperor."

Of course, it was Hannibal who is remembered for saying, as he prepared to cross the Alps:

"Let's get those elephants over the Alps!"

But that's the way it is with the famous sayings of famous men. Some day, they'll be debating whether it was Daley of Chicago who said:

"Let's all get in the deal!"

August 2, 1976

Hefner's Back—Or Wait, Is He?

There was a brief, but depressing, story about Hugh Hefner in one of the papers a few days ago.

It described a recent visit to Chicago by Hefner, who now spends most of his time at his California estate.

His Chicago friends marveled at how fit and well he looked.

They also noted that the formerly reclusive Hefner went out dancing. And he wore a suit, instead of the casual clothing he used to prefer.

Hefner did not explain these changes, but his regular companion, the shapely Barbi Benton, went into detail:

"He blows his hair dry rather than coming out of the shower and letting it do what it wants.

"He's more aware of what kind of shape he's in now than he ever was, because I'm always exercising, making him feel guilty if he doesn't get out and play tennis every so often.

"Next week in Los Angeles, we're going to start riding bikes again."

So that's what happens to famous playboys when they get to be over fifty.

It used to be that Hefner, more than any other man in America, did what he wanted. All of him.

Now his hair can't even do what it wants after a shower. He's got to subject it to a blast from the hot air blower, to give it that youthful poof-poof.

Here's a man who persuaded two generations of American males that they shouldn't feel guilty. Just have at the weak creatures, cast them aside, and giggle about it. (Actually, most of his disciples never got a chance to do anything to feel guilty about anyway, but he made them feel better when they dreamed about it.)

Now he feels guilty if he doesn't join the youthful Barbi to huff and puff about the hot tennis courts. I can't bear the thought that this man, who once decided alone which body was perfect enough to be the centerfold, now stands before his bedroom mirror looking for signs of his own sagging muscle tone.

Bike riding next week? This from the guy who would spend days on end lounging on the world's largest round bed?

As I read the story, Hefner kept reminding me of someone else, but I couldn't place the other person.

Then it came to me. It was Old Charlie, who owned the hard-ware store on the corner near where Slats Grobnik lived. He was one of the most admired old men in the neighborhood.

Old Charlie, a bachelor, always did what he wanted to. He wanted to wear overalls, house slippers, and a Cub cap in his store, and anyplace else, so he did. He even wore that outfit to weddings and wakes.

He wanted to go to ball games, play poker, drink boilermakers, go muskie fishing in Wisconsin, pick mushrooms, play the horses, and get in fights in the tavern, so he did.

He was something of a playboy in his lifestyle.

In the living room of his flat, above the hardware store, he had his own jukebox, which was filled with records by his beloved Spike Jones.

His kitchen pantry contained a large collection of rare old vin-tage bootleg whisky, left over from Prohibition days.

In his closet hung his entire wardrobe from World War I, in-cluding a genuine gas mask, which he always wore while march-ing in patriotic parades.

And on the wall, above the headboard of his bed, hung his most precious possession—a forty-one-pound muskie baring its long teeth.

This muskie, while being dragged into the boat, had bitten off Old Charlie's thumb.

So Charlie, great sportsman that he was, had not only the mus-kie mounted, but the thumb, too, and it was on the same wall.

Charlie was the envy of old men in the neighborhood, and some of the younger ones as well.

Then everything changed. He took up with Slats Grobnik's Aunt Wanda, the beautician, who also gave future readings in tea leaves, palms, stars, and streetcar transfers.

It began when she bought a rat trap in his store, which was innocent enough. But then she asked him to her flat to help remove a dead rodent.

Soon he was visiting her place so often that the neighborhood ladies estimated that there couldn't be a rat alive between here and Rockford.

Before long, Old Charlie's appearance changed. Instead of overalls and his Cub cap, Aunt Wanda had him wearing a yellow straw hat, a powder blue suit, two-toned shoes, and a tie that glowed in the dark.

She changed his leisure habits. No more taverns, mushroom

picking, fishing, and fighting. She had him take her to the Aragon Ballroom's Over-40 Night. She even taught him the tango—a man who had always referred to Rudolph Valentino as "that sneaky greaseball dancer."

She even talked him into taking down his trophies from the bedroom wall, saying they weren't romantic. She replaced them with a genuine oil painting of some nude Greek god that she bought at Nelson Brothers. Old Charlie didn't think that was very romantic, either.

And she put Vaughn Monroe records on his jukebox.

After all that, nobody was surprised when they got married. The neighborhood ladies smiled knowingly. Considering Old Charlie's advanced years, it was considered only a matter of time until Wanda became a well-to-do widow. Especially when she forced him to take her to the roller rink, as well as dancing.

I remember the funeral.

Wanda looked terrific, in an expensive dress, fancy hairdo, and new earrings.

Standing there sniffling, Charlie looked down at her and said: "I thought she'd hold up better than that. Too much dancing."

Then he went home, put on his overalls, and hung the muskie and thumb back on his bedroom wall.

Keep that in mind, Barbi.

December 21, 1976
(Mike wrote this column the day of Mayor Daley's sudden death.)

Daley Embodied Chicago

If a man ever reflected a city, it was Richard J. Daley of Chicago.

In some ways, he was this town at its best—strong, hard-driving, working feverishly, pushing, building, driven by ambitions so big they seemed Texas-boastful.

In other ways, he was this city at its worst—arrogant, crude, conniving, ruthless, suspicious, intolerant.

He wasn't graceful, suave, witty, or smooth. But, then, this is not Paris or San Francisco.

He was raucous, sentimental, hot-tempered, practical, simple, devious, big, and powerful. This is, after all, Chicago.

Sometimes the very same Daley performance would be seen as

both outrageous and heroic. It depended on whom you asked for an opinion.

For example, when he stood on the Democratic National Convention floor in 1968 and mouthed furious crudities at smooth Abe Ribicoff, tens of millions of TV viewers were shocked.

But it didn't offend most Chicagoans. That's part of the Chicago style—belly to belly, scowl to scowl, and may the toughest or loudest man win.

Daley was not an articulate man, most English teachers would agree. People from other parts of the country sometimes marveled that a politician who fractured the language so thoroughly could be taken so seriously.

Well, Chicago is not an articulate town, Saul Bellow notwithstanding. Maybe it's because so many of us aren't that far removed from parents and grandparents who knew only bits and pieces of the language.

So when Daley slid sideways into a sentence, or didn't exit from the same paragraph he entered, it amused us. But it didn't sound that different from the way most of us talk.

Besides, he got his point across, one way or another, and usually in Chicago style. When he thought critics should mind their own business about the way he handed out insurance business to his sons, he tried to think of a way to say they should kiss his bottom. He found a way. He said it. We understood it. What more can one ask of the language?

Daley was a product of the neighborhoods and he reflected it in many good ways—loyalty to the family, neighbors, old buddies, the corner grocer. You do something for someone, they do something for you. If somebody is sick, you offer the family help. If someone dies, you go to the wake and try to lend comfort. The young don't lip off to the old, everybody cuts his grass, and takes care of his property. And don't play your TV too loud.

That's the way he liked to live, and that's what he thought most people wanted, and he was right.

But there are other sides to Chicago neighborhoods—suspicion of outsiders, intolerance toward the unconventional, bigotry and bullying.

That was Daley, too. As he proved over and over again, he didn't trust outsiders, whether they were long-hairs against war, black preachers against segregation, reformers against his Machine, or community groups against his policies. This was his neighborhood-ward-city-county, and nobody could come in and make noise. He'd call the cops. Which he did.

There are those who believed Daley could have risen beyond politics to statesmanship had he embraced the idealistic causes of the 1960s rather than obstructing them. Had he used his unique power to lead us toward brotherhood and understanding, they say, he could have achieved greatness.

Sure he would have. But to have expected that response from Daley was as realistic as asking Cragin, Bridgeport, Marquette Park, or any other white Chicago neighborhood to celebrate Brotherhood Week by having black gang leader Jeff Fort to dinner. If Daley was reactionary and stubborn, he was in perfect harmony with his town.

Daley was a pious man—faithful to his church, a believer in the Fourth of July, apple pie, motherhood, baseball, the Boy Scouts, the flag, and sitting down to dinner with the family, and deeply offended by public displays of immorality.

And, for all the swinging new lifestyles, that is still basically Chicago. Maybe New York will let porn and massage houses spread like fast-food franchises, and maybe San Francisco will welcome gay cops. But Chicago is still a square town. So City Hall made sure our carnal vices were kept to a public minimum. If old laws didn't work, they got new laws that did.

On the other hand, there were financial vices.

And if somebody in City Hall saw a chance to make a fast bundle or two, Daley wasn't given to preaching. His advice amounted to: Don't get caught.

But that's Chicago, too. The question has never been how you made it, but if you made it. This town was built by great men who demanded that drunkards and harlots be arrested, while charging them rent until the cops arrived.

If Daley sometimes abused his power, it didn't offend most Chicagoans. The people who came here in Daley's lifetime were accustomed to someone wielding power like a club, be it a czar, emperor, king, or rural sheriff. The niceties of the democratic process weren't part of the immigrant experience. So if the Machine muscle offended some, it seemed like old times to many more.

Eventually Daley made the remarkable transition from political boss to father figure.

Maybe he couldn't have been a father figure in Berkeley, California; Princeton, New Jersey; or even Skokie, Illinois. But in Chicago there was nothing unusual about a father who worked long hours, meant shut up when he said shut up, and backed it up with a jolt to the head. Daley was as believable a father figure as anybody's old man.

Now he's gone and people are writing that the era of Richard J. Daley is over. Just like that.

But it's not. Daley has left a legacy that is pure Chicago.

I'm not talking about his obvious legacy of expressways, high-rises, and other public works projects that size-conscious Chicagoans enjoy.

Daley, like this town, relished a political brawl. When arms were waving and tempers boiling and voices cracking, he'd sit in the middle of it all and look as happy as a kid at a birthday party.

Well, he's left behind the ingredients for the best political donnybrook we've had in fifty years.

They'll be kicking and gouging, grabbing and tripping, elbowing and kneeing to grab all, or a thin sliver of the power he left behind.

It will be a classic Chicago debate.

He knew it would turn out that way, and the thought probably delighted him.

I hope that wherever he is, he'll have a good seat for the entire show. And when they are tangled in political half-nelsons, toeholds, and headlocks, I wouldn't be surprised if we hear a faint but familiar giggle drifting down from somewhere.

February 17, 1977

Why Do Purveyors of Hate Go Untouched?

A few days before that muscle-bound Nazi went berserk and killed five people in New Rochelle, New York, he was urging acquaintances to read a newsletter called *Thunderbolt.*

Thunderbolt has been around for a long time. It is published by and for people who hate Jews, blacks, and other minorities.

Every so often, some moron will send me a copy and urge that I absorb its wisdom so I will know the truth and the truth will make me a moron.

It's not the only publication of its kind. Anybody who wants printed material that will feed a racial or religious bigotry has a wide range of choices. The grim-lipped crazies apparently exchange reading lists, and if a person subscribes to one, the others will soon offer a veritable library of foam-lipped paranoia.

For those devout bigots who have trouble reading, and that is not an uncommon problem, they need merely turn to their telephone. Several hate peddlers provide a daily tape-recorded message for anyone who dials the number.

The telephone service is perfectly legal. The phone company says it has no choice but to provide the Nazis and others with a forum.

For that matter, so are the magazines such as *Thunderbolt.* The Anti-Defamation League, which monitors these publications, says it can't recall any prosecutors, local or federal, ever trying to take legal action against them.

In fact, a spokesman for the Anti-Defamation League says he isn't sure what possible legal grounds a prosecutor could pursue. While it isn't nice to encourage people to believe that blacks are a subhuman race or that Jews got what they deserved when Hitler turned on the gas jets, it isn't illegal.

Nor can anyone say for sure if these publications cause someone like the pathetic hulk in New Rochelle to pick up a gun and start killing. Someone might argue that the hate publications helped drive him into a homicidal frenzy. But someone else could argue that he was nuts already, and the newsletters only supported his deranged thoughts.

But it is interesting that we are so indifferent to publications like *Thunderbolt,* while we never get over our fear that a magazine like *Hustler* is a terrible threat to our moral fiber.

As a nation, we seem to believe that pubic hair is a greater threat than anti-Semitism or racism.

In Cincinnati, a zealous prosecutor has managed to obtain a conviction against Larry Flynt, the thirty-four-year-old publisher of *Hustler* magazine, which is generally acknowledged to be the most tasteless of the many popular skin magazines.

Flynt has just been sentenced to serve 7 to 25 years in prison for publishing *Hustler.*

The prosecutor in this case must be credited with having a creative mind. He nailed Flynt under Ohio's "organized crime" law.

Most of us, when we think of "organized crime," assume it has to do with people like Tony Accardo, Al Capone, Carlo Gambino, and other crime syndicate figures.

But in Ohio, the law says that if five or more people get

together to engage in an illegal activity, this is considered "organized crime."

Thus, the prosecutor argued that because Flynt, Flynt's wife, and several other people worked together to put out a dirty magazine, they had violated the organized crime law.

I don't care for *Hustler* magazine, and if I knew Larry Flynt, I probably wouldn't like him either.

But it does seem inconsistent that society would decide that Flynt should be put away for 7 to 25 years for peddling sex fantasies, while at the same time permitting other publications to peddle Nazi fantasies.

That's the way the prosecution mentality seems to function in many parts of this country.

They'll go to any lengths to jail a Larry Flynt, or put a Weird Harold out of the book business.

Yet, except for a brief flurry of recent activity, the government has made virtually no effort to move against the many known Nazi war criminals who live in this country.

It's OK for magazines to preach genocide. But it is a threat to us to display a lady's bottom side.

I'm not sure what Larry Flynt's hangups are. But it seems to me that some of the prosecutors are the guys with the real problem.

July 26, 1977

Image May Change, But City Keeps Its Traditions

Chicago's national and worldwide reputation has been changing in recent years.

Because of Sir Georg Solti and the Chicago Symphony Orchestra, it is now thought of as one of the great centers of classical music.

To others, it is the city to visit for the nation's boldest urban architecture.

Thousands of people have come here this summer to see the King Tut exhibit and to take advantage of our many other cultural attractions.

Visitors go away talking about the amazing variety and quality of our dining places. Some say the best of our French restaurants equal those anywhere.

Our plazas have blossomed with the creations of such artists as Picasso and Chagall. Our lake swarms with more and more yachts and sleek sailing craft. Our ultra-chic shops and new stores display the newest and most expensive fashions.

Saul Bellow has brought us a Nobel Prize in literature and the attention of the nation's literati.

And, of course, our new mayor jogs, plays tennis, and has taken a former debutante as his bride.

But at the same time that we become known for our more sophisticated qualities, we do not forget our heritage and the activities that first made the rest of the world sit up and take notice of us.

It is fine to become cosmopolitan, cultured, refined, and debonair. But we also have managed to maintain those traditions that gave us a certain flair and style that is all our own.

What I mean is, the stiffs are still plopping down all over the place.

Visit our museums, yes. But don't forget our morgue. Even for Chicago, the proliferation of professionally ventilated bodies is truly amazing.

For all of its snooty-nose bragging, its Cosa Nostra, its Godfather movies, I have yet to see New York have a week-and-a-half like we've had lately.

Just consider these events.

First, there was the ever-popular Maeshe Baer, loan shark and former purveyor of LaSalle Street's finest corned beef sandwich with pickle, being found in the trunk of his car. The cops said it was meant to be a warning. I don't know what kind of warning. Knowing Maeshe, a kick in the shins would have impressed him just as much.

A few days later, Mark Thanasouras, a former police commander turned crook turned stoolie turned bartender, died of what has now become a natural cause in Chicago. He met a man on the street with a shotgun. The next morning a knowing radio commentator said: "His past caught up with him." You can say that about a guy who died of gout.

Thanasouras barely had cooled when a lady opened an elevator in an office building and found the bodies of four slick businessmen who apparently had been involved in some kind of fast buck scheme.

A detective was asked: "Why do you think they were left on the elevator?"

He said: "They were probably too much to carry down the stairs."

The police quickly announced that they were looking for a guy named Sam Annerino because they believed that he knew something about the four dead bodies.

But before the police could find him, somebody else found Annerino first. And he was turned into a dead body, too.

So now the police are looking for two men who wear ski masks and carry shotguns and squeal their tires when they depart. If my memory is correct, the police have been looking for two men who fit that description for the last ten years and fifty murders.

But by tomorrow, the two men in ski masks might be dead bodies, too, and the police will be looking for three men in Halloween masks who carry bazookas.

The carnage has reached the point where a homicide investigator looked into the trunk of a car and let out a horrified scream.

"What is that," he cried, pointing into the car trunk.

"That's the spare tire," his partner said.

"Oh," said the detective. "I forgot."

April 19, 1978

Bucking Hard for the Equal Rights Amendment

I was talking to an ERA lady recently. She was fretting that the amendment might again fail in Illinois, after all of her hard work.

She showed me a list of about a dozen legislators and asked if I had any idea what kind of approach would work in bringing them around to her side.

I said: "Make the drop."

She looked puzzled and asked: "Make the what?"

"The drop. Give them some money."

She still didn't understand. "Money? For what?"

"Bribes."

She looked horrified and gasped: "Bribes?"

"Well, you can call it a campaign contribution, if it will make you feel better."

Then she laughed and said: "Oh, you're just kidding."

That's the trouble with the ERA crowd and most do-gooders.

They are earnest, diligent, and energetic. But they don't have much sense.

Throughout the history of this state, sly people have been getting what they want out of Springfield. They haven't done it by being honest, earnest, diligent, and energetic. All those qualities get you is laughed at by the legislators and called a goo-goo.

They have done it by throwing a shoebox full of money through the transom of a Springfield hotel room.

But the ERA ladies don't understand that. As I told the lady mentioned above:

"It would be much cheaper, too. You could probably buy the votes of the dozen guys on that list for $5,000."

"I can't believe that," she said.

See? They don't even read about the bribery trials of legislators. They have no idea what a real bargain Springfield can be.

When the ready-mix concrete companies wanted their trucks to carry heavier loads, they bought some legislators' votes for as little as $200. Most of the individual bribes weren't higher than $500. Their total bankroll for cooperation was only $30,000. One legislative leader told the concrete people that he could deliver both sides of the aisle for only $20,000. The fact is, you shouldn't ever offer a legislator too much money. It might scare him. He'll think you want him to commit treason or kill somebody.

In contrast to the concrete people, the ERA forces in Illinois have a war chest of about $200,000.

But how are they spending it? They hire public relations experts and staff members. They print up glossy charts and graphs and pamphlets and hold press conferences. They fly around the state, hold big luncheons, and make long-distance phone calls. They talk, they reason, they cajole. And then the money is all spent and they lose anyway.

It is absolutely sinful to throw money away like that when there are so many hungry legislators in Springfield.

And it is such a waste. I asked a friend of mine, who is an expert in such delicate matters, how much it would cost him to steer ERA through the legislature.

He rubbed his hands as he said: "Give me $100,000 to spend judiciously and discreetly, and I would not only pass ERA, but we would have a contingent of Illinois legislators going to other states telling them how good ERA will be for them, too.

"Naturally, you don't just go around handing money out indiscriminately. That's why they should not try to do this on their own.

"What you do is give lump sums to certain leaders of both parties, so they can distribute it to their individual followers in amounts they think are appropriate. Not every one gets the same amount, you know. That's what democracy is all about.

"It is also essential that everyone who wants something gets something. It can be a disaster if someone is inadvertently left out. That could result in somebody saying:

" 'Did you get your five hunnert?'

" 'Five hunnert? I didn't get no five hunnert. For what?'

" 'The ERA vote. I got five hunnert.'

" 'You got five hunnert? Why, those dirty crooks. They got my vote for nothing!'

"That's the kind of careless planning that causes hard feelings and grand jury investigations.

"Part of the $100,000 would also go for a few study trips. We'd fly some legislators to somewhere like Sweden, to show them how nice equal rights work there. And maybe Hawaii, which is for ERA, to show them how being for it makes people happy and suntanned.

"On the way back we might stop in Las Vegas for a day or two to let them get over their jet lag."

That is what the ERA supporters could get for $100,000, if they had even the sense of a ward heeler, which most of them probably think is somebody who repairs shoes.

And if they wanted to blow the whole $200,000, which they are going to do anyway?

My friend the expert looked dreamy as he said:

"For $200,000? For that we would not only pass ERA by a landslide, but they could probably get something else."

Such as?

"For that much money, I think I could get them a highway."

July 7, 1978

Don't Let Food Bug You

The lady had been eating a box of raisins when she found two bugs. So she put them in a jar and brought it downtown for me to see.

"Look," she said. "You can see them in there. Two bugs."

I peered into the jar, and she was right. They were tiny and appeared lifeless, but they were there, all right.

"You're right," I said. "There are two bugs in your jar."

"Well, what do I do about it?" she said.

"There are a lot of old vaudeville jokes about finding bugs in your food. Should I tell you one?"

"I'm serious," she said. "This has happened to me with food before. Hasn't it ever happened to you?"

It may have, but I've never noticed. I try not to look at food that closely, just so I'll avoid knowing too much about it.

Or even thinking about it. I had a friend who used to think about his food too much. He'd sit at lunch, munching a sandwich, and say things like: "You know, I'm calmly chewing on a piece of ham that came from the dead body of a poor creature that, in its own simple way, once enjoyed living. It had feelings. It knew fear, sexual cravings, fatigue, the pleasure of a good simple meal. And here I am, devouring its body. And we consider ourselves civilized?"

Once, when he was eating a lamb chop and poignantly describing the sweet, gentle nature of little woolly lambs that happily frolic in the green meadow, I demanded to know why he didn't just shut up and become a vegetarian.

"Because they spray chemicals on vegetables," he said, "and I've already got enough to worry about eating meat."

So it's best not to think about such things. But to get back to the lady with the bugs in her raisins:

"Who can I complain to?" she asked.

"The people who package the raisins," I suggested.

"What good will that do?" she said. "It's their product, so you can bet that they know they have bugs in it without my telling them."

"But they'll probably give you a free box. Maybe a whole case of boxes. Ralph Nader has made them all nervous."

"I don't want a free box of this buggy stuff," she said. "I want to get them in trouble for this."

Ah, then there is only one place to go for that. To the federal government. If there is anything our government loves, it is causing trouble for private corporations. It is now estimated that the federal government does more in one week to slow down our national productivity than all of the German saboteurs did during World War II.

"Who do I see there?" she asked.

I had no idea, never having complained about bugs myself. But there had to be a federal agency that did nothing but count bugs in our food, and I urged the lady to go find it.

She called a couple of days later. "It didn't work," she said. "It wasn't above the defect level."

The what?

"They have levels of how many bugs are allowed. This wasn't above it."

I had trouble believing that, but it is true. I've since checked and found out that there is a bug guideline put out by the federal government.

It is called "Food Action Levels—current levels for natural or unavoidable defects in food for human use that present no health hazard."

Under each of the foods listed, there is a "defect action level." Anything below this level the Food and Drug Administration considers "no hazards to health."

And under raisins, it says: "Insects: 10 whole or equivalent insects and 35 drosophilas eggs per eight ounces of golden bleached raisins."

Since the finicky lady had found only two insects in her package, she still was eight whole or equivalent insects short of having a grievance. Plus those 35 drosophilas (fly) eggs. She hadn't found any of those. What was she complaining about?

In case you are the kind of person who studies food closely, looking for tiny black specks and other things that will upset you, here are a few other "defect action levels."

Apple butter: "Average of more than four rodent hairs per 100 grams of apple butter or average of more than five whole or equivalent insects."

(Don't ask me why they allow fewer insects in apple butter than in raisins, but more rodent hairs. I guess it's a matter of taste.)

Fig paste: "Over 13 insect heads per 100 grams of fig paste in each of two or more subsamples."

(That's another puzzler: In fig paste, you count only the insect heads. But what does a person do if he finds 13 pairs of insect feet in his fig paste? Or 13 pairs of insect ears? Is he supposed to just overlook it? It seems to me that the federal government is splitting insects, if not hairs.)

Peanut butter: "Average of 30 or more insect fragments per 100 grams, or, average of one or more rodent hairs per 100 grams, or, gritty in taste and water-insoluble inorganic residue is more than 25 mg. per 100 grams."

(No wonder most people also use jelly.)

Frozen broccoli: "Average of 60 aphids, thrips, and/or mites per 100 grams."

(I've always wondered why I disliked broccoli, and now I know. It wasn't the broccoli; it was all those damned aphids, thrips, and/or mites. Why, you're better off with fig paste.)

I could go on, but why bother? Just try not to look too closely at what you eat. As the Food and Drug people wrote in their defect action level guide:

"It is not now possible, and never has been possible, to grow in open fields, harvest, and process crops that are totally free of natural defects. The alternative to establishing natural defect levels in some foods would be to insist on increased utilization of chemical substances to control insects, rodents, and other natural contaminants."

So it is either bugs or spray. And we know what happens if they spray too much. We might turn into bugs ourselves.

As Julia Child says: *Bon appétit!*

August 11, 1978

The Agony of "Victory"

This month marks the tenth anniversary of one of the most controversial political events in this country's history—the 1968 Democratic National Convention.

Before the month is over, millions of words are going to be written or broadcast about what happened, why it happened, what it all meant.

But the question that will be argued longest and loudest is, who was right?

Those who believe they represented established order are saying that they saved Chicago from being overrun by savage hordes of hippies, so some heads had to be cracked in the process.

The anti-war protesters who were beaten, chased, or thrown in jail say they were the victims of mindless bullying by Chicago's politicians and police.

When the anniversary has passed, and the arguing is over, none will have changed views. Both sides will still believe they were right.

But there can be no doubt as to who won. The forces of established order can claim that honor if they want it. By routing the protesters, they not only retained control of two city parks and a few streets, but they also obliterated the issues. The nation wound up arguing about who was right, Mayor Daley and the Chicago cops or the protesters, rather than about whether we should keep sending men to die in Vietnam.

If they claim their victory, however, they really should accept everything that goes with it. Everything that followed, such as . . .

It was May 1969. Ralph Durain wasn't sure why he was there, or why he was fighting. But he was a young foot soldier in Vietnam.

His infantry unit was in the Central Highlands, held in reserve in case it was needed.

The word came. A battalion was pinned down in a valley. It needed help. Durain's outfit was sent in.

The action became fierce, and Durain's unit began to fight its way out of the valley. Durain was told to be the point for his squad.

Crouching low, he ran ahead. He doesn't remember anything after that, except feeling a blow to his back, as if he had been kicked very hard.

A bullet had struck his spine. His momentum carried him forward a step or two. Those were the last steps his legs would ever take.

July 1978, after midnight. The main street of De Soto, Missouri, a small town an hour's drive from St. Louis, was deserted except for one person in a wheelchair.

It was Ralph Durain, steadily wheeling his chair down the street.

His eyes were slightly glazed. He had been drinking at a friend's house. Durain drinks his share these days. It helps the time pass. There isn't much for him to do. He has no work. His disability check more than covers his needs. But even if he wanted to work, he has no job skills. He was crippled before he was old enough to learn a trade.

He had a wife for a while. But the marriage didn't work out and she went away. So he spends most of his time just killing time. He sees a few friends, does some drinking, and checks into a VA hospital when he isn't feeling well.

That night, after his friend went to bed, he felt like going somewhere. He wasn't sleepy. With his lifestyle, he can sleep days or nights.

So he went out and was taking a slow ride down the street.

A wheelchair must use the street in De Soto. The sidewalks

slant and the curbs are high. But there was almost no traffic, so he wasn't concerned.

He had gone a couple of blocks when a police car came around a corner and caught him in its lights.

The policemen asked him why he was in the street. Ralph told them that he was just taking a ride. Just as people whose legs function would take a stroll.

The policemen said he couldn't do that. He'd have to use the sidewalk.

Ralph got angry. He has a short temper. He berated the policemen for the kinds of high curbs the town has. A wheel chair can't get up those curbs, he said.

The policemen told him he couldn't stay in the street. It wasn't safe, and it wasn't legal. They asked Ralph where he wanted to go. Ralph told them he didn't want to go anywhere with them. He just wanted to be left alone.

So they arrested Ralph, lifting him into the squad car and folding his chair and putting it into the back.

When they got to the station, Ralph said he wanted to make a phone call. He said they told him he couldn't. They put him in a cell and left him there.

During the night, he fell asleep and toppled out of his wheelchair. He couldn't climb back in, so he spent the night on the jail floor.

He has a bladder problem from his war wound. He uses a plastic bag. But the bag filled, and he was unable to go to a washroom all that night, so he developed a bladder infection.

In the morning, they let him out. They told him he would have to appear in court in a few weeks.

He asked them what he was charged with, what law he had broken.

It was a traffic law, and this is what it says:

"Use of coasters, roller skates and similar devices restricted: No person upon roller skates, or riding in or by means of any coaster, toy vehicle or similar device, shall go upon any roadway except while crossing a street on a crosswalk. . . ."

For Ralph Durain, that's what it all came down to in the Central Highlands: roller skates, coasters, toy vehicles—or a wheelchair. Now they're all the same in the eyes of law and order.

And to the victors of the 1968 convention go the spoils: people like Ralph Durain. What else do they have to show for it?

April 4, 1979

Bossy Cows the Party

It seems a long time since the unbelievable day angry Chicago voters reared up and knocked the Machine on its behind—in the process making a national figure out of one Jane Byrne, an unemployed and disgruntled city official who just happened to be in the right place (on the ballot) at the right time (during a record snowfall).

Clobbering the Machine for its arrogant incompetence was foremost in the minds of the voters that day. And it wasn't until the satisfying shock of the February 27 primary wore off that most people actually started taking a longer look at Little Ms. Bossy to see what they were going to get for the next four years.

At first what they thought they saw was someone glistening with independence—someone who owed almost no one anything. No one except the people who elected her.

That vision was nice while it lasted. But it didn't last too long. For me it began ending the day Eddie (The Sewers) Quigley planted a kiss on Ms. Bossy's lips and she neither slapped him nor had him arrested as a public nuisance.

Just the opposite. She has since said that Sewers Eddie is a fine fellow, and that it never even crossed her mind to send him out into the world of free enterprise.

Well, the fact is, Sewers Eddie is not a fine fellow. He is a sly, greedy, vote-stealing bully. The men who work in his sewers department loathe him because he makes a practice of putting the arm on them to buy tickets for his fund-raisers. Some of them hate to come up out of the sewers because they know somebody will be waiting above the lid to force the tickets on them.

After that it was a month-long lovefest between Ms. Bossy and every ward boss and alderman who would slobber on her shoes. By now, it is hard to remember just whom she was so mad at during the primary campaign.

Mayor Bilandic, yes. She was mad at him. And a small handful of people from the powerful 11th Ward organization who worked for him.

But beyond this small group, which will pack up and leave City Hall shortly after the election, she seems to believe that the Machine is made up of a grand bunch of guys.

Remember Francis Degnan, head of Streets and Sanitation? He was the overall boss of snow removal when it wasn't getting removed, and she was howling about it. Now that the snow has melted and she is playing cuddle-cuddle with the cigar-chompers, she sees no reason to put someone else in Degnan's job.

She's going to replace Pete Schivarelli, the shady underboss of snow removal. Sure, but she's going to replace him with Alderman Vito Marzullo's kid. Which shows that it is better to have an alderman as your old man than an aging syndicate head-breaker.

Needing a target during the primary, she vowed to fire James O'Grady, the police superintendent, although he has done a decent enough job. She said he "politicized" the police department. That means he jumped when the mayor's office said jump—just as almost every police chief before him had done.

But while singling out O'Grady, she says she doesn't intend to fire the head of the city's joyously corrupt building department, which is currently leading all other city departments in indictments and convictions. At the rate inspectors are being found guilty of taking bribes, it may take a new prison wing to hold them all.

Almost every property owner in Chicago knows that the building department is in the shakedown business. And in a city of decaying neighborhoods, these parasites are one of the big reasons for the decay.

So if Joe Fitzgerald didn't know what was going on, after years of being in charge, then he is dumb. And if he isn't dumb, then he knew, which is even worse. In either case, he is a better candidate for firing than O'Grady. But Ms. Bossy says he stays.

Oh, yes, I forgot. In her primary campaign, she said there existed an "evil cabal" of aldermen. As it turns out, the evil cabal seemed to consist of Alderman Edward (Fast Eddie) Vrdolyak and his sidekick, Alderman Eddie (Not As Fast) Burke. As fast as they are, two men are a rather small evil cabal.

But apparently they aren't evil enough to hold a grudge against. A few days ago, Ms. Bossy turned up at Vrdolyak's ward headquarters for one of those I-love-you-you-love-me rallies with the precinct captains.

As befits someone who has been rescued from "evil cabal" status, Vrdolyak spoke highly of Ms. Bossy and said that he wanted to forget the past.

And Ms. Bossy echoed that sentiment with a statement that

would have done the late Mayor Daley proud when she said: "The past is past and we should let it remain in the past."

Sandwiched between the smooch from Sewers Eddie and the past-burying with Fast Eddie, there have been numerous appearances at other ward rallies, during which several genuinely seedy candidates for alderman were allowed to pose for campaign photos with Ms. Bossy, hands clasped and held aloft. When asked why she would endorse them she said she hadn't—that they just had their pictures taken together, and she couldn't prevent that. I don't know; she might have just said: "Leggo my hand, creep."

Those who practice the art of practical politics will say that she is simply doing what must be done—trying to pull together the coalition that makes the party system possible.

Yeah, I suppose. But then let us not kid ourselves as to what we are probably going to have for the next four years. Not a populist mayor, as some dewy-eyed types thought. And not an independent, as others hoped for.

She learned the political trade from her hero and teacher, the late Mayor Daley, and I'm sure he taught her that a political machine feeds on patronage and power and is a natural enemy of people who preach independence. The key words in machine politics are loyalty and obedience.

So if you haven't figured out what we bargained for only five weeks ago when the snow was still on the ground, it will be someone who hopes to be the female version of the late mayor.

But if that disappoints you, don't let it. The victory in that memorable primary was yours, regardless of how Ms. Bossy turns out. It will remain yours because you let them know that you did it once, so if the time comes you can do it again.

And that's something for Mayor Bossy to keep in mind.

June 13, 1979

John Wayne's True Grit

During the late 1960s, I had a serious falling out with a liberal friend. He was against the Vietnam War, and so was I. He didn't like Richard Nixon or George Wallace or J. Edgar Hoover, and I didn't either.

But I was a John Wayne fan and he couldn't understand that.

John Wayne, he argued, stood for everything that was wrong. He glorified war, violence, justice by the gun, male chauvinism, simple-minded solutions, and even racism in the casual way he shot down Indians. So how could I like a man who represented all of that?

My answer drove him up the wall and almost ended our friendship. "You're right," I told him. "But I still like John Wayne. His movies make me feel good."

That was about it. I can't remember *not* being a John Wayne fan. Other movie cowboys were more popular than Wayne when I was a kid. But there was something unreal about them. Roy Rogers, for example, never shot anyone, except in the wrist, and seemed to be in love with his horse, Trigger. Gene Autry never shot anyone, except in the wrist, and he played a guitar and sang in an adenoidal voice.

Then John Wayne came along, and he shot people in the heart, and drank whisky, and treated his horse like a horse. In fact, he treated women like he treated his horse. He seemed real because he reminded me of the men in my neighborhood.

I never went to a John Wayne movie to find a philosophy to live by or to absorb a profound message. I went for the simple pleasure of spending a couple of hours seeing the bad guys lose.

And I still refuse to go to movies that have unhappy endings, or movies in which the villain wins, or movies in which the hero whines, or movies in which the hero isn't a hero, but a helpless wimp. If I want to become depressed, why should I spend three dollars at the movies. I can go to work, instead.

That's why the Duke's fans went to his movies. We knew he would not become bogged down in red tape, or fret about losing his pension rights, or cringe when his boss looked at him, or break into a cold sweat and hide in his room, or moan about his impotence, or figure the odds and take the safe way out.

He would do exactly what he did in *True Grit,* my choice as his greatest movie, when he rode out to bring in Dirty Ned Pepper, whom he had once shot in the lip.

As all John Wayne freaks recall, he was alone, as a hero should be, and he was sitting on his horse confronting Ned Pepper across a long, lovely valley. Ned Pepper was accompanied by several villainous friends.

Wayne informed Dirty Ned he was bringing him in—dead if need be.

And Dirty Ned sneered and said something like: "That's mighty bold talk for a one-eyed old fat man."

Who can ever forget the look of thunderous rage that enveloped John Wayne's face. True, he was fat. True, he was old. True, he had only one eye. But did Dirty Ned have to be so rude as to mention it?

Ah, it was a wonderful moment. And it got better when Wayne, in a voice choking with anger, snarled: "Fill yer hand, you son-ofabitch!"

And it got even better when he stuck the reins between his teeth, drew a pistol with one hand, a repeating rifle with the other, and galloped full speed into the valley, steering his horse with his teeth and blazing away with both weapons.

At the time, a movie critic—a man in his thirties—wrote that he was so overwhelmed by that scene that he abandoned his critical poise and stood on his seat in the theater, waving his arms and screaming: "Go, John, go!"

I didn't get quite that carried away, being of a more mature age. I simply stomped my feet and put my fingers between my teeth and whistled as loud as I could.

Foolishness? Maybe. But I hope we never become so cool, so laid back, so programmed, that nobody has that kind of foolish, odds-defying, damn-the-risk spirit.

After all, what makes some firemen drop the hose and run into a burning building to carry somebody down an icy ladder? It's not the pension, or the thirty days of vacation, or the civil service guarantees. What makes one man drop his briefcase, kick off his shoes, and dive off the Michigan Avenue bridge into the Chicago River to try to rescue a prospective suicide, while everyone else just watches? What makes an occasional politician enrage his constituents and risk defeat by damning the consequences and taking a position that is right, but unpopular? What makes some lawyers take on lost causes for no fee, and pound away for frustrating years until they get an ounce of justice?

I don't know the answer, but I'll bet that down deep, they're all John Wayne fans, and would have put the reins between their teeth, too.

Now that he's gone, I don't know what we'll do. I just can't see somebody like Johnny Travolta confronting Ned Pepper.

He'd probably ask him to dance.

September 2, 1979

An Ode to the "Softies"

Because I am known to be a softball freak, I recently received an invitation to Boudreau Stadium, in Harvey, where the national 16-inch softball championship tournament is being held this weekend.

The softball official who called me said: "When the tournament begins, we would like you to appear at home plate so we can give you a plaque for your service to softball and ask you to make a brief speech."

I must admit that I was not gracious. I told the man that he could take his plaque and shove it somewhere that would cause him great pain.

After he stopped stammering, I said:

"If I did make a speech, which I won't do because I won't come to your tournament, I would say that your tournament is a disgrace, an abomination, an obscenity, and maybe even un-American."

Sounding shocked, he said: "But I thought you liked 16-inch softball."

"I love 16-inch softball," I said. "I play fifty games a season despite my crackling knee joints and wheezing lungs. I once played an entire game on a broken leg and got two hits. I intend to play softball until I am seventy-five years old, and have left instructions that I be buried in my softball uniform, spikes and all."

"Then why won't you come to the national championship tournament?"

I gave him my answer in tones filled with as much cold contempt as I could muster:

"Because you let them wear softball gloves."

And it is true. What is billed as the national championship of 16-inch softball is nothing but a sissy event.

Native Chicagoans and those who have lived here awhile know what I mean.

Chicago-style softball is the most heroic, challenging, and satisfying athletic activity ever devised by man, with the possible exception of procreation.

It is unique among games of bat and ball precisely because it is played without gloves.

Wearing a glove in softball would be like using a fishing net to catch a pass in football, or putting the basketball hoop only five feet above the floor.

Chicago is the home of 16-inch softball. It is where 90 percent of all 16-inch balls are sold. It has produced every national championship team, as well as all the second-, third-, and fourth-place teams.

Gloves have never been worn here. One reason is that the game was born and developed in much harder times. It could be played by kids whose parents couldn't afford to buy them gloves. The ability to play without gloves—having "good hands"—became a standard of softball excellence.

There are many other reasons why we play barehanded. But it boils down to this: "It just ain't played with gloves. Period."

So why are they now wearing gloves in the national tournament? To satisfy rustics from other parts of the country who are not skillful or brave enough to play without them.

You see, to have a national tournament, you have to have teams from other parts of the country.

But in almost all other parts of the country, they play 12-inch softball, with gloves, a less challenging game.

So for years, these teams would enter the national 16-inch tournament. And when it was over, they would slink away, moaning about their twisted fingers and the painful booboos on their hands.

They would also moan about having been stomped by scores of 50 to 1 by the Chicago teams.

A few years ago, something called the American Softball Association, which is composed of small-town undertakers and chicken farmers, and which runs the national tournament, looked for a way to give the non-Chicago teams a chance to win.

The obvious solution would be for them to try harder, to practice, to learn how to take a dislocated finger and pop it back into place, to learn to live with an occasional fracture of the thumb or a few popped finger tendons. That is the American way—to improve within the rules.

Instead, these lazy, small-town bumpkins took the easy way: They ruled that everybody could use gloves.

It didn't change the results. Last year, the Chicago teams dominated the tournament, despite the gloves.

But that they are being used at all indicates a further weakening of the American character. In some Chicago suburbs, where they don't know any better, teams now use gloves. In a few Chicago parks there are players so lacking in shame that they wear them.

Only two years ago, a Chicago Park District payroller snuck through a rule saying that gloves could be worn in the huge Grant Park league. He probably knew an alderman who had an interest in a glove factory.

I immediately went into court and filed a suit to prohibit the use of gloves in Grant Park. Fortunately, the case was heard by a judge who had the gnarled fingers of an old Chicago softball player, and I won. The judge sneered at the park district people for trying to degrade the traditions of our unique game.

But this weekend, in the stadium in Harvey, they will be wearing them—the teams from places like Iowa and Arizona, South Dakota and Ohio, Virginia and Colorado. And New York, of course. You can always figure on New York to be involved in anything despicable.

They should be arrested for public indecency. And if any readers go out to the games, I urge you to shout the words of Slats Grobnik, who once saw someone try to get into a neighborhood game wearing a glove.

As Slats put it: "If you're gonna wear a glove, you ought to also wear a bra."

October 5, 1979

(Mike wrote this open letter to his readers a few weeks after his first wife, Carol, died suddenly of a brain hemorrhage.)

Thanks to All of You

It helps very much to have friends, including so many whom I've never met.

Many of you have written to me, offering words of comfort, saying you want to help share the grief in the loss of my wife, Carol.

I can't even try to tell you how moved I've been, and I wish I could take your hands and thank each of you personally.

Others have called to ask when I'll be coming back to work. I don't know when. It's not the kind of job that should be done without full enthusiasm and energy. And I regret that I don't have much of either right now.

So I'm going to take a little more time off. There are practical matters I have to take care of. I want to spend time with my sons. And I can use some hours just to think and remember.

Some friends have told me that the less I look to the past the better. Maybe. But I just don't know how to close my mind's door on twenty-five years. That was our next anniversary, November.

Actually, it was much longer than that. We met when she was six and I was nine. Same neighborhood street. Same grammar school. So if you ever have a nine-year-old son who says he is in love, don't laugh at him. It can happen.

People who saw her picture in this paper have told me how beautiful she appeared to be. Yes, she was. As a young man I puffed up with pride when we went out somewhere and heads turned, as they always did.

But later, when heads were still turning, I took more pride in her inner beauty. If there was a shy person at a gathering, that's whom she'd be talking to, and soon that person would be bubbling. If people felt clumsy, homely, and not worth much, she made them feel good about themselves. If someone was old and felt alone, she made them feel loved and needed. None of it was put on. That was the way she was.

I could go on, but it's too personal. And I'm afraid that it hurts. Simply put, she was the best person I ever knew. And while the phrase "his better half" is a cliché, with us it was a truth.

Anyway, I'll be back. And soon, I hope, because I miss you, too, my friends.

In the meantime, do her and me a favor. If there's someone you love but haven't said so in a while, say it now. Always, always, say it now.

November 22, 1979

A November Farewell

The two of them first started spending weekends at the small, quiet Wisconsin lake almost twenty-five years ago. Some of her relatives let them use a tiny cottage in a wooded hollow a mile or so from the water.

He worked odd hours, so sometimes they wouldn't get there until after midnight on a Friday. But if the mosquitoes weren't out, they'd go to the empty beach for a moonlight swim, then sit with their backs against a tree and drink wine and talk about their future.

They were young and had little money, and they came from

working-class families. So to them the cottage was a luxury, although it wasn't any bigger than the boat garages on Lake Geneva, where the rich people played.

The cottage had a screened porch where they sat at night, him playing a guitar and her singing folk songs in a sweet, clear voice. An old man who lived alone in a cottage beyond the next clump of woods would applaud and call out requests.

One summer the young man bought an old motorboat for a couple of hundred dollars. The motor didn't start easily. Some weekends it didn't start at all, and she'd sit and laugh and row while he pulled the rope and swore.

But sometimes it started, and they'd ride slowly along the shoreline, looking at the houses and wondering what it would be like to have a place that was actually on the water. He'd just shake his head because even on a lake without social status, houses on the water cost a lot more than he'd ever be able to afford.

The years passed, they had kids, and after a while they didn't go to the little cottage in the hollow as often. Something was always coming up. He worked on weekends, or they had someplace else to go. Finally the relatives sold the cottage.

Then he got lucky in his work. He made more money than he had ever dreamed they'd have. They remembered how good those weekends had been and they went looking at lakes in Wisconsin to see if they could afford something *on the water.*

They looked at one lake, then another. Then another. Cottages they could afford, they didn't like. Those they liked were overpriced. Or the lake had too many taverns and not enough solitude.

So they went back to the little lake. They hadn't been there for years. They were surprised to find that it was still quiet. That it still had no taverns and one grocery store.

And they saw a For Sale sign in front of a cedar house on the water. They parked and walked around. It was surrounded by big old trees. The land sloped gently down to the shore. On the other side of the road was nothing but woods. Beyond the woods were farms.

On the lake side, the house was all glass sliding doors. It had a large balcony. From the outside it was perfect.

A real estate salesman let them in. The interior was stunning— like something out of a homes magazine.

They knew it had to be out of their reach. But when the salesman told them the price, it was close enough to what they could afford that they had the checkbook out before they saw the second fireplace upstairs.

They hadn't known summers could be that good. In the mornings, he'd go fishing before it was light. She'd sleep until the birds woke her. Then he'd make breakfast and they'd eat omelets on the wooden deck in the shade of the trees.

They got to know the chipmunks, the squirrels, and a woodpecker who took over their biggest tree. They got to know the grocer, an old German butcher who smoked his own bacon, the little farmer who sold them vine-ripened tomatoes and sweet corn.

They were a little selfish about it. They seldom invited friends for weekends. But they didn't feel guilty. It was their own, quiet place.

The best part of their day was dusk. They had a west view and she loved sunsets. Whatever they were doing, they'd always stop to sit on the pier or deck and silently watch the sun go down, changing the color of the lake from blue to purple to silver and black. One evening he made up a small poem:

> *The sun rolls down*
> *like a golden tear*
> *Another day,*
> *Another day*
> *gone.*

She told him it was sad, but that she liked it.

What she didn't like was October, even with the beautiful colors and the evenings in front of the fireplace. She was a summer person. The cold wind wasn't her friend.

And she saw November as her enemy. Sometime in November would be the day they would take up the pier, store the boat, bring in the deck chairs, take down the hammock, pour antifreeze in the plumbing, turn down the heat, lock everything tight, and drive back to the city.

She'd always sigh as they pulled onto the road. He'd try to cheer her up by stopping at a German restaurant that had good food and a corny band, and he'd tell her how quickly the winter would pass, and how soon they'd be there again.

And the snow would finally melt. Spring would come, and one day, when they knew the ice on the lake was gone, they would be back. She'd throw open all the doors and windows and let the fresh air in. Then she'd go out and greet the chipmunks and woodpeckers. And she'd plant more flowers. Every summer, there were more and more flowers. And every summer seemed better than the last. The sunsets seemed to become more spectacular. And more precious.

This past weekend, he closed the place down for the winter. He went alone.

He worked quickly, trying not to let himself think that this particular chair had been her favorite chair, that the hammock had been her Christmas gift to him, that the lovely house on the lake had been his gift to her.

He didn't work quickly enough. He was still there at sunset. It was a great burst of orange, the kind of sunset she loved best.

He tried, but he couldn't watch it alone. Not through tears. So he turned his back on it, went inside, drew the draperies, locked the door, and drove away without looking back.

It was the last time he would ever see that lovely place. Next spring there will be a For Sale sign in front and an impersonal real estate man will show people through.

Maybe a couple who love to quietly watch sunsets together will like it. He hopes so.

PART THREE

THE EIGHTIES

Mike Royko's fans responded with an extraordinary outpouring of letters and telephone calls after his wife's death. Readers didn't simply like his column—they also loved him. Their reaction surprised and moved him, and it spurred him on to give them what they wanted no matter how heartsick he felt. He attacked the 1980s, his third decade in the column business, with some of his most brash, funny, and provocative writing. "A Poll Cut on the Bias" is typical. Offensive? Well, what can you expect from a fellow named Phil T. Slobb? To complainers who couldn't or wouldn't get the satire in this and other columns, he sometimes wrote back offering to refund their 25 cents or 35 cents or whatever the newspaper cost at the time.

His humor zinged current fads and foibles, as in the portrait of the newly tamed Agent 007 in "Time Weakens the Bond" and the trendy lakefront dweller in "Mike Royko—High-Rise Man." Occasionally it was just plain zany, as in his diatribe against his most hated appendages, "These Feet Are Made for Nothing."

But there were changes in his work. The themes of love and loss recurred, often in the form of artful little essays written immediately after he learned of the death of someone he had admired. In the process, he would reveal as much about Mike Royko as about his subject (see "Fred Astaire Was a Class Act until the End"). Readers adored "A Lovely Couple, Bound with Love" and "A Pact to Cherish," which was an open letter to Prince Charles and Lady Diana on the day of their wedding. "A Pact" was destined to be another of his classic columns published widely in magazines, books, and other newspapers. Mike's readers have long memories; requests for copies poured into his office again when the royal couple split.

The old Chicago Democratic machine, already teetering when Mayor Richard J. Daley died in 1976, was beaten down by federal court decisions that severely restricted hiring and firing for political reasons. Television commercials replaced the precinct captain. Local politics simply weren't as much fun to write about anymore, although Mike did regale readers with bizarre anecdotes of city government under Mayor Jane M. Byrne, a feisty Daley protégée whom he quickly dubbed "Mayor Bossy." When Harold Washington defeated her in the Democratic primary election early in 1983, it seemed as if half of Chicago—the white half—was in shock over the prospect of a black man running City Hall. That inspired Mike to produce another of his classics on the night of Washington's primary victory, "Give Washington a Break," with its memorable opening line: "So I told Uncle Chester: Don't worry, Harold Washington doesn't want to marry your sister."

Washington went on to win the general election April 12, but by only 51.7 percent of the vote—the tiniest margin since the Democrats took over Chicago's City Hall fifty-two years earlier. He was a genial political pro and a populist whose attempts at reform were constantly in the news, but he was not fodder for the Royko column. Mike seldom wrote about Mayor Washington. There was abundant inspiration, though, in the administration of President Ronald Reagan and its humungous military budget, its homage to affluence, its Lt. Col. Oliver North. Where but in Washington in the 1980s would you find carnations sprinkled at appropriate intervals in the toilet bowls of a hotel ladies' room? And who but Mike Royko could write about it so exquisitely as in "A GOP Function Flush with Luxuries"?

The growing political influence of religious conservatives inspired "Slats Mistakes GOP for GOD," with Mike arguing that Jesus was too much of a social radical to have been a Republican. This column marked a significant departure. Slats was now an adult, not just a gawky pal in Mike's nostalgic trips back to his boyhood. The mature Slats had a new role: the level-headed but anxious Everyman, in need of reassurance to cope with the vagaries of the day.

The *Chicago Sun-Times,* like the *Daily News* before it, included the Royko column in the package of news and features it sold to other publications. Mike was not syndicated individually, as were most Washington-based columnists. This made his column more expensive to other newspapers (and less financially rewarding to Mike), but the number of papers that wanted him grew steadily. The Royko column became the linchpin of the *Sun-Times* package. Understandably, the *Sun-Times* management did not want him to break away and sign with a syndicate that would sell his column separately. He didn't want it, either; he still feared he might flop out there alone, that he couldn't generate enough good material for a national audience—even though by the early 1980s the strictly local columns were a minor part of his work.

Mike had formed some close friendships among *Sun-Times* reporters. Two of them, Pam Zekman and her husband, Rick Soll, changed his life in 1982 by arranging a blind date with Judy Arndt, who ran the *Sun-Times* public service bureau. She was smart, witty, and beautiful. They shared a passion for sports and for politics (she had worked in Washington for a congressman and for the public-interest group Common Cause). A tennis pro, she gave him lessons. He taught her to play golf. In 1979 he had told friends he knew he must go on living and working, but he could never be happy again; in 1985 he and Judy were married, and for the rest of his life he marveled at his good fortune. Their son, Sam, was born in 1987 and their daughter, Kate, in 1992.

The *Sun-Times* was a financial as well as professional success, so the staff was shocked when news circulated in 1983 that the Field brothers, Marshall and Ted, had decided to sell it. Both wanted the capital for other ventures—Ted to produce movies, Marshall to invest in real estate. It was even more of a blow when word leaked that the Fields would sell to Rupert Murdoch, the Australian media tycoon notorious for his trashy, sensationalized newspapers. Mike lobbied frantically with Marshall Field to sell instead to a Chicago group that included Jim Hoge, the *Sun-Times* publisher. Field said it was too late, the agreement he had signed with Murdoch was legally binding. Mike responded by signing a contract with the *Chicago Tribune,* which had been yearning for him for a dozen years. His departure was hardly a surprise; when the Fields first revealed their intention to sell to Murdoch, Mike announced in a television interview that "no self-respecting fish" would consent to be wrapped in a Rupert Murdoch paper. His first *Tribune* column appeared the day Murdoch became the official owner of the *Sun-Times.*

Strangely, a Royko column also appeared in the *Sun-Times* that day. Murdoch insisted that Mike's *Sun-Times* contract barred him from moving to a competitor, so he ordered the paper to rerun old columns. Mike's lawyer argued that the sale voided that contract. A Cook County judge agreed, and after a few days the *Sun-Times* stopped the reruns. The entire episode, naturally, gave Mike some delightful *Tribune* columns, including the pungent rebuke "In Alien's Tongue, 'I Quit' Is 'Vacation.' "

Mike had never before worked on a newspaper as big and financially secure as the *Chicago Tribune.* He was no longer subjected to the frequent assertion that the well-being of his paper depended on his column, a concept he detested. But the fun of being surrounded by a scrappy staff reveling in its role of under-dog also was gone. A number of his friends, though, had left the *Sun-Times* for the *Tribune* when Murdoch took over, and Mike's new assistant was Hanke Gratteau, who had done previous tours of duty with him at the *Daily News* and the *Sun-Times.*

Switching to the *Tribune* was not a difficult choice. "I used to beat up on it years ago," Mike told interviewer Chris Rob-ling. "It was the big Republican right-wing monster. But it had changed. . . . By the time I went over to the Tribune, you had a wild-eyed populist, Jim Squires, running the paper, and he hired a number of really fine people. . . . So I didn't have any trouble at all going there. The only trouble I had was figuring out their computer."

Mike's misgivings about Rupert "The Alien" Murdoch turned out to be justified. The *Sun-Times* rapidly deteriorated into sen-sationalism and chaos. Its editor, managing editor, editorial page staff, financial editor, city editor, and other key people left, as did a sizable portion of its readers. After a few years Murdoch sold the paper, and it began a long struggle to regain its credibility and standing in the community.

At the *Tribune,* Mike resurrected a festive event he had begun at the *Sun-Times:* rib-cooking contests in the lakefront's Grant Park, huge community parties so popular that succulent aromas—and haze—hovered over the downtown area.

The Royko column did not change in style or substance. His inimitable brew of toughness and mischief, sentiment and wisdom continued. There was a dramatic change, though, in his status. Tribune Media Services syndicated his column, so for the first time other newspapers could buy it individually, not as part of a package deal. The response was enormous. Within a few years, he was appearing in about 600 papers, an extraordinary number for a general-interest column.

His attacks on bureaucratic stupidity, which helped launch his career, remained an important part of his repertoire. Sometimes the result was hilarious, as in "A Grave Report from Medicare," the saga of a professor who could not convince the system that he was alive. Sometimes Mike's fury fairly steamed up from the page, as in "If This Isn't Danger, What Is?" This account of judicial in-difference toward a horribly battered baby brought results. But, as Mike wrote in a subsequent column, "Abused Baby 1, System a Big 0," he felt that no matter how often he wrote about this issue and forced action in one particular case, he accomplished "noth-ing more than a Band-Aid for a massive hemorrhage."

By the late 1980s, Mike rarely wrote about Chicago politics. One exception was "Daley the Elder and Daley the Younger," which found eerie similarities in the careers of the father and the son. Four months later, Richard M. Daley was elected mayor of Chicago, as Mike had predicted. And, although he didn't mention it in this column, the father's most famous critic had a major role in the ascendancy of the son. Mike was fond of him, and his columns had helped the younger Daley become Cook County State's Attorney, his stepping stone to the mayor's office.

June 3, 1980

A Poll Cut on the Bias

The national polls show that an overwhelming majority of Americans oppose admitting any Cuban refugees into this country.

I've conducted my own poll, and it has the same results.

My poll was limited to only one person—my friend, Phil T. Slobb. I didn't have to poll anyone else because he has always been an accurate barometer of public opinion.

The poll consisted of the following questions and his answers:

Should this country have let in the Cubans?

"Hell no. We should never let in any kinds of foreigners."

None?

"That's what I said."

What are your feelings about Poles?

"We shouldn't have ever let them in. The big dummies can't even speak English. I got on the Milwaukee Avenue bus a few nights ago, and it was loaded with a lot of scrub ladies going home and they were all jabbering in Polish. Why do we let them come here and scrub the floors of our office buildings when we could hire good Americans to scrub floors? Did you hear about the two Polacks who hijacked a submarine? They asked for a million dollars and two parachutes. Hah!"

What about Italians?

"If we had kept them out we would never have wound up with Al Capone and Paul Ricca and other bums like that. We should never let in another Italian. Hell, what do we need them for? We can cook our own spaghetti. You know why Polish jokes are so short? So Italians can understand them."

And the Irish?

"Are you kidding? The Micks are nothing but a bunch of political crooks. What have they ever done except run for office so they can steal my tax money. And the ones who didn't run for office became cops so they could shake me down. All the Irish ever contributed to this country was municipal corruption. By the way, do you know why Irish wakes last three days?"

Why?

"So they can make sure the guy is dead, and not just drunk."

Do you have any feelings about Lithuanians?

"Yeah. They're almost as dumb as the Polacks, and they're twice as mean. The day we let the first Loogin in this country, the average IQ dropped by ten points. Do you know how a Lithuanian pilot navigates an airplane?"

How?

"By reading street signs."

How about Bohemians?

"Look, those people are all the same—Bohemians, Serbians, Yugoslavians, Latvians, Hungarians, Slovaks. They're cheapskates, and all they want to do is stick a lamb on a stick and roast it, drink beer, and play loud music on their mandolins. You can't even pronounce their names. They're as bad as the Polacks and Loogins. You know how you can tell the mother-in-law at a Bohunk wedding? She's the one on her knees, picking up the rice."

I don't suppose you care much for the Greeks?

"What do I need a Greek for? I know how to make a hamburger. I went in a Greek restaurant once and they were all jumping around to that Zorba music and snapping their fingers, and when I ordered some cheese they set it on fire. You know how many Greeks it takes to screw in a light bulb? One to put in the bulb and the other one to burn the place down for insurance."

And the Chinese?

"No gooks of any kind. Chinks, Japs, Koreans, Vietnamese, none of them. We're always having a war with one kind of gook or another, so why do we let them in? And the rats have screwed up our economy with their little cars and TV sets. I say, no more gooks. You know what sound a Japanese camera makes? Crick."

What are your feelings about Jews?

"What do you think my feelings are? Every used car I ever had, I bought from a Jew and they were all clunkers."

What about the French?

"Those people eat snails, and anybody who eats a snail is a creep."

I won't even ask you about blacks.

"Don't bother. You couldn't print it."

But they didn't ask to come here.

"Then they should leave."

I don't suppose you care for other Hispanics, besides the Cubans. Mexicans? Puerto Ricans?

"That's right, I don't care for them. You know why a Puerto Rican can't use a checkbook? Because it's too small for him to spray his name on. Hah! Pretty good, huh?"

Hilarious. I gather, then, that you think this country should not have let anyone in except the early English settlers.

"I wouldn't have let them in either. What do you think the hillbillies are? If the English hadn't come here, we wouldn't have nearly as many hillbillies as we have now. We've had hillbillies in this country for 200 years, and what have they contributed? They invented stock car racing and the demolition derby, that's all. If we hadn't let the English in, we wouldn't have that peanut picker in the White House."

Then there's nobody you like.

"I like Americans."

What kind?

"The kind that are already here. Like me."

June 27, 1980

Demolition Derby

We've been trying to get an answer to a simple question: Who actually demolished Carlos Rodriguez's beautifully renovated house?

We already know that the City of Chicago's legal department went to court and got a demolition order because it thought the house was still an empty, dangerous wreck.

And we know that the U.S. Housing and Urban Development Department stupidly agreed to let the house be demolished, even though it had sold the house to Rodriguez, who spent a year renovating it.

But we don't know which private demolition company the city hired to do the job.

This would be worth knowing because we'd like to ask the demolition contractor how he could be so dumb as to go to a house that looked like it was brand new—new roof, new siding, new porches, new wallboard, new plumbing, new carpet, new furnace, new tile, new everything—and still demolish it.

You would think that it might occur to him that when a house looks new, the paint smells new, and there are still tools inside, a mistake might have been made.

You would think that he might go to a phone, call the city's demolition department, and say: "Say, this house looks new. It's beautiful. Are you sure you want it demolished?"

But a mystery exists. Nobody will admit knowing which contractor did the demolition job.

Records in the city's demolition department are supposed to show who the contractor is for every demolished building.

But when we called Sam Schiro, the supervisor of demolition for the city, he looked up the file on the demolished building and we had this rather bizarre conversation:

Who did the demolition work?

"Let me explain the way we work first. HUD authorizes a building to be demolished. When we receive their consent orders, we advertise for competitive bids. The lowest bid from a contractor gets the job."

Yes, but I'm mainly interested in what happened at 260 W. 106th Street. Why can't you find a demolition contract or demolition permit for that property?

"Because the building was taken off the list of those buildings which HUD told us to demolish. A contractor was not told to demolish that building because it was not on the list."

Why was it removed from the list?

"Because in November, HUD telephoned and canceled the consent [for demolition]."

And so the property was removed from the demolition list?
"Yes."

And no permit for demolition was ever issued?

"Not for demolition, because HUD voided their consent."

Then how did the building get torn down?"

"Someone tore the building down."

Yes, but who did it?

"Who did it? I don't know. But they left a pile of debris. And now we're advertising for bids to get the pile of debris removed."

You are saying your department didn't have anything to do with having this building demolished? That some unknown persons just went in and demolished it on their own?

"We have this problem throughout the city."

Pardon me. Demolishing buildings is widespread?

"Well, we have a problem with brick stealers. With bricks so expensive, some derelict-type people see a building that's open, maybe from a fire, and they'll pull up, put a chain around a wall, and pull out the whole thing."

Uh, this was a frame building, with aluminum siding.

"But brick stealing does exist. We have even issued an order to the police department to apprehend any people who are stealing bricks."

Do you have any theories as to how the Rodriguez building was demolished?

"I dunno. It seems like a police matter to me."

That is one of the damndest things I have ever heard come from the lips of a payroller or bureaucrat.

The man is actually proposing that some mysterious people, for unknown reasons, took it upon themselves to totally demolish a building.

I know that we have many vandals in this city. But I've never heard of vandals so enthusiastic that they completely flatten a building.

Nor have I heard of any vandals who bring out their own heavy equipment, which neighbors of the demolished building said was used.

But there are many things I have never heard of, so maybe Mr. Schiro is right. Maybe we now have super vandals in Chicago.

If so, I would like to make a public plea to these super vandals:

Hey, guys, I have a real challenge for you. Go demolish City Hall.

And be sure not to miss Mr. Schiro's office.

November 18, 1980

Time Weakens the Bond

(Recent news item: The literary executors of the late Ian Fleming's estate have decided to bring Secret Agent James Bond back to life. Another mystery writer has been chosen to write three books about Bond. Fleming died in 1964, after writing fourteen books about the dashing British agent. Author John Gardner, who will write the new Bond books, said Bond, whose adventures took place during the 1950s and early 1960s, will be brought into the 1980s. He will have more modest personal habits and will be sensitive to such modern developments as women's liberation.)

Upon learning that Bond was returning, I phoned him and arranged for us to have dinner. He suggested we meet at his club. He arrived at 6:30 P.M. and strode purposefully into the dining room.

"Sorry I'm late," he said, "but I had trouble finding a parking place."

"How is it running?" I asked.

"What?"

"Your car. I can still see it. One of the last of the great four-and-a-half liter Bentleys, with the supercharger by Amherst Villiers. Battleship gray, I recall, and a convertible. Capable of cruising easily at 90 miles an hour with another 30 miles an hour in reserve. Do you still retain the same devoted mechanic who tunes it for you?"

"Good Lord, no. I got rid of that thing years ago. Couldn't afford the gas. Eight miles to the gallon. I'm driving a VW Rabbit these days."

"A VW Rabbit? You? But how could you ever outrun an agent from SMERSH, the dreaded killer agency, in a Rabbit?"

"Not that difficult. Most of them are driving Honda Civics. We just keep going until one of us runs out of gas, actually. Best m.p.g. survives."

The waiter came to take our drink order. Before Bond could speak, I interrupted:

"Let me order, James. I think I remember your favorite before-dinner drink down to the tiniest detail. Waiter, bring Commander Bond a dry martini. But serve it in a deep champagne goblet. You will make it with three measures of Gordon's Gin, one measure of vodka, half a measure of Kina Lillet. Shake it very well until it is ice cold, then add a large, thin slice of lemon peel. If you have a vodka made with grain instead of potatoes, it will be even better. Do I have it right, James?"

"Yes, but I think I'll skip the martini tonight."

"Of course. Then you prefer a double bourbon on the rocks. That was one of your favorites, too."

"Uh, no bourbon tonight. I think I'll just have a glass of white wine."

"What? White wine? You? At least have the Brut Blanc de Blanc 1943, if they have it, which you considered the finest champagne in the world. I distinctly remember your telling that to the beautiful Vesper Lynd the first time you and she dined at Casino Royale."

"Please, just white wine. Or even Perrier. I'll be truthful: Do you remember all those people I killed? Do you know why I killed them?"

"Of course I do. You were Agent 007. The 00 designation gave you license to kill."

"Actually, that's not entirely true. The reason I killed them was that I was loaded to the gills most of the time. Bourbon before lunch, crazy martinis before dinner. Champagne. Then cognac after dinner. By the time I got around to my job, everybody I met looked like a Russian spy to me. I think the last five people I shot were all innocent bystanders."

"Didn't know that, James. Then let's skip the drinks and order dinner."

As we looked at the menus, I studied Bond's appearance.

For evening wear, he used to wear a thin, double-ended black satin tie, a silk shirt, and a single-breasted dinner jacket.

"Do you still have the same tailor?" I asked.

"No. Inflation. Can't afford it anymore. This suit is from the Johnny Carson line. Double knit. Do you like it?"

"Oh, yes, of course."

He took out a cigarette and lit it. He caught me staring at the cigarette.

"Something wrong?" he asked.

"Well, as I recall, you used to smoke your own brand. A Turkish and Balkan mixture made to your specifications at Morland on Grosvenor Street. They had three golden bands. Those don't appear to be the same."

"No, they're not. These are called Breath. No tars, no nicotine. Made of dandelion, actually. Couldn't take those Morlands anymore. Every time I tried to sneak up on some Russian agent to kill him, he'd hear me coughing and wheezing a mile away."

"I see. And I notice your lighter. That isn't your old black oxidized Ronson?"

"No. It's a Cricket propane. I buy them in packages of three at the discount store. Lost my Ronson."

The waiter appeared for our dinner order.

"At least we can eat the way you used to, James. Ah, what a gourmet you were. Let's see if I remember some of your favorite dishes. We shall have the Beluga caviar, with thick hot toast. Then possibly some stone crab legs with faintly burnt butter in which to dip them. And you would like rare tournedos with sauce bearnaise and a coeur d'articaut. Will that do?"

"Uh, I really would prefer broiled whitefish with some cottage cheese on the side. And a salad with just some lemon."

"James! You, cottage cheese? What about prime rib? Or the cold langouste? And some pâté de foie gras? You never ate cottage cheese in your life."

"And I wound up with a fifty-two-inch waistline. The Russian agents used to laugh at me and call me Agent Double-O-Tubbo. I was a wreck. Actually, I think I'll just have the California Fruit Salad with yogurt."

"Well, you still look trim, so the diet must help. Tell me, James, are you still the same ruthless cad with the women? I remember how you put it when a female agent was assigned to work with you. You said women were for recreation. On a job they got in the way and fogged things up with sex and hurt feelings and all the emotional baggage they carried around. One had to look out for them and take care of them. Then, of course, you slept with her."

"Well, uh, no. I now have a significant other."

"A what?"

"A significant other. That's someone with whom you live and have a meaningful relationship to the exclusion of others."

"I see."

"Yes, we jog together. Ten miles a day, although she can do twelve."

"James, why did you come back?"

"Damned if I know."

January 20, 1981

Epitaph for Jimmy

It's just not Jimmy Carter's day. Or week. Or year. Or decade.

Even though it appears that just before leaving office he will finally manage to get the American hostages released in Iran, he's not going to receive much credit for it. The coach whose team wins the Super Bowl will be a bigger national hero.

Already people ranging from national commentators to the man in the street are saying that Carter should have pulled it off a long time ago, or that he should not have paid such a stiff ransom, or that he should have been much tougher all along, and that the taking of hostages shouldn't have happened in the first place.

Some people are even trying to give President-elect Ronald Reagan credit for the hostage release. Among others, William

Mike at a book-signing for one of his early collections. Pictured with him are author Studs Terkel (left), book dealer Arlene Wimmer, and author Nelson Algren.

Mike at a fund-raiser in the 1960s. Pictured behind him is John Belushi, who would later become famous on *Saturday Night Live*.

Mike stands on an overpass against a backdrop of the downtown Chicago skyline in the early 1970s. Courtesy AP/Wide World Photos and *Chicago Tribune.*

Sam Sianis, owner of Billy Goat's Tavern, and Mike were as close as brothers. Here they are shown at a party in 1971 celebrating the publication of *Boss.* Courtesy Chicago Sun-Times, Inc.

Mike gets ready to pitch in 1971 for his beloved *Chicago Daily News* softball team. Courtesy Chicago Sun-Times, Inc.

Mike waves a rubber chicken over his special barbecue sauce as his assistant, Helene McEntee, stirs the pot in 1982 at the First Royko RibFest, a competition that drew thousands of contestants and spectators. Courtesy AP/Wide World Photos and *Chicago Tribune*.

Mike and Mayor Harold Washington got along well. Here they are pictured in 1983 at the Second Royko RibFest.

Mike strikes a dapper pose for a fashion layout in the March 21, 1986, edition of the *Chicago Tribune:* "Mike Royko, a Chicago tastemaker and rib connoisseur, models Oxxford worsted wool suit, $950; Neiman-Marcus private label cotton shirt, $42.50; Turnbull & Asser silk tie, $40; Churchill Ltd. homburg, $78; Neiman-Marcus private label lace-up shoes, $125; Brigg umbrella, $85. All available at Neiman-Marcus." Photograph by Tony Berardi. Courtesy *Chicago Tribune.*

Mike and Studs Terkel swap stories of the neighborhood tavern in a 1991 segment of the PBS series *The '90s*. Courtesy Studs Terkel and *Chicago Tribune*.

Safire, the *New York Times* pro-Reagan columnist, says that because Reagan called the Iranians a few nasty names a couple of weeks ago, they were frightened into dealing with the milder Carter while they still have the chance, rather than facing the terrors of the Reagan administration.

Maybe they're right. I don't know, because I've never seen anything that lends itself to second-guessing the way the hostage situation has.

But I do know that once the hostages were taken, the most important things that had to be done were to keep them alive while working to bring about their release.

Right from the start, though, there were those who said that preserving our national honor was of equal importance to freeing the hostages.

To preserve our national honor, we would have had to impose a strict deadline and if the hostages weren't out in time, we would have had to go in shooting.

That's what it would have eventually required because it was obvious that the religious fanatics who were running Iran weren't going to be swayed by economic sanctions, tough talk, or even the threat of death. It's hard to frighten someone who is convinced that dying for a cause will provide a one-way ticket to heaven.

But the national honor fever grew, fueled by nightly doses of irresponsible network TV coverage of frenzied but harmless (and staged) demonstrations outside our embassy in Iran. It reached the point where people who had spent the Vietnam War hiding behind deferments were now talking about bombing Iran back to the Stone Age.

And the national honor fever finally got to Carter, goading him into committing the one genuinely stupid act of the entire affair, which was when he sent in the helicopters for a dramatic rescue attempt that failed and caused needless deaths.

From the beginning, the question of our national honor shouldn't have had any place in our thinking, any more than police honor and community honor and any other kind of honor has any place in dealing with domestic kidnappers and hostage-takers. Have you ever heard the parents of a kidnapped child talk about preserving their honor?

And how could we talk about honor when our involvement in Iran goes back to the dishonorable act of propping up the rule of a vicious thief like the late shah? (Americans fume when one of our politicians retires from public life with a million or two more than when he began his career, but we weren't able to understand the feelings of the Iranians about a ruling family that stashed billions of dollars in foreign banks.)

How comforting would a sense of unsullied national honor have been if the price had been dead hostages, dead Iranians, dead American troops, and even worse chaos in the world?

But right up to the past weekend there were still those who were talking about declaring war on Iran, going in shooting, and other nonsense.

Well, revenge always feels good. But that's not the way things work in the real world.

For example: I no longer hold grudges against the Chinese because they wanted to kill me during a nervous year in Korea. When Richard Nixon ate egg rolls with them, and said it was time we acted polite toward each other, I went along with it.

Our streets now teem with Japanese and German cars, and Japanese and German tourists. And not too long ago, they gave us a much harder time than the Iranians have.

In less than a full lifetime, our enemies have become our buddies, our buddies become our enemies, and our buddies-turned-enemies become buddies again.

So there's not much point in fantasizing about revenge on the Iranians. Because of the hostages, they've already made a shambles of their own economy and it might take years for them to straighten themselves out.

Who knows, it might not be long before Americans are taking midwinter vacations in sunny Iran.

Meanwhile, as Jimmy Carter heads quietly back to Georgia, it's only fair to note that his approach, slow as it was, got the job done.

It's not much of an epitaph, but as a friend of mine put it: "Well, he finally did *something* right."

March 17, 1981

These Feet Are Made for Nothing

With some people, the problem is always the back. With me, it's feet.

So I wasn't really surprised during the past weekend when I suddenly found myself howling and hopping on one foot around my kitchen. The thought went through my mind: "It figures, it figures."

The reason I was hopping on one foot was that I had been cooking some spaghetti. But instead of pouring the boiling water into the sink, I aimed badly and poured it on my bare foot.

On the way to the hospital, I watched without sympathy as my foot changed colors.

If it hadn't been for the pain, I might have pointed a finger at it and said: "Foot, you got exactly what you deserve."

The fact is, I dislike my feet. At times the feelings border on hatred. As far back as I can remember, they've been nothing but trouble.

You might wonder how a person can hate his own feet. I don't think that's unusual. Some people hate their own noses. Or their teeth.

At least they can go to a plastic surgeon and get a nose job, or get their teeth capped.

But when you hate your own feet, there's not much you can do about it except try to ignore them or swear when you happen to see them.

And that's one of the problems with feet. They're hard to ignore. The first thing I see every morning are my feet, sticking up at the other end of the bed.

So I start each morning by saying: "Hello, you lousy, ugly, gnarled, painful b————s. I hate both of you!"

That's not the best way to begin the day, I suppose, but it does get me into the proper frame of mind for my job.

As I lie there looking at my feet, I'm always struck by how ugly they are.

Most feet aren't very good looking. I can't remember anybody being renowned for his or her stunningly attractive feet, although there are strange people whose pulses race at the sight of a toe. Or so they say when they write about their fantasies to Penthouse Forum.

But for ugliness, mine have always been in a class by themselves.

When I was born, the first thing my mother said to me was: "He takes after his father. Look at those feet."

She was right. My father had size 12 feet. And so did I—on the day I was born.

And the doctor later said that I was the only infant he had ever seen come into the world with calluses and corns and cracked toenails.

My toes are longer than most people's fingers. If the toes were extended, I'd probably wear a size 20 shoe. But they curl under about three times so they look more like large, clenched fists than feet.

They're also very wide. They might be as wide as they are long, which has always made it difficult for me to find shoes that fit properly.

When I was a kid, we'd spend hours at the shoe stores looking for shoes that were wide enough. One salesman finally gave up and said:

"Lady, the only place you'll find a shoe that fits this kid is at a blacksmith's shop."

We finally found something that fit perfectly. They were comfortable, but a lot of people looked twice when they saw someone walking around with two baseball gloves on his feet.

Then there's the arch. Basically, there are two kinds of arches.

The normal arch curves upward, providing the foot with flexibility and acting as a shock absorber for the spine.

The flat foot has little or no curve.

Mine is in a class by itself. The arch curves downward, sort of like the bottom of a rocking chair.

This makes it difficult for me to stand up without swaying back and forth, which has led to considerable misunderstanding, especially in bars.

When I was in the service, we'd all be standing at attention. Then the wind would blow. With my arms stiff at my side, I'd sway forward, then backward. Pretty soon, I'd be going back and forth like a rocker, first my nose, then the back of my head grazing the ground.

The commanding officer didn't know what to do with someone like that, so he finally assigned me to the base orchestra, where I was the metronome.

You can learn to live with feet like mine, but you have to take certain precautions.

For example, I took a vacation at the seashore once. In the evening, I'd take long, barefoot walks along the beach.

One morning, I noticed a crowd of men studying my footprints in the sand. They were from the police, the conservation department, and the local zoo.

One of them shook his head and said: "I don't know what kind of creature it is, but we better post some armed guards here at night."

My feet have probably sensed how I've felt about them, and they've retaliated by getting themselves stubbed and stepped on every chance they get. I don't even take it personally when someone steps on my foot anymore. I just say: "Don't apologize, he had it coming. Step on the other one, too. He's just as bad."

And I wouldn't have even gone to the hospital when I burned my foot, except that I have to live with it.

When the doctor came into the emergency room, he asked me what happened.

"I just poured a pot of boiling water on it."

He shook his head and said: "Boy, it really does look awful."

"Doc," I said, "it's the other one."

May 13, 1981

Algren's Golden Pen

I remember almost to the moment the first time I saw the name Nelson Algren.

It was in a tent in Korea about three decades ago. The guy in the next bunk flipped a paperback book at me and said: "Hey, here's a book about Chicago. You want it?"

I glanced over the blurbs on the cover to see what it was about. One blurb said something to the effect that this book was set in a "slum" in Chicago. And it described the slum as being the Division Street area.

Slum? I was offended. That was no slum. That was my neighborhood.

Curious, I went ahead and read the book, and I was stunned. It was the first time I had read a novel that was set in a place I knew. And Algren, with *The Man with the Golden Arm,* had captured it. He had the people, the sounds, the alleys, the streets, the feel of the place.

It's a strange sensation to read a novel about a place you know well. It had never occurred to me, growing up in that neighborhood, that it contained the stuff a great book can be made of. The great books, as they were force-fed to us in the schools, were about other countries, other cultures, other centuries. And the duller they were, the greater they were.

But here was somebody named Nelson Algren writing about Division Street and Milwaukee Avenue, and the dope heads and boozers and the card hustlers. The kind of broken people Algren liked to describe as responding to the city's brawny slogan of "I Will" with a painful: "But What If I Can't?"

I didn't know it then, but many Chicagoans weren't pleased by Algren's book, even though it won the first National Book Award for fiction, sort of an Oscar for writers.

Among those who were displeased were the so-called leaders of the city's Polish community—people who were big on joining the Polish National Alliance and other such organizations.

They believed that because many of his characters were Polish, Algren was presenting them in a poor light. I guess they would have preferred that he write a novel about a Polish dentist who changed his name and moved from the old neighborhood to a suburb as soon as he made enough money.

So for years they sniped at Algren, tried to keep him out of the libraries, and made themselves look foolish. As one of them—an insurance broker—once said to me: "I didn't know anybody like the characters in his books." Well, I did. And I saw some of them off when they went to prison or the morgue.

After reading my first Algren novel, I made a point of finding his other works. He had done other novels, and a wonderful prose poem about Chicago called *Chicago: City on the Make.*

But my favorite of all his writings was his collection of short stories called *The Neon Wilderness.* Bitter-sweet stories. Funny-sad stories. I think they're among the finest short stories written by an American.

I told him that the first time I met him, about seventeen years ago. He had invited me to a gathering in his walk-up flat overlooking Wicker Park, near Damen, North, and Milwaukee.

That's where he lived for most of his years in Chicago. It's a funny thing about the rewards of the writing trade in this country: You can pick up *People* magazine and see this or that commercial, best-selling hack lounging by his pool in Beverly Hills, or swaggering about his estate on Martha's Vineyard. Or you can read about some wordsmith who stole the plot of *Moby Dick,* turned the whale into a white shark, and made a fast million or two.

Meanwhile, someone like Algren never got out of Wicker Park and couldn't always make the rent until a small check for a book review came in the mail.

But, he would have to admit, that's the kind of thing that always happened to the losers in his stories, so why not to the author of those stories?

Not that he ever beefed about life around Wicker Park. It had many advantages.

For one, there were the Luxor Baths on North Avenue, once considered the finest steam bath joint in town. When it opened in the 1920s, Mayor Big Bill Thompson himself showed up to honor it by accepting a squirt of steam on his big gut.

Although I always argued that the Russian Baths on Division Street had more class, Algren preferred the Luxor and would spend many hours soaking up steam and listening to the bookies, loan sharks, precinct captains, and his other favorite creatures discussing events of the day.

He could always find a poker game in the back of a barber shop or saloon, or an ex-prizefighter to describe how he almost became a contender.

And when there was nothing else going on, he could sit on his third-floor porch and watch the passing scene—which often included somebody with a brick chasing somebody with a wallet.

In many other countries, a writer of Algren's stature would have been given a chair at a university, assured of a reasonable income, and asked only to write to his heart's content. They do that in this country, too, but usually for dull writers who know how to play university politics and act properly at the dean's wife's teas. Algren tried it briefly, but he talked too tough for them, and I think he pinched a few coeds, so they asked him to go away.

He moved from Chicago a few years ago, and had a great time announcing that he no longer liked this city, and that it had never appreciated him. Neither statement was true, and he knew it. But he liked saying such things to create a controversy. We had dinner the night before he left and the fact was, he was moving because he felt like moving.

He tried New Jersey for awhile, and finally wound up in a pretty, old whaling town on Long Island, New York. That's where he died a few days ago and was buried on Monday.

If the mayor and some of those stiffs in the city council can see their way clear, it would be a nice gesture for them to rename one of the little streets around Wicker Park after him. Algren Court, or Algren Place. Nothing big. He wouldn't expect it.

And if you get a chance, you might want to read some of his writings. Any good bookstore can probably order them for you.

You might even come across a 1967 printing of those short stories I mentioned, *The Neon Wilderness*.

If you do, check the printed dedication. As I said earlier, the first time I met him, I told him I thought the short stories were the best things he ever wrote. I was afraid he might be offended, since he considered himself foremost a novelist. But he listened, nodded politely, and said: "That's interesting."

A few years later, a new, hardcover edition of the short stories came out. He had a little party to celebrate, and when we went home, he handed us each a book.

It wasn't until a few days later that I opened it and saw the printed dedication. It said: "For Mike Royko."

It's still one of the nicest things anyone ever did for me.

May 15, 1981

Dear God: Why?

To: God
Address: Somewhere in the Universe

Dear God:

I know how busy you must be with a whole universe to worry about. That's why it occurred to me that you don't have time to read our papers and your TV reception might not be good. So I thought I'd drop you a note about how things are going here.

Well, things couldn't be going any better, at least as far as your image is concerned. You wouldn't believe how well loved you are on this planet today and how much is being done in your name.

I hardly know where to start, there's so much going on. So I might as well start in Northern Ireland, where you've always been very big. Ah, what religious fervor can be found there.

The Irish Protestants are so devoted to you that they do everything possible to make life miserable for the Irish Catholics, because they don't think the Irish Catholics have the right approach toward worshipping you.

And the Irish Catholics do what they can to make life miserable for the Irish Protestants for essentially the same reason.

In their great love for you, they shoot at one another, bomb one another, set one another afire, and kill little children, bystanders, cops, soldiers, and old ladies, and some are now committing suicide by starvation.

Then each side buries its dead, goes to church, and gives fervent thanks to you for being on its side. It is very touching.

And one thing about these people: Their devotion to you is unshakable. They've been doing this for about 400 years. So it's a good thing that you have an entire universe at your disposal, because I don't know where else you could find room to accommodate the souls of all the people who have died there in your name.

You're also highly regarded in a country called Lebanon, where just about everyone believes in you, although they don't agree on what you should be called.

In that country, there are Moslems and Christians and they've created different sets of rules for worshipping you. Naturally, they say you have sent the rules down to them. I don't know if that's true or not, but if I may make a suggestion: If it's true that you gave them the word, it would really simplify things if there were only one set of rules. It would cause less hard feelings.

But such details aside, they are expressing their devotion to you by killing each other by the hundreds. I guess they figure that if one side can wipe the other side out, it will prove that their way of worshipping you is correct, and you'll be pleased with them.

So every day, they lob shells at one another and blow up the usual men, women, children, bystanders, old ladies, and stray dogs. And every day, they take a few moments out to thank you for your support and to promise that they'll continue their efforts in your behalf.

Now, not far from there are countries called Iraq and Iran. The Moslems in those countries basically agree on what to call you, but they disagree on some details concerning how best to worship you. So they're killing one another, too.

It's more than a little confusing, though, because in Iran there are people who call themselves Baha'i, and they, too, have their own way of showing their respect for you. Unfortunately for the Baha'i, their way doesn't include killing others who don't share their point of view. So that makes them patsies, and the Moslems in Iran, in their love for you, have been kicking the Baha'i around pretty good.

Just a short missile ride away, there's a lot of religious action going on between a country called Israel and just about everyone else in that neighborhood.

The people in Israel also have their own set of rules for worshipping you, which they say you passed on to them. And they claim that you look more favorably upon them than upon anyone else. This has always caused a lot of hard feelings because a lot of other groups figure that *they're* your favorites. (It must be hard being a father figure.) Israel's claim that they're No. 1 has also made some people wonder this: If the Jews, after all they've been through over the centuries, are really your chosen people, what do you do to somebody you *don't* like?

Anyway, the Jews and their Moslem neighbors—both of whom claim your complete support—have been going at it for about thirty years. But I don't think they'll ever equal Ireland's record because they'll all eventually have nuclear bombs. Boy, when they start throwing those around, will you have a crowd showing up.

Oh, and I can't forget to mention this final item. Somebody just shot the pope. As you know, he's the leader of one of your largest groups of followers here. A very peaceful, nonviolent man, by the way, although his followers have been known to shed a few million gallons of blood when their tempers are up.

Anyway, the man who shot him apparently did it because of *his* devotion to you. It's not completely clear, but this fellow seems to think the pope was in some way responsible for somebody invading the sacred mosque of his religion in a place called Mecca. That, of course, was an insult to you, so he got even in your behalf by shooting the pope.

Well, I know you're busy, so that's all for now.

P.S. I never believed any of those stories going around a few years ago that "God is dead." How could you be? We don't have one weapon that can shoot that far.

July 30, 1981

A Pact to Cherish

Dear Prince Charles and Lady Diana:

The trumpets have stopped blaring. The incredible crowds have dispersed. Satellite TV has taken a rest. You two have walked up the aisle in the most publicized and widely seen wedding in history.

And now you are what you are: A young married couple.

That simple fact seems to have been overlooked by most of the world because you, Charles, are a future king of England, as meaningless as that title might be. And you, Diana, are going to be a queen or whatever the wife of a king is called. As an American, I don't keep track of such things.

But I do know that you are a man and a woman and have just entered into—as corny as some may find this statement to be— the most serious arrangement, agreement, contract, relationship, or whatever else someone might want to call it, of your lives.

It's not really that important that you, Charles, are a prince and king-to-be. And that you, Diana, are a queen-to-be. What I see is something far more important.

You are a couple of people who just got married.

That gives you something in common with all the young lovers, and older lovers, of a world that sometimes seems loveless.

You're really no different from the kid from the Southwest Side of Chicago, who is assistant manager of a pizza joint, and his bride from Oak Lawn, who is going to nursing school. They might not have had the trumpets and the audience of millions. But their vows and their commitment are no different from yours.

That's because when all the guests have gone home from your wedding; when all the gifts have been given; when all the wedding photographs have been taken; when all the wedding songs have been played; when all the relatives have expressed their optimism or pessimism, it boils down to the same thing: It's just you and her. Or her and you, to provide balance.

It's the most wonderful thing in the world. And don't let anyone tell you otherwise. And if you don't realize that, then you're missing out on life's most glorious experience.

That experience is very old. It goes back beyond recorded history. It goes back to some time, before man could write or scratch pictures on walls, when a female and a male found themselves in a cave or in the crook of a tree, surrounded by the dark of the night, giving each other comfort, warmth, and security.

This, somehow, became translated into something called love.

Nobody is really sure what love is. Shrinks mess around with trying to define it, and just make it sound more complicated than it is. Poets, as neurotic as they are, do a much better job.

I'm not sure what it is myself, except that it leaves you breathless, makes everything else seem unimportant, and can cause you ecstasy and misery and drive you crazy. And also drive you happy.

I hope, despite your cool, English manners, that this is what you feel. I hope both of you feel crazy and happy.

Be warned: It's not going to be all kissy-face and patty-fingers and the nibbling of earlobes.

There will be times when she's going to be mad as hell at you. If not, she's yogurt or you're a saint. And there will be times when she will drive you up a wall. I hope so, for your sake, or she or you will be about as exciting as a bowl of goldfish.

When that happens—yell. That's right, yell. Tell her you're mad. And tell him you're mad. Then get it out of your systems, glare out the windows, breathe loudly through your nostrils, mutter under your breath, take a walk around the block, call a close friend and complain about how impossible he or she is. Sit and brood about how you got yourself into such an impossible relationship. Daydream, if you must, about the perfect man or the perfect woman you *could* have had.

Then call it a day, say you're sorry, go to bed, hold each other in your arms, do whatever else is called for, and wake up at the first chirp of the birds glad to be alive, and with each other.

You'll find that to be one of the sweetest moments of your life. Almost as sweet as awakening at 3 or 4 o'clock in the morning and seeing the other lying next to you, the moonlight playing on the other's body, and reaching out and gently putting your hand on the other's hand.

I must warn both of you: You aren't going to spend the rest of your life, Charlie, lean, youthful, and clear-eyed. And you, Diana, are not always going to have that fresh, ripened-on-the-vine look.

One of these days, Charlie, you're going to be shaving and you're going to look and look again and say: "By George, I have a receding hairline. And I have bags under my eyes. And a trace of jowls. And my waist seems to be damned near as big as my chest. Can I be getting old?"

And you, Diana, are going to step out of the shower and notice that the proportions of your hips, your waist, and your etc., etc., are no longer as perfect as they are now. And you will have crow's feet in the corners of your eyes. And the sheen of your skin will be something more like the texture of cottage cheese.

But if you haven't become fools, she will say to you that you are even more handsome now than you were before; and you'll tell her that she's more beautiful and desirable than she was then. And you'll mean it. And if you mean it, then it will be true.

You are really lucky, you know. Not because you're young and rich and famous. Those are strictly fringe benefits.

You are lucky because, I assume, you are in love and are beginning a life together. And that's more important than anything else you do, your work, your place in history, or the opinions, approval, or disapproval of others.

Now when you're down, someone will take your hand and help you up. When you're crying, someone will dry your tears. When you're frightened, someone will hold and reassure you. When you're alone, someone will tell you you're not.

That, young prince and young lady, matters more than all the ringing of the bells and the blowing of the trumpets. It's something almost everybody wants, and not everybody has.

So, kids, good luck and don't blow it.

And remember: Squeeze the toothpaste tube from the bottom.

November 22, 1981

Mike Royko—High-Rise Man

Because it's already been the subject of an exposé by Walter Babytalk, a Chicago TV commentator, I might as well make a full confession.

Yes, I have moved into a condominium along Chicago's lakefront. As Walter indignantly raved, I am no longer a resident of one of the city's inland neighborhoods.

However, Walter, despite all his angry bouncing, failed to explain why I have moved to the lakefront. So I'll explain:

In anthropological terms, I was born Bungalow Man. Or Bungalow Baby, to be more precise.

Later, during a period of family hard times, I became Basement Flat Child.

Still later, I became Flat Above a Tavern Youth.

For a while, I was Barracks Man.

Then, in early manhood, I was Attic Flat Man. Then Two-Flat Man.

Most recently I was Bungalow Man again.

From childhood on, I never lived more than staggering distance from Milwaukee Avenue, and thought I never would.

But in recent decades, a new kind of creature has evolved in Chicago. I was the first to name him High-Rise Man.

As an amateur anthropologist, I was familiar with the ways of Two-Flat Man, Bungalow Man, Tavern Man, and all the other species that form the general classification of Neighborhood Man. That's because I was one, from my shot glass to my long underwear from Sears to my new linoleum.

And I had an extensive understanding of such mutants as Suburb Man and such lesser creatures as Downstate Man.

High-Rise Man was a different matter. I could study him only from afar, getting a fleeting glimpse as he jogged past or whizzed by on his 10-speed bike. Or try to gain insights by eavesdropping as he ordered a Perrier and lime, or spoke his quaint pidgin French to a waiter.

But it was difficult to gain a solid understanding of High-Rise Man's culture because he is such an elusive creature, flitting from

trend to trend, dashing from disco to country bar, from Baltic ethnic restaurants to French restaurants to Szechwan restaurants to pasta parlors.

I decided to follow the example of Margaret Mead, the late social anthropologist, whose method was to be part of the tribal culture she studied.

So to study High-Rise Man, I set out to join the Lakefront Tribe and become High-Rise Man.

Like Margaret Mead and other anthropologists and explorers, I couldn't embark on my expedition without proper equipment. The outfitters for this expedition included Gucci on Michigan Avenue, The Season's Best on Michigan Avenue, Robert's on Walton Street, Morrie Mages, and Shutter Bug.

The result can be seen in the picture that accompanies this column, which shows me in my new High-Rise lifestyle, with many of the trappings of High-Rise Man.

They are numbered for identification purposes.

1. The magazines include *People,* the Gucci catalog, and, of

course, *Chicago* magazine, the bible of those who seek new experiences and the perfect pesto sauce for their pasta.

2. High-Rise Dolly. (Also known to some anthropologists as Disco Dolly.)
3. Vidal Sassoon blow drier.
4. Pasta-making machine.
5. Mega-vitamins. High-Rise Man needs strength.
6. Video recorder.
7. Gold Rolex watch.
8. Peugeot 10-speed bike, for those mad dashes through Lincoln Park.
9. Irish walking hat, for those melancholy strolls through Lincoln Park.
10. Trak Nowax cross-country skis, for those invigorating treks through Lincoln Park.
11. Perrier water.
12. Soft contact lenses. The better to see you, High-Rise Dolly.
13. Funny little cigarettes.
14. Vegetable steamer. High-Rise Man must be lean.
15. Racquetball racquet. High-Rise Man must be fit.
16. Harvey's Bristol Cream. (Or Amaretto on the rocks, if you prefer.)
17. Another High-Rise Dolly. High-Rise Man always carries a spare.
18. His and hers roller skates. High-Rise Man swoops and spins.
19. Useless little dog. They're very good, by the way, on a Ritz cracker.
20. Cognac-colored, reverse-leather Gucci loafers, at $185 a pair. High-Rise Man loafs in style.
21. Nike jogging shoes. For running off the calories of the perfect pesto pasta.
22. Head jogging suit. For looking suave while running off the perfect pesto pasta sauce calories.
23. Funny white powder for High-Rise Dolly's nose. Inside of nose, not out.
24. High-Rise Man's credit cards and membership card for East Bank Club, in greedy clutches of High-Rise Dolly.
25. Gold chain and medallion, to accent High-Rise Man's manly chest.
26. Sony Walkman portable stereo. High-Rise Man must hear beauty wherever he jogs, bikes, glides, or strolls.

There is much more, of course, such as the Tony Lama boots, the Calvin Klein jeans, bomber jacket, goose down vest, keys to BMW car, coffee bean grinder, Cuisinart, microwave oven, futon mattress, Eames chair, George Kovacs lamp, L. L. Bean catalog, and glassware and other doodads from Crate and Barrel. I didn't want to show them all because High-Rise Man doesn't want to appear ostentatious.

So that's the story of my evolution from Bungalow Man to High-Rise Man. Or my decline, if you prefer.

I will have regular scientific reports on my findings of various aspects of this culture. Is there a perfect pesto sauce? Does walking a useless little dog help High-Rise Man meet High-Rise Dollies who are also walking useless little dogs? Can a French 10-speed bike outdistance a Chicago high-speed mugger? Does potential class war exist between Coho salmon snaggers and High-Rise joggers?

Meanwhile, I must go. My cappuccino machine is hissing at me.

March 7, 1982

My Belushi Pals

Like so many Chicagoans, last Thursday night I was watching a rerun of the Original "Saturday Night Live" show.

I was rewarded when John Belushi came on to do one of his outrageous skits.

As happened whenever I saw John perform, I felt a mix of emotions.

Amusement, of course. All he had to do was lift a brow and curl his lip and he could make me laugh.

I go a long way back with the Belushi family. John's late Uncle Pete was one of my closest friends and was godfather to my first child. John's father and I were also friends. I first set eyes on John when he was about five years old, running around his uncle's backyard while I devoured his Aunt Marion's wonderful Greek cooking. I don't remember that he was very funny then. But he and the other Belushi kids were sure noisy.

So when John became successful, I suppose I felt something like a distant uncle and was proud for him.

But as I watched him on my TV or in a movie theater, I always felt puzzled. Where had this incredible comic instinct come from?

His parents were good people, but not visibly humorous. Yet they produced two sons, John and Jim, who have the rare gift of being able to make strangers laugh.

I remember when I first learned that John had become an entertainer. It had to be, oh, a dozen years ago and I was at an independent political rally at a big restaurant on the South Side. A young man came up to me and, in a shy way, said: "Uncle Mike?"

I guess I blinked for a moment because he said: "You don't remember me?"

I said: "I know you're one of the Belushi kids by your goofy face, but I'm not sure which one."

He laughed. "I'm John. Adam's son."

I asked him if he was there because he was interested in politics.

"I just joined Second City. We're going to be doing a few skits here tonight."

I was impressed. Second City was already a nationally known improvisational theater group. I wish I could say that after I saw him perform, I knew he would one day be a big star. But I didn't. I could see he had a flair, but I wouldn't have bet you money that by the time he was thirty, he'd have one of the most familiar faces in America. A lot of people are funny, but very few have a talent that might be called genius.

As I said, I always had a mix of feelings when I watched John. And last Thursday night, I also felt a twinge of sad nostalgia.

That's because he was playing Pete the Greek, the owner of the short-order diner. You know the one: "Chizbooga, chizbooga, cheeps, cheeps, cheeps."

Whenever I watched him do that character, it was like flipping back in time almost thirty years.

I'd be sitting in a short-order diner in Logan Square, waiting for my wife to finish work upstairs in a doctor's office. The diner was where Eddie's Barbeque now stands, just across the side street from where the old L terminal used to be.

John's Uncle Pete would be at the grill, slapping cheeseburgers on the grill, jiggling the fries. Marion would be serving the food and coffee and handling the cash register.

I don't remember if Pete said "chizbooga" and "cheeps" exactly the way John later did. His thick accent was Albanian, not Greek. But it was close.

And somewhere in another neighborhood, in another short-order joint, Adam Belushi was slapping cheeseburgers on another grill. Everybody in the family was chasing the American dream.

And they were doing it the way immigrants have always done it: whatever works—and never mind how many grease burns you get on your arms.

If it was a Friday, we'd probably wind up in Pete's third-floor flat or my attic flat, drinking Metaxa and talking about the things we might do some day. If I ever got off that weekly neighborhood newspaper and he and Adam could pyramid those short-order grills into the restaurant of his dreams.

We were all together the night a few years later that the dream restaurant opened. Adam, Pete, and me and our wives. The place had thick carpets and cloth wallpaper, oil paintings, a piano player in the bar, and the best prime rib I've ever had. Maybe you remember it—Fair Oaks, on Dempster, in Morton Grove. It's now a big Mexican restaurant.

We toasted their success. It was a long way from tending sheep in Albania, and they had earned it. It didn't stop there, either. Before long there were other businesses. Pete figured he might as well go on and become an American tycoon.

But life has a way of giving you the glad hand, then slamming you with a fist.

A few years ago, Pete, still in his forties, died. At the funeral, we talked about John and how he had gone to New York and was starting to make a name, and how proud everybody was.

And the last time I saw John, we talked about those times and my friend Pete. It might surprise those who saw him only on the TV or in movies, but he was still shy and often quiet. And he had not let his success and wealth turn him into a jerk. He was still a genuinely nice kid.

That was the night his movie *Continental Divide* opened in Chicago and there was a party after the show. A reporter for *Rolling Stone,* who covered the evening, later wrote that as the evening ended, John and I were hugging.

I guess we were. When you feel like a proud uncle, and see the kid up there on a movie screen, you ought to give him a hug.

This column seems to have rambled. I'm sorry, but I just heard about John's death a few hours ago, and I have difficulty writing when I feel the way I do right now.

He was only thirty-three. I learned a long time ago that life isn't always fair. But it shouldn't cheat that much.

March 16, 1982

Don't Write Off Belushi

The moment it was determined that drugs caused John Belushi's death, they snatched up their pens and paper to express their self-righteousness.

"You have been caught with your pants down!" was the triumphant message from Mrs. Martha McMinn, of Portland, Oregon.

I assume Mrs. McMinn means that because I wrote a column expressing sadness at the sudden death of a friend, I should now be embarrassed because of the circumstances surrounding his death.

She went on to say: "Life was certainly not unfair to Belushi. He had fame, money, adulation, and he blew it on dope and a broad who was not his wife.

"He got what he deserved!

"Sincerely . . ."

And I'm sure Mrs. McMinn is sincere. At least I would sincerely hope that people would not be *insincere* when expressing what almost amounts to glee at someone else's death.

Mrs. Pauline Olson was not exactly bubbling with compassion, either. She said:

"Boy, I'll bet your face is red! You give us a song-and-dance about what an All-American kid your friend Belushi was. But now it turns out that he was just another show business dope user.

"Frankly, I never liked him much on TV. He was fat and crude, so I'm not surprised that he came to such a bad end.

"He was not deserving of our sympathy, and I think you owe your readers an apology for portraying him as a decent person when he was no such thing."

There were many others, and their letters are still coming in, but you get the idea.

Well, I hate to disappoint Mrs. Olson and Mrs. McMinn and all the others, but no, I'm not embarrassed and, no, I'm not going to apologize.

When I wrote about Belushi, he had been dead only a few hours and nobody knew what had caused his death. Later, I was surprised to learn that he had been using drugs. When I had seen him in Chicago last fall, he appeared to be leading a clean life. Soft drinks, a sensible diet, regular exercise, no outward evidence of drug use.

Had I known about his drug use, I wouldn't have been any less sad. If anything, I would have felt worse because of the wastefulness of his death.

Nor does the way he died mean that he was, as Mrs. Olson so harshly contends, not "a decent person."

The fact that he stuck needles in his arms could mean that he was capable of stupidity; that he might have been weak, self-indulgent, or guilty of whatever character flaws make otherwise intelligent people perform self-destructive acts. But that didn't make him a monster.

Belushi hurt no one but himself, and his family. But until his family condemns him for their pain, I think outsiders like Mrs. McMinn ought to reserve their condemnation.

Actually, I have more difficulty understanding the workings of the minds of people who are so quick to dance on somebody's grave. Obviously, no sensible person approves of drug use. But Belushi wasn't exactly selling the stuff to kids in schoolyards.

I wonder if they fire off notes like that whenever somebody they know dies.

If you think about it, the opportunities are always there. Drugs aren't the only form of self-indulgence that can lead to death.

For example, one could write a note like this:

"Dear Lucille:

"I was saddened to hear of the untimely death of your dear beloved husband, Rudy. Because I was out of town at the time, I could not attend the funeral.

"However, I must say that Rudy brought it on himself! And you didn't help, either.

"As your friend for many years, I could not help but notice that Rudy was always thirty or forty pounds overweight. Lugging around all that fat couldn't have done his heart any good. And you must share the blame for cooking him all those high-calorie meals.

"Dietitians keep warning that being overweight can shorten a person's life. But did Rudy stop shoving food in his mouth? Noooooo!

"So as much as I can sympathize with you in your time of sadness, you and Rudy got exactly what you deserved!

"Sincerely, your friend . . ."

Or one could always write a note like this:

"Dear Mary:

"I didn't want to bring this up at John's funeral because you were busy greeting mourners.

"But I have to say that I can't understand why you and everyone else were so surprised that John dropped dead so suddenly.

"After all, he did smoke two packs a day, and any idiot knows that the U.S. Surgeon General has warned that smoking is dangerous.

"If he had had the willpower that my William has, and had quit the filthy habit, he'd probably be alive today. And his teeth would have been much whiter. But, nooooo, he just kept on puffing away.

"So in your time of sorrow, I just want you to know that John got what he deserved!

"Sincerely, your friend . . ."

Or this one:

"Dear Lucille:

"Just a note to let you know that we are thinking about you in your time of sorrow.

"But as I was telling my dear Ed the other day, it was just a matter of time.

"Your George just wouldn't slow down, would he? Sure, all that drive and aggressiveness got you a big house, and two cars, and those fancy clothes, and expensive vacations. But it also got George hypertension, anxiety, and high blood pressure!

"So you and George got exactly what you deserved!

"Sincerely, your neighbor . . . (We're the ones in the much *smaller* house, with the *older* car, and the *cheaper* vacations. But at least my husband is still around!)"

So Mrs. McMinn and Mrs. Olson and all you other gravedancers, feel free to use any of the above letters when the occasions arise.

Or have you already been doing it?

April 11, 1982

Survival Talk Stinks

Suddenly there's all this serious talk about civil defense planning and how many people could survive a nuclear war.

Whenever that subject comes up, I recall a conversation I once had with Carl Sandburg, the great poet, when I was a young reporter.

It was about twenty-two years ago, when the Cold War was

really frigid and digging fallout shelters was one of this country's most popular pastimes.

Sandburg was visiting Chicago and I was assigned to interview him.

Before I left the office, I was called aside by an editor who was building his own home fallout shelter.

He said, "I want you to ask Sandburg what he would stock a fallout shelter with."

"Why should I ask him that?" I asked the editor.

"Well, he's a brilliant, world-famous man, and I think a lot of people would be interested in knowing what somebody like him would think was important to have."

When I put the question to Sandburg, we were in a dining room with some of Chicago's wealthiest, most socially prominent citizens, who were honoring him.

He pondered the question for about twenty or thirty seconds, pursing his lips and looking toward the sky, while everyone sat silently awaiting his profound thoughts.

Then, in that dramatic, rumbling voice, he said very, very slowly and deliberately:

"I would be sure [pause] to take with me [pause] a sufficient number of receptacles [pause] to hold that [pause] which Norman Mailer [pause] calls shit."

At the sound of that word, all the fine ladies in gowns and fine gentlemen in dinner jackets gasped. Sandburg stifled a grin.

"Is there anything else?" I asked.

"No," he said, "that is what comes to mind when someone talks about survival after nuclear war."

I returned to the office, wrote the story, and turned it in. The editor yelped, "We can't print this!"

"Why not? He said it."

"Because it's crude."

"But I think Sandburg was trying to make a point."

"Well, I don't understand his point and it's not going into this newspaper."

And it didn't.

But I've always remembered it because Sandburg pretty well summed up in that one blunt word what all of these serious discussions about crawling into holes or evacuating the cities really amount to: It is just a crock.

It was a crock back then, when millions of frightened Americans stocked their basements with bottled water, canned foods, and first-aid kits, and politicians donned civil defense uniforms and blew off sirens to show that they were ready for anything.

And it's a crock now, as the Reagan administration unleashes a double-barreled propaganda barrage.

Propaganda Barrel one: We are woefully behind the Russians in nuclear strength, so we have to have a huge military buildup costing billions of dollars.

This buildup, of course, terrifies many people. We build more bombs and the Russians build more bombs. So we build more and they build more. And along the way, a lot of other, smaller countries build their bombs. And one of these days, poof!

So that's where Propaganda Barrel two comes in. It goes something like this:

Don't worry about the nuclear buildup. The more bombs everybody builds, the safer we'll all be. Besides, we *can* survive nuclear war. Not nearly as many people would die as we might think. Sure, millions would not make it—but many, many more millions would survive.

All we have to do is be prepared with plans to evacuate the cities. Then when we see the Russians evacuating their cities, we will know they are going to attack us, and we can evacuate our cities.

Or something like that.

This kind of talk is almost funny when it comes from those eccentric people who call themselves survivalists and plan for the day when they will barricade themselves in their vacation homes and wait with shotguns cocked to blast the looters who want their homes.

But the talk isn't funny when it comes from officials in the present White House administration.

They talk about evacuating the cities. Every day at about 4 P.M., people get in their cars to go home from work. Every day there is a huge traffic jam.

And that's with only a small fraction of the population being on the move.

What would happen if *everybody* tried to get away at the same time?

Nothing would move. It would be chaos.

Ah, but Washington tells us that wouldn't happen because we would have about four days in which to evacuate the cities.

I don't understand why they think there would be a four-day grace period before we and the Russians began bombing each other. Maybe they have an optimistic computer.

But even though it's ridiculous to think there would be time to evacuate the urban areas, let's go along with this crazy thinking and assume there would be time.

We would have 200 million people wandering around the countryside with no food, no shelter, no medical care, no organized society.

Then when the bombs went off and the radiation and fallout got to them, they could die slowly instead of quickly. And those who survived the blasts and radiation could die of the diseases that would quickly spread.

Since most experts on the subject agree that planning for survival is a waste of time, why is there so much official talk about it?

The answer is that if the government wants to engage in a nuclear buildup that we don't need, since we are already as powerful as the Russians, it has to soothe us into thinking that we can survive a nuclear war.

That is supposed to make the buildup, and the possibility of nuclear war, less frightening to us.

It's a sales job. Even worse, a con job.

All they're doing is talking a lot of that which Carl Sandburg said Norman Mailer described as. . . . Well, you know what they're talking.

February 23, 1983

Give Washington a Break

So I told Uncle Chester: Don't worry, Harold Washington doesn't want to marry your sister.

That might seem like a strange thing to have to tell somebody about the man who will be the next mayor of Chicago. I never had to tell Uncle Chester that Mayor Daley or Mayor Bilandic wouldn't marry his sister.

On the other hand, no other mayor, in the long and wild-eyed history of Chicago, has had one attribute of Washington.

He's black. It appears to be a waste of space to bother pointing that out, since every Chicagoan knows it.

But you can't write about Harold Washington's victory without taking note of his skin color.

Yes, he is black. And that fact is going to create a deep psychological depression in many of the white, ethnic neighborhood people who read this paper in the morning.

Eeek! The next mayor of Chicago is going to be a black man! Let's all quiver and quake.

Oh, come on. Let's all act like sensible, adult human beings.

Let us take note of a few facts about Harold Washington.

First, Washington was born in an era when they still lynched people in some parts of the United States. By "lynched," I mean they took a black man out of his home, put a rope around his neck, and murdered him by hanging. Then they went home to bed knowing they were untouchable because the sheriff helped pull the rope.

Washington suffered through it. God knows how he did that. I think that most of us—white, privileged, the success road wide open to us—might have turned into haters.

Washington didn't turn into a hater. Instead, he developed a capacity for living with his tormentors and understanding that in the flow of history there are deep valleys and heady peaks.

He fought in World War II. Yes, blacks did that, although you don't see them in many John Wayne movies. He went to college and got a degree. Then he went to Northwestern University's law school, at a time when blacks were as common as alligators there.

Had Washington been white, he would have tied in with a good law firm, sat behind his desk, made a good buck, and today would be playing golf at a private country club.

But for a black man, even one as bright as Washington, an NU law degree meant that he was just about smart enough to handle divorce cases for impoverished blacks.

Being no dummy, he gravitated toward politics. And the Democratic Party. It may have been pseudo-liberal, but the Democratic Party did offer a black lawyer a chance, meager and piddling as it might be.

And he went somewhere. Come on, admit that, at least, even while you brood about a black man becoming your next mayor.

He became a state legislator. Then a United States congressman.

I'm still enough of an idealist to think that most people who become members of Congress are at least a cut or two above the rest of us.

And even his critics say that as a state legislator and as a U.S. congressman, he was pretty good.

So I ask you: If Jane Byrne is qualified to be mayor of Chicago after holding no higher office than city consumer affairs commissioner, what is the rap on Harold Washington?

And I also ask you: If Richard M. Daley is qualified to be mayor after being a state legislator and state's attorney of Cook County, what is so unthinkable about a man holding the mayor's office after being a state legislator and a U.S. congressman?

The fact is, Washington's credentials for this office exceed those of Byrne, Bilandic, Richard J. Daley, Martin Kennelly, Ed Kelly, Anton Cermak, and most of the others who have held the office of mayor of Chicago.

Byrne was a minor bureaucrat. Bilandic's highest office was alderman. Richard J. Daley was the county clerk. Kennelly was a moving company executive. Kelly was a sanitary district payroller. Cermak was a barely literate but street-smart hustler.

All became mayor. And nobody was horrified.

But this morning, the majority of Chicagoans—since this city's majority is white—are gape-jawed at the prospect of Representative Washington becoming mayor.

Relax, please. At least for the moment. There is time to become tense and angry when he fouls up as mayor—as anybody in that miserable job inevitably will do.

Until he fouls up, though, give him a chance. The man is a United States citizen, with roots deeper than most of us have in this country. He is a sixty-year-old Chicagoan who has been in politics and government most of his life.

He is a smart, witty, politically savvy old pro. He is far more understanding of the fears and fantasies of Chicago whites than we are of the frustrations of Chicago blacks.

The city isn't going to slide into the river. The sun will come up today and tomorrow, and your real estate values won't collapse. History shows that real estate values in a town like Chicago go up and up, over the long haul, no matter who is mayor.

He'll fire a police superintendent, hire a new one, and the earth won't shake under us.

He might hire some jerks. I haven't seen a mayor who hasn't. They don't learn. Two days before Lady Jane was elected, I wrote: "How she does will depend on the kind of people she surrounds herself with."

She surrounded herself with Charlie Swibel and other bums and got what she deserved.

If Washington is smart, which I think he is, he'll surround himself with the very best talents and minds available. And they're available. If not, we'll survive and we'll throw him out.

Meanwhile, don't get hysterical. As I wrote four years ago, if we survived Bilandic, we can survive Jane Byrne.

And if we survived Jane, we easily can survive Harold Washington.

Who knows, we might even wind up liking him.

November 2, 1983

(Mike wrote this column the day after George Halas died.)

Halas: A Classic of Grit

In recent years, I've found myself sitting around with other Chicago Bears fans and defending—or at least trying to explain—team owner George Halas.

You wouldn't think that it would be necessary to have to speak up for a man who was a towering giant in his field.

To those of us who are old enough to have seen him in his prime—and fortunate enough to have known him personally—no defense was necessary.

But to the late-coming fan—those who took up football-watching when it became a TV spectacular—Halas was just a penny-pinching relic of a past that they didn't know or care about.

"All he wants to do is make a buck," the fans would bellow after another Bears loss.

Actually, that wasn't true. But if it had been, would that have made Halas any different from the average Bears fan? I mean, how many of them devote their lives to the unselfish betterment of their fellow man?

"He's too old and ought to sell the team to somebody who knows what they're doing," they'd shout.

Just like that. A man devotes his life to building a business. *His business.* He does the hard work, takes the risks, puts his money and his imagination on the line, and builds something. Nobody gives it to him. It's *his.*

But when he starts getting old, the cry goes up to shove him aside, get him out of the way, let him fade from sight and mind.

There are societies that honor and value their old people. There are other societies that push them out into the cold to die. I'm not sure which kind of society we are.

I first got to know Coach Halas about twenty years ago. Of course, I had known *about* him as far back as I can remember. What Bears fan didn't? He was the man who brought us those great bruising, bristle-chinned teams, with players who had fearsome names like Bruno and Bulldog.

But when I got to know him, I realized there was much more to admire than his success in football.

He was, in many ways, a classic Chicagoan. Like most of us, he was an ethnic. He came out of a working class family on the West Side and hustled and scrapped and worked his way toward success. He might have heard of the eight-hour day, but he didn't get close enough to it to pick up any bad habits.

Like this city, he could be tough, even almost brutal at times. He could be shrewd and conniving, pushy and loud, arrogant and overbearing.

But he could also be generous, compassionate, and direct. If he had something to say, he said it to your face, nose to nose and eyeball to eyeball.

Can you imagine somebody like Halas ever coming out of a city like Los Angeles or San Francisco? He would have caused the natives to swoon.

That, I'm sure, is why he had a lifelong attraction to players like Dick Butkus, another Chicagoan with soot behind his ears and cinders under his nails.

But in any recent argument about Halas, no matter what you said, somebody would slam the table and repeat: "So what? He was still a loser."

In recent years, sure. We all know that his Bears haven't been what they were in the old days.

The question is why? And the answer is something that those who admired and respected the old man—which would include just about everybody who knew him—would not talk about because it would have hurt him.

The Bears slid not because Halas was cheap, or because he lost his sharpness, or any of the popular explanations.

They slid because he was very human.

Halas had a son, Muggsy. And like many men who build successful businesses, Halas dreamed of his son taking over the business someday.

The day came in the late 1960s, when Halas decided to step aside for his son. Halas had already done everything that somebody in his work could ever hope for. He had won a world championship in 1963, when he was almost seventy. He had won more titles and games than anyone in the history of his sport— and still has.

So he turned the team over to his son, just as businessmen do all the time.

It became clear that Muggsy didn't have his father's genius for football. That is sometimes the case in any line of work.

It would be easy to say: "Well, then he should have told his kid to move aside and put somebody else in there." That would be easy to say, especially for somebody who isn't a father.

So Halas didn't push back in. He waited and hoped. But instead of the success he hoped for, tragedy came in its most devastating form. His son died.

Halas could have shriveled from grief. Instead, like the old oak he was, he withstood the pain. And then he came back.

I think that if there had been more time, if his old body had held up, he might have pulled it off one more time. At least I prefer to think so. I was at a small party for him on his eighty-seventh birthday and he was crackling with enthusiasm, hope, and ideas.

But the clock ran out before he could do it again. Too bad, but it really doesn't matter.

What matters about those losing years is that Halas knew what was really important in life—and it wasn't happening on a football field.

January 12, 1984

In Alien's Tongue, "I Quit" Is "Vacation"

A Chicago politician called today and chortled: "Congrats, you're one of us now, you sly devil, you."

One of you? What are you talking about? I've never been indicted, convicted, or even nominated.

He chuckled knowingly and said: "C'mon, you turned out to be a real double-dipper."

A double-dipper? Me?

"Sure. And you remember how many times you've rapped us for double-dipping, don't you?"

You mean for somehow managing to be on two payrolls at the same time?

"Right, you slicker, you. But now you've done it yourself. When are you going to run for alderman? Believe me, you've got all the instincts."

Despite my protests, he was still chuckling when he hung up.

A moment later my Uncle Chester called and said: "I want to

apologize. I just told your aunt that you're not as dumb as I always thought you were."

I appreciate that. But what changed your mind?

"Because I see that you managed to get two papers to print your stuff at the same time. How'd you swing that? I was always amazed that even one would do it."

Me, too, but this isn't my idea. I'm against it.

"Then I'm wrong. You really are dumb."

Let me explain.

"Don't bother. You probably don't understand it yourself. G'by."

He might be right, but I'd like to try to explain this bizarre situation anyway.

As people who read both Chicago newspapers might have noticed, my columns have appeared in both of them the last couple of days.

The columns in this paper are new. The ones in the other paper are reprints of columns that were written and published in past years.

The reason there are new columns in this paper is that I now work here.

The reason old columns are appearing in the other paper is that I don't work there anymore. But The Alien who now owns it doesn't seem to understand that. So he keeps printing my old columns and saying that I'm on vacation.

I don't know why The Alien is doing that. Maybe it's a custom in his native Australia, which is about 6,000 miles from Chicago.

If so, it is a very strange custom.

I mean, in this country, most employers know when somebody does or doesn't work for them.

Around here, if somebody walks into the boss's office and says something like, "You're kind of a disreputable character and I don't want to work for you, so I quit and here is my resignation," the boss would surely understand.

And the boss would say something like: "Good riddance. Turn in your key to the underlings' washroom."

But apparently it doesn't work that way in The Alien's native land. There, I suspect, when a person quits and walks out, the boss smiles brightly and says: "Ah, he has gone on vacation."

If so, they must have some really confused payroll departments.

Or maybe there's another explanation. It could be that The Alien, in trying to learn about our customs, has been studying City Hall.

If that's the case, then I can understand why The Alien is acting so strangely.

In our City Hall, it's always been difficult to tell if people are working, on vacation, retired, or even dead or alive. And it's made little difference. The work level has been about the same.

There have been documented cases of aldermen's young nephews being hired as city inspectors and immediately vanishing, not to be seen again until they showed up for their retirement party.

It is said that a City Hall supervisor once showed up at the wake of a foreman from Streets and Sanitation. As he stood over the coffin, somebody said: "Did you know him well?" The supervisor said: "He worked for me for thirty years, so I came here to see what he looked like."

But if that's what The Alien believes, somebody should straighten him out. That's the way it is done in City Hall, but not in the private sector. The custom is for the rest of us to work in order to support our ancient political tradition.

I suppose this is the kind of confusing problem that we're going to have to get used to in this modern world, with rich foreigners running in and out of each other's countries to buy up each other's businesses.

And it could be worse. As an anthropologist friend said:

"It's a good thing for you the other paper wasn't bought by somebody from the wealthy but distant and remote nation of Manumbaland."

Why?

"It is the custom there that when somebody resigns from his job, he is beheaded."

I guess I was lucky.

But there's still time.

March 2, 1984

A GOP Function Flush with Luxuries

A fascinating tidbit about Washington high society caught my eye the other day.

It had to do with a spectacular weekend of fancy balls, black-tie dinners, parties, and a fashion show luncheon—attended by the Reagans, top people in government, and hundreds of wealthy industrialists, tycoons, and movie stars. Sort of a Republican rainbow coalition.

Some of them wore such heavy gold objects that they set the Secret Service's metal detectors to howling.

They paid $5,000 a person to attend all the events, less if they wanted to be choosy. But it went to a worthy cause—the Princess Grace Foundation, which will provide arts scholarships.

Actually, this is routine recreation for rich Washington Republicans. They don't go in much for Saturday Night Bingo.

But one fact struck me as unusual. It was tucked down in a story in the *Washington Post.*

It said that at the fashion luncheon, carnations were sprinkled in the toilet bowls in the ladies' room.

When the ladies came in and used the toilet bowls and flushed them, a maid (presumably a Democrat) would scatter more carnations in the bowl.

Naturally, this item set my social conscience to quivering with thoughts of poverty, the jobless, homeless, and foodless, and cutbacks in social programs.

In the midst of this suffering, there were all these Republican ladies having flowers scattered, not at their feet as is traditional, but at their . . . well, you know.

And what Republican ladies. The guest list included Mr. and Mrs. James Baker of the White House, Mrs. Alfred Bloomingdale of the New York store, Clare Booth Luce, Mr. and Mrs. Caspar Weinberger, Margaret Heckler, who is the secretary of Health and Human Services (flowers in the can are some human service), and about 120 others.

So I decided to track down the full story and find out why they put carnations in the toilet. I mean, I entertain, too, and I've always thought that Ty-D-Bol, that blue stuff, is pretty classy. And much cheaper. Carnations go for a buck each. And with that many people at the luncheon, if they had weak kidneys it could deplete an entire floral nursery.

Well, it turns out that things are not always as they appear.

A call to the Princess Grace Foundation brought a response from a spokeswoman who was almost trembling with indignation.

She said: "Neither the foundation nor the White House had anything to do with the carnations being put in the toilet bowls."

Then who did it? A volunteer?

"No. It was the hotel's idea. They thought it was a gracious thing to do. But the *Washington Post* didn't mention that. Oh, I could kill the reporter who wrote about the carnations. But that's off the record, of course."

Of course. By the way, have you any idea how many carnations were used?

"How would I know that? You'll have to ask the hotel."

The manager of the Loew's L'Enfant Plaza Hotel, where the luncheon was held, was also oozing indignation.

When he was asked about the flowers, he said.

"You mean my overkill? Hmmmph. That's what the reporter for the *Washington Post* called it.

"They were also inaccurate. They said we put chopped carnations in the toilet bowls. They were not chopped. We used only the petals. We pulled the petals off and dropped them in."

Good grief, that really is irresponsible journalism. But what was the idea in the first place? What's wrong with Ty-D-Bol?

"It is not new. It is a practice we have used for VIPs long before this. We have been doing this for four years. We did it for a reception for the mayor of Washington and for many others."

He was also miffed that the *Post* mentioned that the hotel answered its phones by saying "bonjour" and "bonsoir."

"This hotel has been here for fourteen years, and we always answered the phones by saying bonjour before 5 P.M. And bonsoir after 5 P.M."

Of course. Who doesn't? But to get back to flowers. How many carnations did you use?

"Oh, I doubt if we used any more than a dozen for that event."

The luncheon lasted three hours, so those Republican ladies must have the bladders of camels.

"By the way," he added, "we normally use roses. But carnations were Princess Grace's favorite, so we used them instead."

What a beautiful tribute.

So that's the story. Flowers in toilet bowels are definitely not a regular part of gracious living among Washington Republicans.

But even at one hotel, it does raise a question about sex discrimination.

If you are going to sprinkle carnation petals in the ladies' toilets, in the spirit of fairness and equality, should there also be something put in the men's urinals?

The trouble is, I can't think of anything appropriate for a man's urinal.

Well, maybe there is something. For all those rich Republicans, how about a five-dollar cigar?

March 9, 1984

Slats Mistakes GOP for GOD

I could tell something was wrong. President Reagan had been on the TV at the end of the bar for ten minutes. But Slats Grobnik hadn't said even one unkind word.

Normally, Slats hoots, jeers, snorts, hisses, or puts his thumb to his nose and wiggles his bony fingers at any Republican—especially a Republican president.

As he once said: "That's why I love TV. My father was a lifelong Democrat, just like me. But he didn't have the same advantages. There was nothing but newspapers and radio in his day, and it wasn't nearly as much fun thumbing your nose at the front page or a radio dial."

But this time Slats sat silently staring at his beer and occasionally glancing at the TV screen. I finally walked over and asked him if something was wrong.

He nervously cracked his knuckles, then said: "I got a problem. It has to do with my soul."

Your what?

"My soul. You know, that thing inside ya."

Oh, your soul. What's the problem with it?

"I'm worried about losing it or having it burn in hell or something. Look, you know how I am about politics. I was born a Democrat. I never voted for a Republican even once. I always figured that with all my other vices, I don't need one more."

Yes, we all know that.

"But now I'm thinking about voting for. . . . Gee, I hate to even say it. Let me whisper. I'm thinking of voting for Reagan."

And you think you'll lose your soul if you do?

"No, I'm thinking that I might lose it if I don't."

Why should that happen?

"Well, what if God is a Republican?"

That's ridiculous.

"You think so. Then tell me. Who's Reagan's running mate?"

It will surely be Vice President George Bush.

"No it won't. Take it from me, it's God."

What are you talking about?

"Just listen to Reagan. Every speech lately, who does he talk about? God. Do you remember any president who talked about God as much as he does?"

Now that you mention it, no.

"And what gets me is that he talks like he knows God and knows exactly what He likes or doesn't like. I mean, sometimes Reagan sounds like God is his campaign adviser."

It does sound that way.

"And look how he's got Congress spending its time. All they do these days is argue if God wants the kids to pray out loud or pray quiet or to pray at all, and who writes the prayer. You'd think it was some kind of Bible meeting instead of a bunch of politicians cutting deals."

But that's just politics. Reagan and the Republicans are trying to hustle the fundamentalist vote. Don't worry, God is not a Republican.

"You don't think so? Well, tell me this. I'm not religious, but I always heard that God is all-powerful, right?"

True.

"And you break His rules and—bam—you're in big trouble, right?"

Some people believe that, yes.

"And if you goof up, He's liable to smite you with His mighty and swift sword, right?"

So it has been said.

"Well, if that don't sound like a Republican to me, I don't know what does."

But what about God's son? Do you think Jesus was a Republican? Or a conservative?

"Well, Republicans usually pass it on. I think in Lake Forest, they put it in their wills with the stocks and bonds."

Would a Republican have said, blessed are the poor in spirit, the meek, the merciful, and the peacemakers?

"If he wanted to get elected in the suburbs, he wouldn't."

And what about all this silly business of organized, vocal, school prayer? Would a Republican have said he was against it?

"You're not saying Jesus was against it?"

Some people think he might have been. He said: "But thou, when thou prayest, enter into thy closet, and when thou hast shut thy door, pray to thy Father which is in secret; and thy Father which seeth in secret shall reward thee openly." Does that sound like something Reagan's supporters are screaming at congressmen to pass?

"No. And I'm all for putting a lot of those noisy kids in closets, too."

And if Jesus was a Republican, would he have spent most of his life hanging around with the poor, the afflicted, the social riff-raff of his day, and raising hell with the government, the rich, and the powerful?

"No, that doesn't sound like something Ed Meese or Jim Watt would go in for. Unless they just wanted to see the poor and the afflicted so they could tell them that they brought it on themselves."

And one more thing. Would any Republican have said this: "And again I say to you, it is easier for a camel to go through the eye of a needle, than for a rich man to enter into the kingdom of God"?

"A Republican? That sounds to me like somebody whose phone they would have tapped."

All right, then stop worrying.

"I think you're probably right. Except for one thing. About the camel going through the eye of the needle."

What about it?

"With all their money, I figure they'd just build a bigger needle."

September 17, 1985

A Grave Report from Medicare

It was last February when Professor George Blanksten became aware of a very sad event in his life.

He had reason to visit his physician. Nothing serious. But a blood test was required.

The physician sent the bill for the blood test to Medicare, since Blanksten is sixty-eight years old.

A few weeks passed, and Blanksten received a letter from the Social Security Administration, which administers the Medicare program, and it contained shocking news.

"They told me that I was dead," Blanksten says, "and therefore they could not honor the bill."

Obviously, Blanksten was surprised. Although he isn't a kid anymore, he feels pretty good—even spry on his better days.

He's alive enough to teach political science, specializing in Latin American politics, at Northwestern University.

Along with the letter—which had been addressed to Blanksten's "estate"—was a form that he could fill out if he wanted his alleged death reviewed.

Naturally he filled it out and sent it in, since he didn't want word getting around that he was dead any sooner than is absolutely necessary.

Soon his estate received another letter. Once again, it was a blank form, the very same form he had already filled out.

So he filled it out again and sent it in.

Apparently, he had engaged either a bureaucrat or a computer in some kind of duel.

He would send in the completed form. And it or he or she would respond by sending him another blank form to fill out.

This went on for months, with him filling out the form and them or it sending him the same blank form to fill out. He finally contacted his congressman's office, and somebody there said they would look into it.

That finally brought him a response from Social Security.

The agency said: "As requested, we have reviewed your entire claim to decide whether our original determination was correct. . . . A specially trained person reviewed the claim. This person did not take part in the original review. . . . We have found the decision made on this claim was correct. Our reason for this decision is as follows: According to our records, the date of death occurred prior to the date of the service."

In other words, he still was dead. Why, he was dead even before he went in for the blood test. Some doctor.

Even worse, he doesn't know when he died or what it was that did him in.

"That part really gets me. I asked them for the date and circumstances of my death, and they won't tell me."

Hoping that a face-to-face meeting might help, the professor went to the Social Security office in Glenview. He took a number and a seat on a bench and waited to be called.

When his number came up, he tried to explain to a female bureaucrat that he was not dead.

"That's what you say," she said, leading him to believe that they must get a lot of dead people posing as the living. And she gave him more of the forms he had already filled out.

But he hopes that there still remains a chance that he might be allowed to return to life.

The last letter—the one in which he was declared dead by an impartial, "specially trained person"—did hold out one slim hope.

It said, "If you do not agree with our findings, you can request a fair hearing within six months of this date."

So he sent them a letter, asking for a fair hearing.

"I haven't heard anything from them yet, but I'm hoping for a fair chance to convince them that I am alive."

He hasn't decided what he'll do at a hearing to show them he isn't a cadaver. Possibly a soft shoe dance or, if the hearing officer is a female, a lascivious grin or even a pinch on her bottom.

In the meantime, he is thinking of taking legal action under the Freedom of Information Act.

"It bothers me that they won't tell me anything about the circumstances of my death. So I might take action on that.

"The least I should be able to do is visit my own grave."

October 17, 1985

If This Isn't Danger, What Is?

The year-old child was in terrible shape when her grandmother brought her into Cook County Hospital.

Her arms were broken in three places. Her face and jaw were bruised. She had a concussion. There were burn marks on one arm. Hundreds of what appeared to be pinch marks covered her abdomen.

She was in shock, her blood count was dangerously low, and she was having trouble breathing.

She was rushed into surgery. When they opened her belly, they found bleeding. Her liver had lacerations. Her pancreas was bruised and bleeding. She had 10 centimeters of dead bowel.

After surgery, she was put in the intensive care unit. That's when doctors discovered old fractures of both arms that were beginning to heal.

The doctors reported their findings to the Illinois Department of Children and Family Services, the state agency that investigates suspected cases of child abuse.

A caseworker went to the family's home on Chicago's South Side and asked the young mother and the grandmother what happened to the child.

They were hostile and defensive and refused to concede that anybody had done the baby harm. Nothing had happened. The baby just got sick.

When they came to the hospital, the caseworker tried again, talking to them separately, hoping they would be honest. Again they refused.

But somebody at the hospital picked up a clue. The baby has a three-year-old brother. And the little boy told a doctor that the mother has a boyfriend, a fellow named Calvin. He said Calvin sometimes hit, choked, and pinched him.

And the mother finally admitted that when she had left the home for a few hours, taking her son with her, she had left the baby in the care of the boyfriend.

Doctors noticed something else. When the mother visited the baby in the hospital, Calvin came along. At the sight of him, the baby became hysterical, screaming, and thrashing. Calvin was ordered to stay away from the hospital.

There was enough evidence of child abuse for Children and Family Services to take the case to juvenile court and ask for temporary custody of the child.

As a medical expert says: "There was no question that the baby had been abused. From all the medical records, and just looking at her, it was obvious. Cut and dried."

A doctor testified and told about the broken bones, both old and new, the facial bruises, the burn marks, the internal bleeding.

Then the mother and grandmother testified. Amazingly, they said that nothing had happened to the baby while she was home.

"Nobody done hurt my child ever," the mother said.

Then how, she was asked, did the child suffer such terrible and extensive injuries?

She and the grandmother offered a remarkable theory. They said that if the baby was injured, it must have somehow happened while she was in the hospital.

After the lengthy testimony about the child's condition, everybody turned to Judge Ronald Davis to hear his ruling.

According to those who were in the courtroom, Judge Davis said that, yes, it did appear that there was an "injurious environment" in the child's home.

But, he said, there did not appear to be an "urgent or immediate danger."

So he refused to give temporary custody of the child to the Department of Children and Family Services.

Or, put another way, he said the child should be returned to her mother.

And in another week or so, that's what will happen. A source at the hospital says: "She's getting better. Her teeth are budding out now. She was starved at home; didn't get enough calcium. She's still missing part of her bowel, but her two broken arms are mending. Her liver has been sewn up. And her concussion is gone. She's coming along nicely.

"But we can't keep her here for more than another week or two. Then we have to return her to the mother. We don't want to do that, but we have no choice."

They have no choice because of Judge Davis' ruling that there is no "immediate danger" in the very place where the child wound up looking like she had been run over by a truck.

When asked to explain his ruling, Judge Davis said:

"Juvenile proceedings are confidential. We are not allowed to discuss them. We're not permitted to discuss them under the law. We have to maintain confidentiality."

Well, that law doesn't prevent me from discussing such cases. And I promise Judge Davis that if the child is returned to her mother, it will be discussed further.

And if Judge Davis' judicial superiors happen to read this, maybe they would like to discuss why the hell somebody like Judge Davis is dealing with the lives of children.

Can't they find a nice, harmless parking ticket court for him?

November 14, 1985

Abused Baby 1, System a Big 0

I suppose I should take satisfaction out of the fact that Lashaunda, the battered baby I've written about, is finally going to be placed in a foster home where it's unlikely that she'll have any more broken legs, concussions, burns, internal injuries, and other miseries.

Judge Ronald Davis finally made that decision Wednesday after a lot of ridiculous delays by the public defender who represented Lashaunda's mother.

Until the very end, the public defender was trying to portray the doctor who blew the whistle on this case as the villain.

It also can be considered good news that Judge Davis, who initially botched this case by refusing to take the baby out of a dangerous environment, is being whisked away from juvenile court to another assignment, where he can ponder such things as contracts or parking tickets. Things that don't bleed and cry out in pain.

And it's encouraging that the last thing Judge Davis did before ending his stint in juvenile court was to put Lashaunda's three-year-old brother in temporary custody of the state, pending an investigation to see if he too should be put in a foster home.

But there's really not much reason to feel more than a passing satisfaction from the way this case turned out.

Oh, it's fine that this one baby, and maybe her brother, is being protected from potential harm.

But what it amounts to is nothing more than a Band-Aid for a massive hemorrhage.

If I learned anything from this case, it's that the legal system that has been set up to protect children like Lashaunda is a frustrating, disastrous failure.

Sure, Lashaunda is now safe. But not because of the system. She's safe because one doctor had the courage to speak out and because stories about the case aroused public anger. Despite what judges say about being above outside influence, their ears can quiver when the public raises hell.

If the system had followed its course, with lawyers going through the motions of doing something while actually doing nothing, Lashaunda would still be home. Or maybe she'd be in a tiny coffin.

So there can't be any satisfaction when there are hundreds and hundreds of other Lashaundas out there that we don't know about—and the system hasn't protected.

And that it isn't capable of protecting.

What's the problem? There are lots of them.

For one thing, there is a state agency, the Illinois Department of Children and Family Services, that is supposed to be responsible for checking on cases of child abuse.

You think the CIA is secretive? You should try dealing with this outfit.

Throughout this entire case, every time I tried to get even a speck of information from Family Services, all I heard was the whiny response:

"Oh, we're not permitted to discuss these matters."

If somebody was known to be eating babies on a sesame roll with mustard and onions, their response would be: "Oh, we're not permitted to discuss these matters."

We're supposed to take it on faith that this agency does its job. But if there's anything I've learned during thirty years in this business, it's that you can have as much faith in bureaucrats doing their job as you can in the warranty offered by the guy selling jewelry out of a shopping bag in a gangway.

Then we have court hearings being run on an adversary basis, like a personal injury case or a murder trial.

The result was that the mother's court-appointed lawyer tried to put the doctor on trial, suggesting that the doctor who diagnosed the injuries wasn't qualified, even implying that maybe the doctor was somehow responsible for the kid being mauled and maimed.

And that led to a two-week delay so that the imaginative public defender could find a doctor who could testify to . . . damned if I know to what. That the kid broke her own legs? That some clumsy nurse dropped her a dozen times? That, as Mom suggested, the baby inherited broken legs, concussions, burns, etc.?

After the two-week delay, the public defender couldn't find a doctor, or even a Gypsy fortuneteller, to be her expert rebuttal witness.

All that legal jockeying is to be expected in courtrooms where the fates of dope peddlers, throat cutters, jackrollers, and porch climbers are decided.

But in this case, there were only two questions: Had the baby been bashed around? And should she be returned to the place where it obviously happened? (I say "obviously" because most one-year-old kids don't sneak out of their cribs and toddle down to the street corner for a brawl.)

Those questions could have been answered in a day, if that long.

Then there is the judge. Not just this particular judge, but any judge in juvenile court. The question might sound silly, but why is the final decision left to a lawyer who, through political connections, happens to be wearing black robes?

I'm sure that his legal training has made him a whiz at contracts, writs, motions, and knowing when to overrule an objection. But how does that background qualify him as an expert in the field of child abuse?

Why not, instead of a judge—or in addition to a judge—a panel that might include a doctor, a psychologist, and a streetwise social worker?

I'm not an expert in this field, just as I'm not an expert in automobile engines. But I don't have to be an expert to know that when you turn on the car engine and it sputters, spits, howls, and clunks along, something is wrong.

And the whole juvenile protective system needs more than a tune-up.

December 24, 1985

A Lovely Couple, Bound with Love

The conversation at the bar got around to Christmas trees. Somebody had mentioned how much they cost today and what a pain in the neck it is to go out in the bitter cold and shop around for a good one.

"Nah," said Slats Grobnik. "There's nothing to it; not if you know what you're doing."

What makes you an expert?

"I used to work in a tree lot when I was a young guy," said Slats. "My uncle used to sell them in the vacant lot next to his tavern. And that's when I learned the secret."

What secret?

"The secret of having the most beautiful tree you ever saw."

That's easy. The secret is to go out with a pocket full of money and spend what it takes to buy the best tree.

Slats shook his head. "Uh-uh. Money's not the secret."

So, tell us the secret.

"Awright. It was a long time ago, maybe thirty years. I was in the lot and it was the night before Christmas Eve, about a half hour before I was going to close up. I hadn't seen a customer in two hours.

"I had maybe a couple dozen trees left, and most of 'em weren't much to look at. By the time you get that close to Christmas, they've been picked over pretty good.

"So I'm standing by the kerosene heater when this young couple comes in and starts looking at the trees.

"I don't know 'em by name, but I know they live down the street in the basement of one of the dumpiest three-flats in the neighborhood.

"He's a skinny young guy with a big Adam's apple and a small chin. Not much to look at. She's kind of pretty, but they're both wearing clothes that look like they came out of the bottom bin at the Salvation Army store.

"It's cold as a witch's toes, but neither of them have got on gloves or heavy shoes. So it's easy to see that they're having hard times with the paychecks.

"Well, they start lifting the trees up and looking at 'em and walking around 'em, the way people do. They finally find one that was pretty decent. Not a great tree. But it wasn't bad. And they ask me the price.

"It was about $8 or $9. They don't say anything. They just put it down.

"They keep looking. They must have looked at every tree in the lot. Like I said, there weren't many that were any good. But every time I gave the price on a decent one, they just shook their heads.

"Finally, they thank me and walk away. But when they get out on the sidewalk she says something and they stand there talking for awhile. Then he shrugs and they come back.

"I figure they're going to take one of the good trees after all.

"But they go over to this one tree that had to be the most pathetic tree we had. It was a Scotch pine that was OK on one side, but the other side was missing about half the branches.

"They ask me how much that one was. I told them that they'd have a hard time making it look good, no matter how much tinsel they put on it. But they could have it for a couple of bucks.

"Then they picked up another one that was damned near as pathetic. Same thing—full on one side, but scraggly on the other.

"They asked how much for that one. I told them that it was a deuce, too.

"So then she whispers something to him and he asks me if I'll take $3 for the two of them.

"Well, what am I going to do? Nobody's going to buy those trees anyway, so I told them they had a deal. But I tell them, what do you want with two trees? Spend a few dollars more and get yourself a nice tree.

"She just smiled and said they wanted to try something. So they gave me $3 and he carried one of them and she took the other.

"The next night, I happen to be walking past their building. I look down at the window and I can see a tree. I couldn't see it all, but what there was looked good.

"The lights are on, so I figure, what the heck. I knock on the door. They open it and I tell them I noticed the tree and I was just curious.

"They let me in. And I almost fell over. There in this tiny parlor was the most beautiful tree I ever saw. It was so thick it was almost like a bush. You couldn't see the trunk.

"They told me how they did it. They took the two trees and worked the trunks close together so they touched where the branches were thin.

"Then they tied the trunks together with wire. But when the branches overlapped and came together, it formed a tree so thick you couldn't see the wire. It was like a tiny forest of its own.

"The two of them looked so happy with it that it made me feel good the rest of the week.

"And thinking of those two orphan trees, which would have been tossed out if they hadn't come along, made me feel good, too.

"So that's the secret. You take two trees that aren't perfect, that have flaws, that might even be homely, that maybe nobody else would want.

"But if you put them together just right, you can come up with something really beautiful.

"Like two people, I guess."

January 29, 1986

These Seven Were Special People

Pick up this or any newspaper, and there will be a page of death notices and obituaries. People die every day. Some die young; more die old. Some suddenly, some after long illness. Rich, poor, unknown, and famous.

We pay little or no attention to most of them. In smaller cities, people might look a little closer at the obits because there's more likelihood that they'll know someone.

But in the big cities, most people don't even give them a glance. Or if they do, they just skim the names. And nobody says that this or that death is a great tragedy, a terrible loss. We don't say that about the death of strangers. People die. That's part of life.

Yet, millions of people around the world were plunged into deep sadness Tuesday because of the death of seven individuals who were strangers to almost all of us.

On the streets, you could find ordinary people staring into store windows at TV sets that showed the explosion of the space shuttle Challenger and weeping at the sight.

People phoned me, most of them shaken, subdued, depressed, just wanting to talk to someone about the tragedy.

I asked one elderly woman, who had surely seen much death in her lifetime, why she was so moved at the deaths of people whose names she wasn't sure of.

She said: "It's because they were doing it for us. They were representing us up there weren't they? They were special."

And I suppose that's part of it. Yes, they were representing us. The human race is going to explore space because it's in our nature to go where we've never been. And maybe we have to if we're going to survive. But we can't all do it. We have to delegate. And they are our explorers. They push back the boundaries for the rest of us.

In a sense, it's the same reason we mourn strangers in the uniforms of cops and firemen who die while doing their jobs. It's because they're representing us. We delegate, and they do our dirty and dangerous work.

And there was truth in what the elderly woman said about the seven being special.

They're special because they were among that small minority who don't do what they do for the paycheck.

They were the fortunate ones who have the brains, the drive, the vision, the physical gifts, to accomplish things that the rest of us can only marvel at. In Tom Wolfe's phrase: "the right stuff."

So it's doubly shocking when we see such special people die literally before our eyes, when we see a great, inspiring adventure turned into a video horror.

And it's a jarring reminder of our mortality. How sure are any of us that there will be a tomorrow when even the very special, the very gifted, can be gone in an instant; when all the dazzling technology, the brilliant minds of the space agency, the meticulous planning, the countless safeguards can't guarantee that a disaster won't occur?

It was a tragedy, yes. But I can't help but think that even in death, maybe they were still among the lucky ones.

I've known so many people, and you probably have too, who have quietly slipped away after lives of frustration, drudgery, failure, disappointment, and sickness. People who never had a chance to climb the mountains of their souls. Or who had no mountains.

The seven people on the spaceship, including the schoolteacher, had all chosen to climb. They wanted to walk the edge, with all the risks it involved.

I'm not sure that the risk wasn't worth it. Maybe it wouldn't be for you and me and most of us who prefer to play it safe. But the next time a spaceship is launched, there will be people aboard who believe that what they're doing is more than worth the chance. There will always be such people, and all of them will tell you that they consider themselves lucky, no matter the outcome.

So in feeling grief, remember that the seven were special in what they did with their lives, right up to the end.

As someone once put it: "If I reach for the stars, I might not touch them. But I won't come up with a handful of dirt."

February 11, 1986

Sorry, Reggie, You Struck Out

From time to time, I make note of the alarming tendency of many well-known public figures to babble about their private lives. I call this the People Magazine Syndrome, for which there is no known medical cure, except tearing their tongues out, which is illegal, although it shouldn't be.

The most recent example of this affliction is Reggie Jackson, the wealthy baseball player and hot dog.

A publicity man for a magazine has sent me a news release announcing that in the current issue of the magazine, "Reggie Jackson Speaks Out On His Sex Life."

What first caught my eye were the words "speaks out."

This term is not uncommon in the writing of news. But it's usually reserved for when someone of importance takes a stand on a grave issue in which there is assumed to be considerable public interest.

You'll see headlines that say "Governor Speaks Out On Tax Hike," or "President Speaks Out On Philippine Vote," or "Medical Chief Speaks Out On Malpractice Suits."

So I thought it a bit presumptuous of the publicity man to use the words "speaks out" in the context of how a baseball player says he does it, when he does it, and with whom he does it.

It's true that some men do discuss their sex lives, although not as entertainingly as their golf scores. But you'll seldom hear someone in a bar or locker room say: "Hey, guys, listen because I'm going to speak out on what happened Friday night after I hit on this good looking. . . ."

Such disclosures could be more accurately described as bragging, lying, fantasizing, or BSing; but not "speaking out."

The magazine's publicity man went on to quote Jackson as saying:

"I'm active sexually, but not as much as people think."

The key phrase there is "people think." Obviously, Jackson believes that a considerable segment of the American people has given thought to his sex life.

And that widespread curiosity is probably what persuaded him that the time had finally come for him to *speak out.*

The human brain is an incredible organ. In any given day, even the dumbest of us will have thousands of thoughts, impressions, images, memories.

But as hard as I racked my brain, I couldn't recall even once thinking about Reggie Jackson's sexual activities.

Out of curiosity, I asked the first thirty people I spoke to if they have ever thought of Jackson's sex life, and, if so, what they thought of it.

The responses to my informal survey might have a depressing effect on Jackson's ego.

A middle-aged man said: "To be honest, no, I have never given it any thought. But, then, I don't watch much TV."

A man of the Yuppie persuasion asked: "No, is there something unusual about it? I mean, does he wear his uniform and fielder's mitt?"

Another's indignant reply was: "Of course not. Why should I bother? Does that palooka ever think about *my* sex life? I have my needs, too, you know."

A young woman said: "I'm afraid not. I've always been a Cub fan. Do you want to ask me about Ryne Sandberg?"

A middle-aged woman said: "I'm sorry, but I haven't paid attention. I really try to keep up with current events, but there are only so many hours in the day."

Not even one of thirty people I surveyed could remember ever having even a fragment of a thought about Jackson's sex life.

Of course, this survey was taken in Chicago. So I suppose it's possible that in southern California, where Jackson has been playing baseball for several years, people might have been thinking about his sex life.

But knowing southern California, that's unlikely, unless Jackson's been doing it while surfing or hang gliding.

So it appears that if Jackson's motive for speaking out was to correct "what people think" about his sex life, there was no need. He might as well have zipped his lip, or his trousers, or whatever.

And if his sex life has gone the way of his hitting, then he shouldn't have been wasting his time talking to a magazine writer anyway.

Maybe a therapist.

June 23, 1987

Fred Astaire Was a Class Act until the End

When a Fred Astaire movie came to the Congress Theatre, we all groaned. It meant that on Saturday afternoon—movie time in the neighborhood—we had to go up Milwaukee Avenue to the fancy Harding, which cost more. Or down the street to the grimy Oak, which ran nothing but the worst B-films.

But anything was better than sitting through a Fred Astaire movie, with their sappy stories, mushy love songs, and dance after dance after dance.

His movies were the worst, the pits. No Errol Flynn boldly sword-fighting with pirates. No rib-busting jokes from Abbott and Costello or Curly, Larry, and Moe. No monsters like Boris or Bela or Lon. Or John Wayne facing down the bad guys. Or Bogart snarling. Sissy movies is what they were.

And Astaire himself. What a geek. Skinny, homely, always strutting about in his fancy clothes and singing in a frail voice. He was a star? Don't make me laugh.

Only Slats Grobnik had the slightest appreciation of Astaire. As Slats said: "If a guy who looks that goofy can wind up with Ginger Rogers, I got to have a chance with Theresa Gabinski, if her fodder don't come out on the porch and catch us."

I don't remember precisely when it happened. Sometime after I started shaving regularly. But I was looking up at a movie screen when it dawned on me that I was watching just about the sharpest, hippest, coolest guy in the world. In my social circle, we didn't use words like debonaire or sophisticated, but that's what we meant.

And one of the most talented. I didn't know that Ballanchine, the dance genius, had said Astaire was the greatest dancer in the world. It wouldn't have mattered because I didn't know who Ballanchine was. But I'd figured that much out myself. If anybody danced better, he'd need an extra leg.

From that point on, I saw every Astaire movie ever made—the new ones when they came out, the old ones when they were on TV or, more recently, in videocassettes.

I still think most of the plots were sappy. In fact, I have trouble remembering the names of the films, or which Astaire movie was which.

But the names and plots aren't important. What mattered was the music, written by the best composers, and Fred Astaire dancing and singing or just looking debonaire. He could stroll across a room with more style than most dancers can dance.

As the years went on, I found something else about him that I admired tremendously. It was that I knew very little about him, other than what I saw on the screen.

I didn't read about his love life or about his punching somebody in a nightclub. I didn't read about him storming off a set, feuding with a director, fighting with the press, or babbling about what he liked to eat, what he liked to drink, snort, or smoke.

In other words, he did his work, went home, closed the door, and said: "That's it, world. You get my performance. The rest belongs to me."

These days, any mediocrity who gets his mug in *People* magazine is considered a "star." If they don't fade into oblivion after two years, they are declared "superstars."

So if Michael Jackson is a "superstar," what do we call Fred Astaire—a constellation?

Monday the guy who, in my boyhood eyes was a skinny geek, died. He went privately and quietly—a class act right up to the end.

So when I finish writing this, I'll go home, have dinner, then get out my videocassette of *That's Entertainment.* I'll fast forward to the part where Gene Kelly tells us about Fred Astaire and his remarkable talents.

For about the twentieth time since I've had that cassette, my wife is going to have to sit and listen to me say: "Will you look at that? He's dancing with a coat rack . . . on the ceiling . . . look at that move . . . look at that timing . . . you know, he's an incredible athlete . . . fantastic."

But when Astaire finishes gliding through "Dancing in the Dark" with Cyd Charisse in Central Park and they almost float into a carriage, I won't say a word. I never can.

July 9, 1987

A True Hero Puts North to the Test

Ollie North got off to a fine start. For a while, it looked as if he was being hounded by a spiteful lawyer and a room full of politicians for nothing more than being a great patriot.

With his boyish good looks, chest full of ribbons, and obvious devotion to God and country, he almost had me saluting the TV set.

But it has started coming apart. By the end of the second day of testimony, all of his flag-waving couldn't hide the fact that handsome Ollie does have a flair for telling whoppers.

Of course, he always had a noble motive for lying, as he modestly admitted. When he lied to Congress or inserted lies into official documents or lied, in effect, by shredding other documents, he was doing it for a good cause. He was fighting the Commies.

So he told lies—time after time, lie after lie. If he were Pinocchio, his nose would have been halfway to the White House.

And what it boils down to is that he and his chums couldn't risk telling members of the Congress of the United States what was really going on at the White House—about the secret arms sales to Iran and the illegal diversion of profits to the *contras* in Nicaragua. Congress would just get in the way. It might even blab all of North's secrets to the world—including the Commies.

He seemed to be implying—while saying that he wasn't—that maybe Congress wasn't as loyal, as patriotic, as security conscious as he and his gumshoe associates were.

I'm sure that seemed reasonable to a lot of people—especially those who are dazzled by a chestful of ribbons.

But after two days of hearing why Congress couldn't be trusted with the truth, it obviously became a bit too much for Sen. Daniel Inouye of Hawaii to handle.

And as Wednesday's session ended, he told North so. Calmly and deliberately, he reminded North that for years he had been trusted with many national secrets and none had ever leaked. And that when leaks came, they were usually from up the street in the White House where North and his people hung out.

I'm not sure whether most viewers were impressed by Inouye, but that might be because they don't know much about him, except what they see. And that's not a very impressive sight.

Inouye isn't nearly as glamorous a TV figure as North. He's kind of pudgy-faced, and he talks in a monotone with a slight accent. He spends most of his time at these hearings sitting there like an inscrutable Buddha.

But when it comes to proven patriotism, he doesn't have to take a back seat to North or Poindexter or any in that crowd. And surely not to their commander in chief.

The cameras don't show it nearly as vividly as they show North's ribbons, but Inouye has only one arm. He left the other one back on a World War II battlefield in Italy when a German hand grenade went off.

That's when he was part of a legendary Army outfit—the

442nd Regimental Combat Team, made up almost entirely of Japanese-Americans.

Many of them had spent time in barbed-wire internment camps until the government decided they could be trusted to spill their blood for their own country. So they said good-bye to their families—still behind barbed wire—and went off to fight.

They became known as the "Go for Broke" outfit and were the most decorated unit in the war.

Inouye received his share of honors. He has the Distinguished Service Cross, which is the nation's second-highest military decoration. Ollie North, by the way, doesn't have one.

Plus the Bronze Star, the Purple Heart with cluster, five battle stars, and a few others. All that and the loss of his right arm before he was old enough to vote.

And he is one of the people whom North didn't find trustworthy enough to know—as our laws require—what kind of cloak-and-dagger stunts North and others were engaged in.

So I can understand why Inouye finally showed a touch of irritation and gave North a rather stern little lecture on loyalty and trust.

I can also understand why North looked more subdued at that point than he has during the entire hearing.

He knew he was being chewed out by a genuine hero.

And that's no lie.

June 27, 1988

When "Prix Fixe" Is Hard to Swallow

While browsing through a restaurant directory, I suggested to the blond that we might try a place that was newly listed.

She asked if it was expensive and I said that it had a "prix fixe" dinner.

"A what?" she said.

I repeated, "Prix fixe."

"How is that spelled?"

I spelled it aloud and again said: "Prix fixe."

"You're not pronouncing it correctly," she said.

Why not? I'm pronouncing it exactly the way it is spelled.

"No, no. If you say it that way, it sounds, well, it sounds obscene."

I said it again: "Prix fixe," the way it is spelled. And she may be right. It did sound like it might be a phrase describing some sort of male surgical procedure.

"The proper pronunciation," the blond said, flaunting her re-fined upbringing, "is pree feeks."

Then why isn't it spelled pree feeks?

"Because it is French. And in French, pree feeks is spelled prix fixe."

How stupid of me. I had forgotten that the first rule of the French language is that almost nothing is pronounced the way it's spelled. When the French invented their language, they rigged it that way just to make the rest of us feel inferior. They also thought that if they had a language that was almost impossible to learn, the Germans might not invade them.

"Pree feeks," the blond said. "It simply means fixed price."

I already knew that much. The question is, why do newspapers and magazine restaurant listings in the United States, where most of us speak one form of English or another, insist on using "prix fixe," which is pronounced "pree feeks" and means "fixed price," instead of "fixed price," which means fixed price and is pro-nounced "fixed price"?

My guess is that the vast majority of Americans do not know how to pronounce "prix fixe." And a great many don't even know what it means.

Why, if you went into some restaurants in Arkansas or Tennes-see and asked if they had a "prix fixe" dinner—pronouncing it the way it is spelled—it's likely that the waiter would bellow, "Ya lowdown preevert," and hit you with a catfish.

This newspaper, I'm sorry to say, is no exception. We have "prix fixes" scattered all through our restaurant listings. I asked a few copy editors, who are experts in such matters, why we don't just say "fixed price." They weren't sure.

One of them said that he thought we did it when reviewing French restaurants.

If so, we're being inconsistent. We may even be discriminating.

For example, when we list a German restaurant, we don't say "fester preis," which is German for fixed price.

Fester preis. It has a pleasant, homey ring. It sounds like the name of somebody who lives deep in the Ozarks. "Howdy, I'm Fester Preis and this here is my brother Lester Preis and my uncle Chester Preis."

In our listings for Chinese restaurants, we don't write "Gu din jia ge," which I was told by a Chinese acquaintance means fixed price. Of course, he might have been pulling my leg. For all I know, it means: "The person who wrote this column is a geek." But I'll take his word for it.

I was going to include the Greek version of "fixed price," but Sam Sianis, who owns Billy Goat's Tavern, said: "Feex price? You crazy? In Greek joints, we no got feex price. We charge what we can get."

Another copy editor told me that "prix fixe" is used so widely that it has become the accepted, common meaning for "fixed price."

That didn't make sense to me, either. I've never picked up the financial pages and read a story that said:

"Three steel companies have been accused by the antitrust division of the Justice Department of prix fixeing. The companies engaged in the fixe, sources say, to drive up the prix of steel."

Years ago, when Chicago was strictly a meat-and-potatoes town, we didn't have such linguistic problems.

I suppose that as we became more sophisticated, this was the prix we paid.

August 9, 1988

Cubs Park Wasn't Always Like This

It was much simpler then. No parking to worry about. No phone calls to Ticketmaster. No crowds or long lines. The nation was not watching.

The kid brother and I would leave the family flat at about 8 o'clock in the morning and start walking the five miles from Milwaukee Avenue and Armitage to Cubs Park.

We walked because it saved the streetcar fare, which then could be used to buy a Coke to go along with the fried egg sandwich, wrapped in wax paper, each of us was packing.

It was a pleasant walk on a summer morning. You could actually pass through neighborhood after neighborhood without risking being shot for not flashing the proper gang hand signals.

When we got to Cubs Park (true fans seldom called it Wrigley Field), we went to a service gate and waited with a dozen or so other kids for The Man to come out.

We always got there early enough so that we'd be up front and chosen by The Man.

Finally he'd appear, a rumpled looking guy who looked a little hung over.

"OK, you, you, you . . . ," and he'd point at us and wave us inside.

We'd go up a ramp and into the ballpark, empty except for the ground crew tidying up the field.

Then we'd start work. It was an easy enough job. In those days, the box seats had folding chairs that had to be set up and put in place.

That was the job. And our pay was free admission to the ballpark, with our choice of grandstand seats.

The choice was unlimited. Chances were that on a good weekday day, only eight or ten thousand people would mosey into the ballpark. Often the crowd was so sparse the upper deck was closed to save the expense of having an usher or two up there.

By the time we finished setting up the seats, the team had drifted onto the field—Pafko, Schmitz, Cavarretta, Waitkus, Smalley, playing catch and a pepper game to loosen up.

Then came what was often the highlight of the whole day. Batting practice. Booming shots into and over the bleachers. We savored every one of them because we knew it was unlikely that we'd see many during the game.

If teams like the Giants, the Cards, or the Dodgers were in town, we'd watch them practice with awe and a sense of fatality. Mize, Musial, Slaughter, Robinson, Campanella, Kurowski, Snider, Thomson—their practice shots soared like golf shots.

But, of course, they had an unfair advantage. The owner of the Cubs, an eccentric named P. K. Wrigley, had won a pennant in 1945 with a collection of athletes judged 4-F, physically unfit for military service. When World War II ended, everybody else signed the able-bodied veterans. Only Wrigley, out of sentiment or indifference, stayed with his collection of 4-Fs.

So the Cubs were losers. When I was setting up seats, they may have been one of the worst teams in the history of the game.

But there were some advantages to that. The price was right, and we had almost any seat in the house. And the law of averages said they'd occasionally win a game. Pafko might hit one out. If he hadn't had too much beer the night before, Schmitz's curve might baffle even Musial. And on the long walk home, we'd go over every play of the game.

Now we're in a new era. History, the sports intellectuals tell us, is being made because lights are being turned on.

For last night's game—the first night game in Wrigley Field—tickets were being scalped for as much as $1,000. The same seats I used to sit in for unfolding a few chairs. The Chicago Symphony Orchestra played the National Anthem. Celebrities flocked to town, pleading for a few moments on the air with Harry Caray.

My kid brother, no longer a kid, drove in from Wisconsin with his kid. We'd been on the phone talking logistics. Where to park? What's the tow zone? Is formal dress required? If we order a beer before the seventh inning ban, must we finish drinking it by the completion of the inning?

I even had a phone call from a former Chicagoan in San Diego. He's outraged because his TV cable service doesn't carry the Cubs games and he's going to miss this monumental event.

And I remember being in the ballpark when there were only about 800 people, including the vendors.

Yes, it is a new era. The only thing that remains the same is that the team stunk then and it stinks now.

And the biggest difference isn't the lights. It's that in those by-gone days, nobody was stupid enough to pay a grand to watch a bunch of losers.

October 5, 1988

Shopping Isn't Everyone's Bag

I still haven't figured out why it is such a big deal that Blooming-dale's, the New York department store, has opened a branch in Chicago.

The newspapers, TV stations, and disc jockeys have become giddy over the arrival of the store.

The silliness may have peaked when a gushy female reporter from the *New York Times* called and asked me to describe my own excitement.

I explained to her that while certain activities excite me, most of which I would not describe to a respectable woman, the open-ing of a Bloomingdale's store is not one of them.

Furthermore, I said, this is not Wyoming. We already have enough famous, high-priced stores in Chicago to satisfy the self-indulgence of every coke-sniffing pork-belly trader in town, as well as their wives, mistresses, or any other sex objects of their choice.

Not easily discouraged, the New York reporter asked: "Are you going to go shop at Bloomingdale's?"

"No," I said.

"Why not?"

"Because I don't shop."

"Everybody shops," she said.

"Not me. I do not shop."

"Then how do you get your clothes?"

An interesting question. So I explained.

About five years go, I was in my closet looking for something to wear that didn't have gravy stains on the lapels.

As I searched the cluttered room, I realized that I had enough garments and shoes to open a men's shop.

That's because I never throw any clothes away. I have suits, shoes, jackets, slacks, and shirts that are more than twenty-five years old.

Some of the trousers are worn thin in the seat. But if you wear shorts that match the trouser color, few will notice. And many of the jacket sleeves have holes at the elbows. But you can get a leather patch sewn on for a few bucks, then pose as a professor of literature.

Most of the shoes have holes in the bottom. But in dry weather it doesn't matter. And for winter I have Luigi, my neighborhood shoemaker, give a few pairs a rehab.

As I went through this ancient but vast wardrobe, counting each item, digging some out from under old luggage, something remarkable occurred to me.

After making a count, I called an actuary and asked him how long I could expect to live. He said that based on my personal habits, a few minutes or maybe an hour. But based on his statistical tables, a few more decades.

I did mental calculations: How many shirts per year, how many shoes, how many slacks, jackets, and so on.

And I realized that if I lived to a ripe, even rancid, old age, I would never again have to buy another garment.

I even set aside my least shiny suit and a shirt with a sturdy collar button to be buried in. (However, that won't be necessary because I have since redone my will, instructing my wife to stuff my remains in a Hefty bag and call the ward sanitation superintendent for a special pickup.)

One of the benefits of having all these old clothes is that every couple of years, some of them come back in style. If I could find my original zoot suit, bought when I was seventeen from Smokey Joe's on Halsted Street, I'd be a sensation in the Hard Rock Cafe.

On the other hand, one of the disadvantages is that I frequently look like a bum. However, there are advantages to that disadvantage. For one thing, if you look as rumpled and frayed as I usually do, you're less likely to be mugged. In fact, when I walk on a street, people who see me approaching sometimes cross to the other side, fearing I might mug them.

Anyway, I explained all this to the New York reporter. Being clever, she said: "Yes, but what about socks and undergarments? You have to shop for them."

Not so. My wife buys them for me, although my favorite brands are becoming harder to find with the decline of Army-Navy Surplus stores.

Sounding amazed, the reporter said: "You're the first person I've ever talked to who never shops. I can't believe it."

So I told her that I wasn't being entirely truthful. I admitted that I sometimes make purchases at a Salvation Army resale shop.

"Ah," the reporter said, "you do shop after all."

Of course, I said, I have loved ones, and I have to get them something for Christmas and birthdays. I'm no Scrooge.

December 20, 1988

Daley the Elder and Daley the Younger

There's something almost eerie about the similarities between the year 1955—a milestone in Chicago's political history—and this year, which could be another milestone.

As 1955 began, Chicago had a mild-mannered, likable, but somewhat ineffectual mayor in Martin J. Kennelly.

Kennelly became mayor in 1947 because reform-minded ex-GIs were kicking out old-time boss rule in city after city.

To avoid that happening here, the Machine trotted out Kennelly, a successful businessman who looked and sounded good.

Their idea was that the silver-haired Kennelly would sit quietly in his office, cut ribbons, go to banquets, be a charming figurehead, and not meddle with the way the aldermen looted City Hall.

For the most part, it worked. But by 1955, the Machine was ready to take back the mayor's office.

So it turned to Richard J. Daley, one of a younger, cleaner breed of Machine politicians.

Yes, despite his later reputation as the boss of all bosses, in those days Daley had rather nifty credentials for a Machine creature.

As a young state legislator, he developed a reputation for being honest, hard-working, quiet, but effective.

He later served ably in the late Gov. Adlai Stevenson's do-gooder cabinet as revenue director, which gave him credibility among Stevenson's liberal-reform supporters.

Then he was elected Cook County clerk, a patronage-rich office that he ran efficiently and without scandal.

So although Daley had spent his life in the Machine, and knew all its tricks, he was seen as superior to the Paddy Baulers, Botchy Connors, Joe Gills, and other cigar chompers.

Although not a wild-eyed reformer, he was considered somewhat progressive. While not a preachy liberal, he was considered a reasonable man on social issues.

Most important, he didn't have firm ties to the many feuding factions in the Machine. He managed to distance himself from their squabbles, while remaining part of the big picture.

So when the Machine decided that it was time to dump nice-guy Kennelly, Daley stepped in, knocking Kennelly out of the primary.

And, of course, the next twenty-plus Daley years are history.

So let us jump forward to the present.

Again, we have a mild-mannered, likable, somewhat ineffectual mayor: Eugene Sawyer.

Like Kennelly, Sawyer was put in that office by Machine types after Harold Washington's death because it suited their short-range survival strategy. One can even say that Sawyer, like Kennelly, was installed to beat back the threat of self-styled reformers; like Washington, Sawyer was black, but he was not a reformer.

But now that his usefulness has been served, the Machine types are looking to replace him with one of their own in next spring's mayoral election. Or someone they hope will be one of their own.

This time it's Richard M. Daley, son of Boss. You like parallels? I'll give you parallels.

Just as his father did, Richard the Younger has been running a county office, that of state's attorney, efficiently and without scandal.

Just as his father did, Richard the Younger has stayed out of the bickering and feuding that has fragmented the Democratic Party. In his dad's day, it was South Side against North Side, as well as tussles within each group. Today, it's whites against blacks with Hispanics getting in their jabs, as well as tussles within each group.

Just as his father did, Richard the Younger has forged political ties with liberals and reformers. This week, a group of them held a press conference to declare that he's their guy.

It's as if the late Daley left a blueprint, titled: "OK, kid, here's how you get to be mayor."

When Daley the Elder ran the first time, Kennelly said it was the forces of graft and evil (Daley) against the forces of goodness and reform (Kennelly).

Daley loftily responded: "Let's talk about the issues. I do not believe in dealing in personalities."

Today, Alderman Tim Evans and his supporters are saying that the choice is between them—the "progressives" (which is more delicate than saying blacks)—and the "conservatives" (which is more tactful than saying whites).

And Richard the Younger, scrambling for the high road, says: "I don't believe in talking about personalities or using labels. Let's talk about the issues."

Both Daleys even have their Eastern European ethnic adversaries, who saw it as a fight to the death.

In the case of Richard the Elder, it was Ben Adamowski, who thought that just because he was smarter, quicker, far more articulate, and better looking, he should be mayor. He quit the Democratic Party and became a Republican in order to carry on his blood feud with Daley.

In the case of Richard the Younger, it's Ed Vrdolyak, who thinks that just because he's smarter, quicker, more articulate, and better looking, he should be mayor. And he's switched parties to better carry on his blood feud. Knowing Eddie, it's liable to last for life.

I don't know how this is all going to turn out, but right now the words of Yogi Berra come to mind:

"It's like déjà vu all over again."

August 15, 1989

Woodstock Was Just a Muddy Memory

I don't remember what I was doing twenty years ago today. Probably what I'm doing now.

But I do know I wasn't wading in mud on a New York farm, running naked in the presence of strangers, puffing on a weed, or popping pills that made me say "wow."

In other words, I wasn't at Woodstock, the legendary rock festival, mass drug party, sex orgy, mud bath, and traffic jam that many of its 350,000 participants and some media philosophers are now trying to turn into an event of great historic and sociological significance.

However, I do remember turning on my TV set and being told that this was the "Woodstock Nation."

My reaction was that if this was some kind of new "nation," we should send them foreign aid, since they obviously were in dire need.

The poor souls were wrapped in blankets, sleeping in muck, and eating in soup kitchens and many of them were being hauled on stretchers to be treated for dope overdose.

Even worse, there was obviously a shortage of toilet facilities. And because there were no motels, couples who couldn't control their passions were forced to engage in the procreative act before cheering spectators.

Despite all this, many of them said they were having a great time, that despite the hardships there was an aura of love and to-getherness, and some had found a new meaning to life.

So I wished them well. But I still preferred a smoky piano bar with a clean john.

Now, twenty years later, it seems as if every publication and TV show in America is looking back at Woodstock, seeking its meaning and talking to those who were there.

The good news is that most of those being interviewed appear to have washed off the mud.

The bad news is that they actually think something remarkable occurred.

The author of a book on Woodstock is quoted in the *New York Times* as saying: "Woodstock was a moment in time that was the culmination of a lot of ideals and sensibilities that were the 1960s for a whole generation of people. . . . Culturally, it helped to define a generation."

There we go with the old defining-a-generation routine.

Well, maybe it did. But if so, I don't think the results were anything to brag about.

Most of those at Woodstock were somewhere between their late teens and early thirties, the majority in their early twenties.

No offense meant, but that generation was the most self-centered, self-indulgent, demanding, pampered, ungrateful generation in this country's history.

They were the children of people who grew up knowing hard times in the Great Depression. And many knew even harder times when they fought World War II.

But for their efforts, these parents were told: "Look at what a terrible world you brought us into. All you think about are material things."

Of course, these crass material things made them the best fed, best clothed, best housed, best educated, and least appreciative generation in history.

"Ideals and sensibilities," the Woodstock author said. Well, yes, I'm sure most of them were against the Vietnam War. Or at least personally taking part in the war. But as soon as they were safe from the draft and the war ended, many of the more ardent peaceniks became furious dollarniks. The peace generation became the "I'll get mine" generation.

And when it came to materialism, they made their parents look like monks. There were no designer labels on ma's and pa's butts.

The "ideals and sensibilities" of that generation also pioneered this country's massive drug habit. It wasn't enough that they zonked themselves out but, even worse, they passed along the idea that it was the way to go to their kid brothers and sisters. And we're still living with it.

One of the Woodstock scholars said that the rock music they gathered to hear could change society, could change the world. That's part of the '60s vanity. I've never quite understood why if the genius of Bach, Mozart, Beethoven, and Brahms didn't change the world, the sight of Joe Cocker twitching through withdrawal on a public stage should be profound.

But I will concede that the world did change for some of the artists who appeared at Woodstock. Three of the top stars soon doped themselves to death. A couple of others wound up in jail and rehab joints. And one made a fast exit using a noose.

Of course, it would be unfair to judge an entire generation by a herd of grass-puffing mud-bathers. There were some from that generation who put themselves on the line in the civil rights movement. But they were a minority.

And that generation included many ghetto blacks, working-class ethnics, and sleepy-hollow Southern boys who couldn't or wouldn't wrangle deferments and wound up in Vietnam. But when they slept in mud, it wasn't any "culmination" of their "ideas and sensibilities."

So spare us the nostalgia. Get back on the phone and sell some stock, or take your BMW in for a tune-up.

Or at least be honest, as one Woodstock veteran was, when he told a reporter:

"What do I remember most? I got the clap. That was it."

PART FOUR

THE NINETIES

From the beginning, the 1990s seemed tailor-made for the Mike Royko column. Politicians in a dither about flag-burning (not that it was happening anywhere). The Rodney King beating in Los Angeles. Tonya Harding and Nancy Kerrigan's smashed knee. A new crop of word police. Even a war to hate, as with Vietnam during his first decade on the job.

If he worried that after nearly thirty years of the daily grind he might run out of ideas or zest, it wasn't apparent in his work. Always relishing his role as a contrarian, he went after the "political correctness" crowd as soon as they announced their intention to scour the media for evidence of insensitivity. Later, it became fashionable for writers to lambast this new form of intolerance. But Mike was at it when much of the nation's news media was cowering. He refused to forgo his brand of satire, remaining an equal opportunity ridiculer no matter how loudly the critics howled.

In one of his early columns on the subject, "A Nose Rub of Sorts for Ditzy Word Jocks," he poked fun at a checklist of possibly offensive words compiled under the sponsorship of the University of Missouri School of Journalism. The conclusion opens with Mike in his gleeful, defiant-kid mode: "Fried chicken, fried chicken, fried chicken. I said it and I'm glad."

He described his feelings toward his correctness critics in his two-hour interview with Chris Robling in the fall of 1993, his thirtieth anniversary as a columnist. "I think and write in the same terms I always did," he said. "Most of the things that people carp about under the guise of political correctness are really kind of dumb. It bothers me that newspapers today are so sensitive to this, including the one that I work on." At this point in his career, he said, his attitude was, "Squawk all you want, pick at me, I don't care; I'm going to say what I want the way I want to say it." If the complainers bothered to actually read his columns, he added, they would find that "my views have not changed at all."

He was right. He wrote some of his most powerful attacks on racial and economic injustice during the 1990s, often couched in savage wit. Offenders received equal Royko treatment, whatever their ethnic backgrounds. Los Angeles Police Chief Daryl Gates was skinned in "Ticket to Good Life Punched with Pain," a commentary on the Rodney King beating, as was rapper Ice Cube in "David Duke Has a Partner in Slime." This column, incidentally, had a bonus for readers: an original Mike Royko rap lyric, written especially for "Mr. Cube," as Mike politely referred to him.

There are layers of wisdom on race relations in this country, accumulated over three decades of dealing with the topic, in the prophetic "Don't Bet on a Guilty Verdict for O. J.," written as opening arguments began in the trial; in "Eloquence and Gall on Washington Mall," his reaction to the Million Man March; and in "Politically Incorrect, But Right on Target," a tribute to Jesse Jackson.

Mike saw injustice, too, in the Persian Gulf War. For the most part, opinion writers and editorial pages around the country were leading the cheers for President George Bush. Mike, though, was pounding out angry commentaries such as "Kuwait's Future Brighter Than Ours," which predicted that Kuwait would be rehabbed and spruced up long before the West Side of Chicago or other ravaged neighborhoods in U.S. cities. Another is the bitterly ironic "It Didn't Take Long to Lose Euphoria." He thought the war in the Gulf would accomplish about as much as the war in Vietnam—in other words, the killing of hapless innocents.

He also had fun in the 1990s, of course, and often with a familiar target: himself. His hatred of his feet surfaced again in "Why Be a Writer? Think of Your Feet." He overcame a terrible fear, albeit on the verge of panic, in "Look, Up in the Sky, It's a Bird . . . It's a Plane . . . It's Mike!" And who could not sympathize with his depression when he realized that the best inspirational saying he could recall in response to a book editor's request was Slats Grobnik's old standby, "Stay out of the trees, watch out for the wild goose, and take care of your hernia"? ("He Could Fill a Book with Pithy Phrases").

Early in his career, Mike developed a talent for writing about an issue that everyone else was writing about, but first turning it inside out and finding its kernel of truth. He would then relay his discovery in such a piquant and comical fashion that readers had to nod in agreement at the same time they were laughing. Two examples, on utterly different matters, are "Whitewater Almost Too Far Out There" and "We Love Her, We Love Her Not, We Love . . ." in which skater Tonya Harding ("a female Dead End Kid," Mike called her) has him spinning like a human top.

The mellow Mike made frequent appearances, too. What sweeter tribute could Michael Jordan have than "A City in Full-Court Depression"? And the image of the father and the boy in "Horrors of the Past Are G-Rated Today"—surely, Mike and his son Sam—is as tender as it is funny.

When computers were introduced in newsrooms, back in the 1970s, Mike swore he would stick with his old typewriter forever. Instead, he became a technology fanatic—as obsessed with the latest electronic gadgetry as he was with softball, golf, baseball statistics, and the Godfather movies. By the early 1990s, Mike had acquired so many adoring fans (as well as garbage-tossing detractors) that he and Judy sought privacy by moving from their busy city street to a quiet North Shore suburb. Mike fashioned a home office on the third floor of their house. With the wonders of technology and his penchant for it, he was able to do much of his writing at home. His two small children often played nearby, which he loved.

It was in this third-floor hideaway that he granted the radio interview to Chris Robling, a rarity for someone who so disliked being probed by others in his business. His assessment of his own work—or, at least, the way he portrayed it to Robling and the public—was pure Mike, wry and cynical and very funny.

Yes, there were certain columns—"anytime I peeled a grape with an ax"—he would not want to read again. "When I was younger, I think I was a little rougher on people than [when] I got a little more mature. You know, you whack some guy, a small timer—a column is a very, very powerful weapon. If I nail him, who have I nailed? His wife, his kids . . ."

He consistently turned down big fees to make speeches and seldom appeared on television for the simple reasons that he didn't like doing them and he didn't care a whit about the celebrity that went along with it. "If they're going to offer me a large sum of money [for speaking], I've got to tell them something worth hearing. Which means I've got to sit there for a few days and write it. I can't just wing it. I don't have a canned speech that I can drag out. People have suggested that I do a canned speech, but I don't know—I just haven't been able to think of one. I stay off television for the most part. I'm trying to set the record for most times by a journalist saying no to Ted Koppel. . . . If I've got something to say, I can say it in my column."

He refused repeated offers to move to Washington because "there's more to my life than work, and in Washington you never get away from it. And I don't want to have to scramble for status, or worry because, gee, I'm not on some TV show, or whatever. I'm not part of the McGoofy [McLaughlin] Group. Ben Bradlee [when he was executive editor of the *Washington Post*] once told me that I had to come to Washington if I wanted to cast a long shadow. And I'm thinking, I never thought about my shadow, how far I can cast it. I know how far I can cast a lure, if I'm fishing. But my shadow? I've never worried about casting a long shadow."

Actually, he said, he did not think in terms of long-range goals. "I just hope my next column is readable, doesn't bore people. I don't have any grand scheme."

But, Robling persisted, what did he think he owed his readers?

"Do I owe them something that will be worth reading 100 years from now? I don't think so. Do I owe them something of the quality of Mark Twain? Nah. Not for 50 cents. I guess what I owe them is, if I write something, believe me, I wrote it because this is what I think. No editor told me to write it. The Trilateral Commission didn't tell me to write it. I'm not doing it because then the *Tribune* editorial page will like it or not like it. So readers can be sure they're getting what I happen to think at that moment. I may change my mind the next day, but it's what I think at that moment."

Robling concluded by asking how it felt to be consistently referred to as the nation's best columnist.

"Like being the tallest midget in the circus. We're not talking about Shakespeare, you know. Big deal. I'm good at writing 900 words a day. It shows I've got the mental equivalent of a strong back. There are people who can out-write me, but they can't out-write me five days a week, or four days a week. One day a week they might."

As Mike turned sixty-four, he and Judy were talking of retirement. He had several ideas for books. They wanted to travel. They bought a condominium on the Gulf in Florida. By this time four more collections of Mike's columns had been published. He had won dozens of awards; in addition to the Pulitzer and the Broun, there was the Ernie Pyle Memorial Award and the first H. L. Mencken Award from the *Baltimore Sun,* named after its own legendary columnist. He was voted America's top columnist by readers of the *Washington Journalism Review* three times—the only times the poll was conducted. Mike Royko was the most widely honored columnist of his time, perhaps in the history of journalism.

On March 21, 1997, just before flying to Florida with Judy and the children for an Easter vacation, he wrote one more time about his Chicago Cubs—"It Was Wrigley, Not Some Goat, Who Cursed the Cubs."

While in Florida, he suffered a brain aneurysm. He survived surgery and flew back to Chicago, where he died on April 29, 1997. He was sixty-four years old.

Mike Royko's memorial service was held on a sunny June day in Wrigley Field.

March 16, 1990

Why Be a Writer? Think of Your Feet

The letter began with a question: "Do you recall an event from your childhood that first inspired you to write?"

The question was posed by a worthy organization called Child's Play Touring Theatre. It's a professional theater company promoting writing literacy among children.

To raise funds, they're asking writers: "Will you please take a few minutes to help the cause of literacy by sharing your own memory with us?" They plan to hold an auction and sell the writers' responses.

I'd like to help their cause. But I have a conflict.

On my wall there is a quotation from Samuel Johnson that I try to live by. It says: "No man but a blockhead ever wrote except for money."

So if I write something free for this worthy cause, I will be a blockhead.

On the other hand, I'd like to help them out. The solution is to answer their question in my column. That way, they will have their answer, and I'll be paid by the *Tribune.*

To answer their question: Yes, I recall several events in my childhood and young manhood that inspired me to become a writer.

When I was a child, my father was a milkman. Those were the days when most people had fresh milk, cream, butter, cheese, and other dairy products delivered to their doors each morning.

Most of his customers lived in three-flats, so he would grab a couple of metal trays, load them with bottles, and run up the back steps. During the summer, when school was out, I went along as his helper. Because I was only seven, he had me handle light first-floor deliveries.

Watching my father dashing up those steps at 5 A.M., sweat pouring down his face, I learned two things: 1. Being a milkman was hard work. 2. I didn't want to be a milkman.

A few years later, when I was about twelve, I became my grandfather's helper. He was an independent housepainter.

So I spent another summer vacation going with my grandfather on jobs, helping him with the dropcloths, ladders, and scaffolds and putting on masking tape and doing some painting myself.

This was before the days of rollers and paint that could be washed off brushes with water. Painters prized their brushes like the fine tools they were. They had to be thoroughly cleaned with chemicals.

Working with my grandfather, I learned several things. Painting walls wasn't bad, although it could get tedious. Doing woodwork and floors was murder on your knees. Ceilings got paint in your face and a crick in your neck.

I also discovered that housepainters drank a lot. My grandfather and his cronies said that was because fumes from the paint were hazardous but shots and beers were an effective antidote. However, one day, my grandfather had too much antidote and fell off a scaffold and broke his leg. So I decided that I didn't want to be a housepainter. Besides, I was a sly scamp and knew that you didn't have to paint ceilings to drink antidotes.

After that, I had other jobs setting bowling pins, working on a landscaping crew, in a greasy machine shop, and in a lamp factory and pushing carts around a department store. I learned one thing from these jobs. They made my flat feet hurt.

So I decided that if I was going to find my life's work, it would have to be something that wouldn't make me run up and down steps, get paint in my face, or give me aching feet.

Then, while still a young man, I read a magazine article about Ernest Hemingway, the great novelist. It described his typical workday.

He would arise, have a bit of breakfast, and write until about noon. Then he and a pal or two would get in his cabin cruiser and spend the rest of the afternoon sipping tall cool ones and fishing.

Except on days when he didn't feel like fishing. Then he would write until noon and go sit at an outdoor café with his pals and sip tall cool ones.

This impressed me as a sensible way to earn a living, and that was when I began thinking about becoming a writer.

But I almost changed my mind. I later saw another article about Hemingway, and there was a picture of him in the act of writing. His typewriter was on the mantel and he typed while standing. According to the article, he always stood while he wrote.

While that wasn't as grueling as running up three flights with six quarts of milk and two pounds of butter, I knew that standing over a typewriter all morning wouldn't do my fallen arches any good.

So I gave up thoughts of becoming a writer and set a new career goal. I would become a disc jockey. I knew that they sat while jockeying their discs. And one of my teachers told me I had a natural gift for that sort of work. Actually, she didn't say I should become a disc jockey. But she mentioned that I often babbled like an idiot, so it amounted to the same thing.

Fortunately, I read still another article about Hemingway. And that one said that he wrote while standing only because he had hemorrhoids and they hurt more when he sat.

That clinched it, and I set out to become a writer. And while I haven't achieved Hemingway's success, the job has never given me aching feet.

On the other hand, I can modestly say that I've been compared with Hemingway. Well, sort of. Readers sometimes tell me that I'm a real pain in the whatchamacallit.

June 1, 1990

A Nose Rub of Sorts for Ditzy Word Jocks

Maybe it's time to wave the white flag. The age of supersensitivity is crushing me.

I started to feel like a beaten man while reading a list of words that I shouldn't use because they might offend someone.

The bad-word dictionary was put together by a panel of news-people on something called the Multicultural Management Program at the University of Missouri School of Journalism.

The introduction to their bad-word dictionary says:

"As newspapers move into the 1990s, there will be more emphasis on including minorities in daily stories—accurately, succinctly, and in good taste. Language usage that has been acceptable in the past may no longer be acceptable.

"The following is a checklist of words, many objectionable, that reporters and editors must be aware of in order to avoid offending and perpetuating stereotypes."

Some of the words on the list are obviously offensive: nigger, chink, faggot. So you don't see them in newspapers.

But "Dutch treat"? "Airhead"? And how about such shockers as barracuda, burly, buxom, dear, dingbat, ditz, dizzy, fried chicken, gorgeous, gyp, housewife, illegal alien, Ivan, jock, johns, lazy, pert, petite, rubbing noses, shiftless, stunning, sweetie, and ugh.

That's right, "ugh." The dictionary says: "A gutteral word used to mimic American Indian speech. Highly offensive."

Why not "Dutch treat"? They say: "To share the cost, as in a date. Implies that Dutch people are cheap."

Shall I go on? It depresses me, but why not?

- Barracuda: "A negative generalization of persons without morals and/or ethical standards or judgments. Many times directed at forceful women."
- Airhead: "Term is an objectionable description, generally aimed at women."
- Burly: "An adjective too often associated with large black men, implying ignorance, and considered offensive in this context."
- Buxom: "Offensive reference to a woman's chest."
- Dear: "A term of endearment objectionable to some. Usage such as 'He was a dear man,' or 'she is a dear,' should be avoided."
- Dingbat: "Objectionable term that describes women as intellectually inferior."
- Ditz: "Objectionable term meaning stupid."
- Dizzy: "Avoid as an adjective for women."
- Fried chicken: "A loaded phrase when used carelessly and as a stereotype, referring to the cuisine of black people. Also applies to watermelon."
- Gorgeous: "An adjective that describes female physical attributes. Use carefully."
- Gyp: "An offensive term, meaning to cheat, derived from Gypsy."
- Illegal alien: "Often used to refer to Mexicans and Latin Americans believed to be in the United States without visas; the preferred term is undocumented worker or undocumented resident."
- Ivan: "A common and offensive substitute for a Soviet person."

- Jock: "A term applied to both men and women who participate in sports. Can be offensive to some."
- Johns: "Men who frequent prostitutes, but not a proper generic term for men or bathrooms."
- Lazy: "Use advisedly, especially when describing non-whites."
- Pert: "An adjective describing a female characteristic. Avoid usage."
- Petite: "Reference to a woman's body size. Can be offensive."
- Rubbing noses: "Allegedly an Eskimo kiss. However, Eskimos don't rub noses and object to the characterization."
- Senior citizens: "Do not use for anyone under 65. . . . Do not describe people as elderly, senile, matronly, or well-preserved. . . . Do not use dirty old man, codger, coot, geezer, silver fox, old-timers, Pop, old buzzard."
- Shiftless: "As a description for blacks, highly objectionable."
- Stunning: "Avoid physical descriptions."
- Sweetie: "Objectionable term of endearment. Do not use."

I've changed my mind. I refuse to knuckle down to the dizzy new-age journalistic airheads in this ditzy Multicultural Management Program.

These dingbats appear to be bigots themselves. They list dozens of words—including fried chicken—that they say offend blacks, gays, or women.

But they don't include "honky," which many blacks call whites, or dago, wop, heeb, kike, mick, herring-choker, frog, kraut, bohunk, or polack. Ain't us honkies got feelings, too?

Whether or not they like it, Ivan Boesky is a Wall Street barracuda. The Chicago Bears' William Perry, who used to be a fat slob, is now merely burly. My wife is petite and a gorgeous sweetie.

If some geezer unzips in a schoolyard, I reserve my constitutional right to call him a dirty old man.

The damn Rooskies have aimed missiles at me for forty years, so maybe I'll refer to a Soviet as an Ivan. I've been called worse.

I'll continue to go have Dutch-treat lunches with my friends and check the bill to make sure the waiter didn't gyp me.

Why not "illegal alien"? It's specific. It means an alien who is here in violation of our immigration laws. But what's an "undocumented worker"? If I come to work without my wallet, I don't have any documents with me, so I'm an undocumented worker. Will I be deported?

If I decide to say "I hit the john," instead of "I visited the room where one disposes of bodily wastes," I'll do so.

When I put together a softball team, I'll recruit real jocks, not a bunch of wimps, nerds, dweebs, or weenies.

And little kids have been rubbing noses and calling it an "Eskimo kiss" as long as I can remember. And that's a long time, since I border on being a geezer, a coot, or a codger.

Fried chicken, fried chicken, fried chicken. I said it and I'm glad. Sue me.

In conclusion, your dictionary is a stunning example of lazy, shiftless thinking.

Ugh.

June 13, 1990

Flag Foes Show No Real Burning Desire

After looking out my window for ominous puffs of smoke, but seeing none, I called the Chicago Fire Department.

"Have you had any reports of anyone burning a flag since the Supreme Court said it was not illegal?"

"Not a one."

So I called the police department. They, too, had no flag-burning sightings.

Something seemed wrong. Here we have President Bush, dozens of congressmen, and chest-thumping political patriots everywhere, gearing up to amend the Constitution.

But in this, the nation's third-largest city, where people engage in all sorts of mischief, nobody had burned a single flag.

Could it be that our dangerous flag burners are just slow on the uptake?

To check that theory, I called Los Angeles, which is often said to be America's setter of weird trends.

No trend there. LA's firefighters had not been called to battle with even one burning flag. Nor had the cops.

So I tried New York.

"What?" a New York official said. "You wanna know what?"

Flags. Are New Yorkers burning flags?

"Nah. And if they do, nobody'd notice. It's not like somebody setting fire to himself. They do that in front of the United Nations."

Finally, I phoned our nation's capital, home to the street-corner crackhead, the congressional meathead, and the bureaucratic rockhead.

As usual, they were burning up our tax money as fast as they could glom on to it. But flags? Not a one.

How strange. Here we have politicians flapping their tongues all over the world of TV about how we must amend the Constitution to protect ourselves from those who would burn a piece of cloth—probably manufactured in Taiwan.

The way they're howling, you would think that the flag-burning menace is right up there with cancer, heart disease, drug addiction, AIDS, murder, rape, child abuse, deficit spending, lousy education, and the savings-and-loan scandal.

But in the nation's three biggest population centers and our nation's capital, not one flag has been burned. At least, not openly. You never know, of course. There might be a timid radical cooking one in his microwave.

How can this be? If nobody is burning flags, why is Sen. Robert Dole demanding that Congress get snapping and pass an amendment to the Constitution so that thirty-eight states can vote on it? Why is President Bush in a flag-protecting tizzy?

We know the answer, of course. They think we're kind of stupid.

They believe that if they can get us all worked up about flag burning—even though nobody is burning flags right now—we're stupid enough to overlook all the things they aren't doing that they should be doing.

For example, we have the Justice Department and other investigative agencies floundering around the S&L mess. President Bush doesn't want us to think about that. Nor do Dole and other members of the rally-round-the-flag gang.

More than 20,000 cases of possible fraud and theft, most of them gathering mildew in the Justice Department files. But we are supposed to be grinding our teeth because some publicity-hungry ninny might burn a flag the day after tomorrow.

If you are Bush or Dole or any of the other backers of the idiotic amendment, that makes sense. Come the autumn elections, they'd rather have us arguing about flag burning than asking them what they're doing about the $500 billion scandal.

Dole prefers that kind of senseless babble to being asked, for example, about a no-vote he cast last April.

But I'd rather talk about that no-vote.

Sen. Alan Dixon had proposed that Congress take $30 million that was supposed to be used to promote tourism in Panama and switch it to a fund to hire more investigators and lawyers to go after S&L crooks.

(You're probably wondering why the heck we're sending money

to Panama to promote its tourism industry. That's another goofy story. But we are.)

Now, what would the response be if you stopped 1,000 average tax-paying Americans on the street and asked: "Should we spend $30 million to catch S&L thieves or to persuade people to vacation in Panama?"

Unless you happened to run into a bunch of Panamanian tourist agents, you'd probably get a 100 percent vote to catch the S&L thieves.

But that's not the way the Senate felt. By a vote of 50 to 48, the funding switch was defeated.

And Dole, a heavyweight Republican leader, was one of those who voted against it. And he was joined by many of his fellow cloakroom patriots who are trying to stir us into a fever pitch over the dangers of flag burning.

To paraphrase a country and western song: Thanks to Dole and his pals, Panama gets the gold mine, and we get the shaft.

Dole wants a constitutional amendment? I think we should give him not one, but two. First, we should have an amendment that requires that the heads of S&L thieves be chopped off, mounted by a taxidermist, and given to the swindle-victims as a trophy.

Second, we should have an amendment requiring that senators who talk nonsense have their tongues plucked out.

July 12, 1990

Message on AIDS Gets Lost in Poster

The last I heard, that controversial advertising poster showing a variety of people smooching had not yet appeared on Chicago Transit Authority buses.

This is the one that shows a man kissing a man, a woman kissing a woman, and a man and a woman of different races kissing.

The printed message says something to the effect that love doesn't kill; greed and indifference kill.

The ad, we're told, was created by a group that wants to dispel myths about how people get AIDS. And kissing is one way you don't get it.

However, some members of the city council and the state legislature saw a different message in the poster.

They said it was nothing more than a plug, a promo, a hype for gay sex or gay lifestyle or the gay community or some such thing.

Since the aldermen have no legal authority over the CTA, all they could do is huff and puff, which is what they do best. And because they're aldermen, nobody pays much attention to them anyway, except for their comedic value.

The state legislature, which takes itself more seriously, decided to pass a bill that would prohibit the displaying of the kissing poster.

The CTA says that it isn't in the business of censoring the advertising it displays and could be sued if it rejects the poster.

So when the legal quibbling is over, the poster will probably be put on display and the people who created it will surely hail it as a victory.

But that doesn't mean that the aldermen and the state legislators were wrong. I'm amazed to find myself agreeing with them.

Yes, the poster appears to be nothing more than a plug for gay sex and lifestyle. And, no, it really has nothing to do with the realities of how people get or don't get AIDS.

Sure, people don't get AIDS by kissing. Nor do they get it by shaking hands, sitting on toilet seats, or eating in restaurants that have gay chefs or waiters.

So they could just as well have created a poster showing people shaking hands, sitting on toilet seats, or eating in a restaurant.

Instead, they show two men kissing. That's not a promo for homosexuality? Come now, even an alderman isn't dumb enough to buy that.

Of course, they shrewdly include an interracial couple kissing. That way, besides accusing any critic of being homophobic, they can toss in the nasty charge of racism.

And I'm a bit puzzled by the statement that love doesn't cause AIDS. Love isn't an issue at all, unless you define love as having anal sex with a stranger in a bathhouse, which would be kind of stretching love's definition.

And whose greed and whose indifference are we talking about?

The ad doesn't say. If they're talking about government indifference, that might have been true at one time. But it no longer is. Vast sums are being spent on AIDS research. Far more per victim than on cancer, heart disease, and other diseases that kill far more people. And as the recent AIDS conference showed, scientists are working frantically to find solutions.

So if that poster is intended to do anything about stopping the spread of AIDS, it's a waste of money. Even worse, it's phony.

A new study has shown that AIDS is rapidly increasing among young women, particularly in New York, New Jersey, and other Northeastern cities.

At first glance, the study is a shocker. Women getting AIDS? That isn't the predictable pattern.

But it becomes less of a shocker when you read beyond the headline. Yes, more young women are getting AIDS. But how? Same old story. Most share dirty drug needles with other addicts. A lesser number get it by having sex with drug addicts.

The greatest tragedy to be found in this study is that some of the women become pregnant, so even before they are born, the infants have the disease and are doomed.

And other studies show that more and more young gay men in San Francisco and New York aren't bothering with safe sex precautions. They're again coupling with strangers and without condoms. So, after all these years of being told how to avoid it, AIDS is being spread again the same old way.

So I suggest that the creators of the poster cut out the con job, with the kissing and the talk of greed and indifference.

You want to do a poster? Show a couple of glassy-eyed fools jamming the same needle into their arms. Or a couple of guys in a bathhouse saying: "Let's get it on, and we can exchange phone numbers later."

Greed and indifference, not love? Why not try: "Love doesn't kill. Stupidity, moronic self-indulgence, and flat-out ignorance kill."

Or maybe a poster showing a dying infant and a line saying: "This baby has AIDS because his mother stuck a dirty needle full of dope in her arm. President Bush didn't stick the needle in her arm. The U.S. surgeon general didn't. Society didn't. You didn't. She did it to herself. So blame her. And if you don't want your baby to get AIDS, don't stick dirty dope needles in your arms."

Now maybe that isn't quite as subtle as a poster showing men kissing men, women kissing women, and blacks kissing whites, but I think it gets the message across.

Or isn't that the idea?

March 12, 1991

Kuwait's Future Brighter Than Ours

Colonel David Hackworth is probably right about the nation's spinal cord. As he wrote in *Newsweek,* "Americans are standing tall for the first time in years."

The retired Army officer, one of the most decorated in history, says he has not seen such national pride since World War II ended.

That's what I'm hearing, too. It's pouring out of radio talk shows, newspaper and magazine editorials, and the mouths of politicians everywhere. We've shaken off the doldrums; we're on the move as a great nation again; pride has been restored, and we're Number One.

Those who opposed the Gulf War are either slinking in dark corners or bowing their heads and pleading: "Forgive me for having been a wrongheaded weenie."

But I'm afraid that Colonel Hackworth has allowed his euphoria to blur his vision. Or maybe it's because since retiring from the Army a couple of decades ago, he has lived in other parts of the world.

Whatever the reason, he goes on to write: "So, let's use our newfound confidence to turn America around. Yes, we need a new world order, but let it begin at home and not just with soaring polls and White House speeches.

". . . The key is to get American priorities right. We need to start with our education system, so our kids can read and write again. We need to take care of the homeless and poor, and attack drugs and crime. We must clean up our environment, rebuild our highways, railroads, and merchant fleet. We must revitalize our industries to the point that Made in America will once again stand for quality. . . . Our vital national interests depend on a stable and secure America. Let's roll up our sleeves and make it that way."

Dream on, colonel, dream on.

In two or three years, Kuwait will be close to looking as it did before Iraq looted and plundered it. But I guarantee that the West Side of Chicago, much of the Bronx, and the slums of Newark, Gary, New Orleans, and other American cities will be the same mess they are now.

That's because Kuwait sits atop an ocean of liquid gold. It can hire the giant Bechtel corporation and other globe-hopping companies to perform a miraculous rehab job. Unfortunately, nobody is drilling gushers on the West Side of Chicago or in Detroit or the Bronx. And Bechtel doesn't take our IOUs.

It's not a matter of rolling up our sleeves. Dedicated teachers in poverty-plagued neighborhoods have been rolling up their sleeves for years. But baring their arm hair doesn't do much when most of their students come from broken families, with illiterate, jobless relatives. The educators talk a lot but they don't know what to do. The politicians blab even more, and they know less.

But don't worry, colonel. Most American kids can read and write—those who live in the better suburbs and prosperous smaller cities. And many will go on to college and better jobs.

Then they'll reflect their parents' attitudes—resentment that they have to pay taxes to support that huge, lazy, welfare-sucking, crime-ridden underclass in the cities.

See, colonel, one of our biggest problems is that Americans don't really like or trust each other that much. They dislike each other for racial, class, regional, economic, and political differences. If we like and trust each other, why do we lead the world in lawsuits? And murders. Yes, there's a bit of friction here.

Of course, they're not going to concede that we have these social problems because the majority of more comfortable Americans long ago decided it wasn't their responsibility. And the federal government is better at creating bureaucracies than finding solutions, while politicians do what they can, so long as it doesn't cost them votes.

Does the good colonel really believe that Richard Nixon and Ronald Reagan were concerned about better education? If so, what did they do? Besides dubbing himself the "education president," what has George Bush done?

It's not going to get better, it's going to get worse. I know that because it's worse today than it was twenty years ago and ten years ago, and there's nothing new in the works.

Take care of the homeless and the poor? (And you might throw in the poverty-level elderly.) Rebuild highways and railroads? Smack down crack, lock up criminals?

That takes manpower, which means money, colonel. If you haven't noticed, we're running up a monster tab just rescuing the savings-and-loan industry, with the banks next. The time to have kind thoughts about the homeless, the poor, better schools, health care for the old, crumbling highways, and collapsing bridges was before Ronald Reagan's crowd napped their way through the white-collar larceny of the bloated 1980s.

And even before then, when American industry became near-sighted while the Japanese and others developed long-range vision. We can roll up our sleeves, but only to dip into our pockets to see if we can cover the juice to all the countries that now act as our loan sharks.

No, all we've proved is that we can win a war. So maybe we should make that our national product. But at a better price. The

Kuwaitis and Saudis, as trembly as they were, would have surely accepted a stiffer bill for our bodyguard and security service.

So the colonel will have to settle for those soaring polls and White House speeches. That's all we'll get.

And in a few years he should compare Kuwait City with Chicago's West Side—the schools, clinics, housing, and job opportunities. With America's sick and elderly. With the wrecks in the Veterans Administration hospitals.

And see how many yellow ribbons will be displayed for them.

March 19, 1991

Ticket to Good Life Punched with Pain

The police chief of Los Angeles is being widely condemned because of the now-famous videotaped flogging of a traffic offender.

But Chief Daryl Gates, while refusing to resign, suggests that the brutal beating might have been an uplifting act that could bring long-range positive results for the beating victim.

As the chief put it at a press conference Monday:

"We regret what took place. I hope he [Rodney King, the beating victim] gets his life straightened out. Perhaps this will be the vehicle to move him down the road to a good life instead of the life he's been involved in for such a long time."

I hadn't thought of it that way, but there could be something in what Chief Gates says.

There's no doubt that King, 25, hasn't been an exemplary citizen, although he's no John Dillinger. When the police stopped him for speeding, he was on parole for using a tire iron to threaten and rob a grocer.

But as Chief Gates said, the experience of being beaten, kicked, and shot with an electric stun gun might be what it takes to "move him down the road to a good life."

Who knows, in a few years when all of this is forgotten, a reporter might drive out to a nice house in a California suburb and find a peaceful Rodney King pushing a mower across his lawn.

The reporter might ask: "Mr. King, what is it that moved you down the road to a good life?"

"That's a good question," Mr. King might reply, "and I'll be glad to explain it to you. You'll have to excuse me if I wobble and drool a bit; my face has nerve damage and my coordination hasn't been the same since they damaged my brain."

"Of course."

"But to get back to your question. I think it was after L.A.'s finest hit me about fifty or fifty-five times with their clubs. As you recall, some of the fillings flew out of my teeth and one of my eye sockets sort of exploded."

"Must have been a tad uncomfortable."

"Yes. And at that point, I'm pretty sure that those nine skull fractures and internal injuries had already occurred, my cheekbone was fractured, one of my legs was broken, and I had this burning sensation from being zapped with that electric stun gun. I was feeling kind of low."

"That's to be expected."

"Right. But as I was lying there, and they were getting in a few final kicks, and then sort of hog-tying my hands to my legs and dragging me along the ground, I said to myself: 'Why not try to look at the bright side?' "

"And did you?"

"Yes. I thought: 'Well, one of my legs *isn't* broken; one of my eye sockets *isn't* fractured; one of my cheekbones *isn't* broken. And although my skull is fractured, my head remains attached to my body; and while fillings have popped out of my teeth, I still have the teeth.' And I said to myself: 'Half a body is better than none.' "

"Very inspiring."

"Thank you. And I had a chance to think about why the police were treating me that way. It was their way of telling me that speeding is an act of antisocial behavior and I had been very bad, bad, bad."

"You have unusual insight."

"I try. And I thought that if only I had led the life of a model citizen, this wouldn't have happened to me. Let's face it. The L.A. police never fracture the skull of the president of the chamber of commerce, the chief antler in the Loyal Order of Moose, or the head of the PTA. No, it was my past history of antisocial behavior that brought it on."

"But they had no way of knowing you were on parole."

"Yes, but I'm sure they could guess just by the look of me. Be honest, I don't look at all like the head of the PTA, do I?"

"True."

"Then, later, when Police Chief Gates said that the beating, although regrettable, could be the vehicle that would get me on the road to the good life, everything became clear. I realized that the beating would turn my life around and be a one-way ticket to the good life."

"The chief's words inspired you?"

"Not exactly. To be honest Chief Gates' words convinced me that he had to be as dumb an S.O.B. as ever opened his mouth at a press conference."

"But you said he helped you to a good life."

"That's right, he did."

"How?"

"When I took his police department to court, that jury awarded me a couple of million in damages, and I've been leading the good life ever since."

"I don't think that's what the chief had in mind."

"I don't think that chief had anything in mind."

April 23, 1991

It Didn't Take Long to Lose Euphoria

That old euphoria. Like the twenty-four-hour flu, it seems to just come and go. And now it's going, going, and might soon be gone.

Only seven weeks ago, *Newsweek* magazine conducted a poll about the Gulf War in which this question was asked: "Saddam Hussein has withdrawn from Kuwait, but remains in power in Iraq. Is this a victory for the U.S. and allied forces?"

Fifty-five percent said, yes, it was a victory. Only 38 percent said it wasn't. The rest didn't know or didn't care.

Now the magazine has done another poll and asked the very same question. But the results are almost a perfect flip-flop.

This time 55 percent said, no, it wasn't a victory. Only 36 percent thought it was, and the rest were watching soaps or something.

If the poll really represents what Americans believe, it means that in only a few weeks, tens of millions of people sprung a major euphoria leak.

This is probably viewed as bad news in the White House, with all the parades and airport greetings still on the schedule.

But the White House shouldn't take it as a disappointment. If anything, it shows that the Bush administration knew what it was doing and did it almost to perfection. Except for one minor glitch, which we'll go into a little later.

The first poll, in which 55 percent said we scored a victory, proved how effective censorship, media manipulation, and skillful propaganda can be in shaping public opinion.

It didn't matter that Saddam, the latter-day Hitler, was still in power. We had won, really kicked butt, with little loss of life to our troops. And to most Americans, that was what counted.

And it had been done so neatly. All the dramatic video bombings and Scud missile interceptions. The generals in their combat fatigues and boots detailing each day's triumphs. (I've always wondered why generals wear combat fatigues and boots to sit in offices.)

Then the lightning fast ground attack that brought Saddam's miserable 4-F's popping out of their gopher holes with their hands in the air.

So we didn't kill or capture Saddam. What's the difference? We stomped him so thoroughly and quickly that it didn't seem to matter. Besides, it was only a matter of time until Saddam's own people would string the villain up for messing up their country. Our leaders told us so.

It was more than even the White House could have hoped for. Wham, bam, thank you, Saddam. All that remained was for the troops to come home to heroes' welcomes and let the festivities begin.

Ah, but then came that little glitch I mentioned.

Once the war was ended, so was the censorship. No more press pools being told where they could go and to whom they could speak. No more carefully staged and filtered briefings. No more ladling out info and carefully chosen bombing-run tapes like thin broth in a soup line.

Anybody with a camera or a notepad was free to go where he chose. And many went into northern Iraq, where the Kurds were trying to pull off a revolution. When Saddam's Republican Guard began slaughtering the rebels, the cameras and notepads followed the masses of fleeing Kurds into the cold and muddy mountains where they hoped to avoid extermination.

Suddenly the pictures on TV weren't neat and pretty anymore. A general blustering at reporters, a bridge in the cross hairs suddenly going "poof"—these images were replaced by those of children with skin blistered and blackened from napalm; their teeth chattering from the cold; their little bodies being wrapped in burial rags; their mothers shrieking their grief.

Of course, it wasn't our fault. We don't napalm Kurdish children. We don't chase them into the cold mountains to die of exposure, hunger, and disease. All we did was leave Saddam in power, with his robust health and evil nature, and the means to engage in mass slaughter.

So Americans, many of whom have soft hearts and get squeamish at the sight of suffering children, began thinking that if this pain was the fruit of our victory, it might not have been our finest hour.

There's a lesson in all of this that our present and future leaders should keep in mind. When you fight a war, don't be too quick to declare it over. Even if you stop fighting, by officially remaining at war, you can keep the censorship going, herd the press pools like sheep, and filter anything that might upset the TV viewer's appetite.

Remember, next time keep the lid on. No burned, freezing, starving, or dying kids.

They can ruin a good show.

July 17, 1991

Sensitivity Pops Up in the Unlikeliest Place

These are such sensitive times. Feelings are easily hurt. You can offend individuals or groups something awful without even realizing that you've done it.

Especially someone such as myself, who has spent almost three decades earning a living by being insensitive and crude.

I've finally realized that it might be time for me to undergo sensitivity training so I can be more aware of the delicate feelings of others.

The decision to change my raucous ways was brought on by the angry and pained reaction to some of my recent writings.

"It felt like a slap in my face," one of the offended readers said.

She was referring to something I wrote about the proper way to adorn a hot dog.

As any native Chicagoan knows, it's a choice of mustard, onions, relish, tomato, and, of course, a dash of celery salt.

And I had written: "What kind of damn fool puts sauerkraut on a hot dog?"

Several New Yorkers demanded an apology, since they make a practice of putting sauerkraut on hot dogs. But, then, New Yorkers have many strange ways.

But the most poignant response came from Betty Manor, of Milan, Michigan.

"I am of Czech ancestry and fifty-five years old. I did not enjoy your statement about those of us who put sauerkraut on hot dogs. It felt like a slap in my face."

Lout I may be, but I don't approve of slapping fifty-five-year-old Czech ladies in the face. And I feel bad that Mrs. Manor's feelings were hurt.

It may be that as someone of Czech ancestry, an ethnic group of notorious sauerkraut lovers, Mrs. Manor puts sauerkraut on everything she prepares. If all that sauerkraut is OK with her husband, it's jake with me.

So I apologize to Mrs. Manor and all others whose sensitivities were offended by my reference to sauerkraut on hot dogs. Put anything you want on a hot dog. It is your right as an American.

And I promise to never again make snide remarks about sauerkraut on hot dogs. Or even ketchup, although Dirty Harry once said that only an (obscenity deleted) would use ketchup.

I also promise to never again use the name "Wanda" in my column.

That's because I have hurt the feelings of Mrs. Wanda T. Larson, of Elkton, Maryland. She noted that from time to time I have mentioned Slats Grobnik's Aunt Wanda. Actually, Slats mentions her more than I do, since he is fond of her and proud of her mystical ability to tell fortunes by reading coffee grounds.

But Mrs. Larson, who is of Polish ancestry, says, "Your use of the name Wanda is degrading and insulting to people of Polish background. It presents a devastating picture of Polish intelligence to those not familiar with the Polish heritage."

She goes on to say: "My name is Wanda. I have been named after one of the most heroic figures in Polish history.

"The great Princess Wanda committed suicide rather than marry the mean Prince Rydygier of Germany, thereby saving Poland from a fate worse than death.

"You should spend a little time studying Polish history."

See? That's what I mean about offending people without realizing it.

I wasn't aware that the great Princess Wanda did herself in to avoid marrying Prince Rydygier of Germany. Nor do I know why she did it. Maybe the prince was a boozer. And in the old days, even a prince didn't take a bath more than once a week. So he might have been a real disgusting guy.

Wait, I take that back about Prince Rydygier having been a disgusting guy. I don't know that to be a fact, since the politically incorrect and insensitive educational system of my youth didn't teach us about him.

And for all I know, this could be read by angry descendants of Prince Rydygier, who will write and tell me that I have insulted them by saying their ancestor was disgusting. And even if he was disgusting, why can't I let bygones be bygones?

Or from angry men who will demand to know why I automatically take the side of the woman (Princess Wanda), and don't consider the possibility that the man (Prince Rydygier) might be getting a bum rap. Maybe Princess Wanda was no prize herself. And why am I insensitive to the feelings of men?

And they would have a valid point. In disputes between the sexes, sometimes the men are right and the women are in the wrong. Not that I'm defending Prince Rydygier. But maybe he had an unhappy childhood and couldn't help being a louse. If he is one, which we really don't know.

Not that women aren't right as often as men. If I appear to have suggested otherwise, I didn't mean it and hope no female sensitivities have been offended.

So I apologize to Wanda Larson of Maryland and to any other female persons named Wanda.

Or, for that matter, to any male persons named Wanda. Now that I'm sensitive, I'm covering all bases.

December 26, 1991

David Duke Has a Partner in Slime

Let's give white supremacist David Duke a rest for a moment and consider the ravings of another prominent bigot.

I'm not sure what his real name is, but he is known to his many fans as Ice Cube.

Mr. Cube is described by his publicists as a "rap artist." I'll take their word for it, although I think that's stretching the word "artist" a bit.

His publicists also say that Mr. Ice Cube likes to use his music, if it can be called that, to make social statements.

One of his recent social statements has to do with the strained relationship that exists between black customers and Korean merchants in Los Angeles.

Many blacks believe, as Mr. Cube says, that the Korean merchants "disrespect" them.

He says that the Korean shopkeepers seem to believe that every black who walks in the door is a potential thief or gunman.

This isn't a new problem. It has flared up in New York, Chicago, and other cities.

So in one of his recent recordings, Mr. Cube has made a social statement. The song includes this thought:

"So don't follow me up and down your market

"Or your little chop suey ass'll be a target . . .

"So pay some respect to the black fist

"Or we'll burn your store right down to a crisp. . . ."

It's no surprise that Koreans were surprised, frightened, and upset by what they took to be a rallying cry for blacks to engage in arson against their property. (Some might also have been offended by the reference to their "chop suey" asses. Mr. Cube is obviously unaware that chop suey is not a Korean dish. In fact, it isn't even a Chinese dish, having been invented in this country. But maybe all Asians look alike to Mr. Cube.) Mr. Cube's publicist says that the Koreans have misunderstood the intent of the song. Mr. Cube wasn't really urging blacks to burn stores. He just wanted to make the Koreans aware of the frustration and resentment many blacks feel at social and economic injustice.

Well, that is a worthy goal, I suppose, but if I were a Korean, I would think that there might be a better way of discussing social and economic injustice than by angrily rapping about my chop suey ass or burning my store down to a crisp.

In fact, if I were a Korean, I would tell Mr. Cube to stop the con job about social and economic injustice, that he is a front-line bigot and is no better than David Duke.

I might also suggest that he stop rapping about disrespect by Korean merchants and give some thought to why Korean merchants are operating stores in black neighborhoods in the first place. That's something I have yet to hear explained.

If blacks don't like the idea of buying groceries, liquor, and other products from Koreans, the solution seems simple enough. Open your own stores and sell the stuff yourself.

Yes, it takes a certain amount of capital to open any business, even a small store. But the Koreans manage to raise the startup money, despite being a minority and, in many cases, having the added handicap of not speaking much English.

Mr. Cube, for example, is a wealthy young man. His rap records are big sellers.

So why can't Mr. Cube finance some ambitious blacks who want to open stores? In fact, if all of the disgruntled rap artists who make social statements would throw some money into a pot, a considerable number of blacks could open their own small businesses. That's how the Koreans do it. Those who are successful create a pool of money and finance those who want to get started.

Mr. Cube might also give some thought as to why Korean merchants might be wary of their black customers. If he wants to check police statistics in Chicago, New York, and L.A., he would find that it isn't unusual for Korean merchants, as well as those of other backgrounds, to find themselves looking into the barrel of a pistol held by a young black man.

In some cases, such as that of a Korean merchant on Chicago's West Side, that gun barrel was the last thing they ever saw in this life.

There are some black merchants who don't feel fully clothed without a pistol in their belt. If they have reason to be cautious, why shouldn't a Korean?

This wasn't Mr. Cube's only social statement about other groups. It seems that he had a spat with his agent over the profit from recordings. Normally, these show biz differences are handled in lawsuits.

But Mr. Cube used his artistic form to air his grievance. It included this lyric:

"Get rid that devil, real simple,
"Put a bullet in his temple.
"Cause you can't get a nigga for life crew
"With a white Jew telling you what to do."

When he was asked why he thought it necessary to mention that his former agent was a Jew, Mr. Cube said it had nothing to do with bigotry; Jew rhymed with crew, so he was just being a poet.

Mr. Cube has inspired me to my first effort at rap. You provide the mindless thump-thump background music, and I'll handle the words.

"Hey, Mr. Cube, you don't like the Jew?
"Say he should be shot for cheatin' you?
"And you got a grudge 'gainst them Koreans?
"Say they should burn for treating you like peons?
"Different reasons and different strokes,
"But you and David Duke hate the same kind of folks.
"You're just another bigot, guilty as sin,
"You and David Duke, brothers under the skin."

September 23, 1992

Next Time, Dan, Take Aim at Arnold

Enough about Murphy Brown and her baby. What about Arnold Schwarzenegger, one of the biggest of all Hollywood stars?

Here we have a staunch Republican, who was appointed by George Bush as chairman of the President's Council on Physical Fitness and Sports.

At the GOP convention, Republicans were tripping over each other to get their pictures taken with Big Arnold. Proper Republican ladies pleaded to be allowed to touch a dainty finger to his bicep.

Ah, but what kind of films does this prominent Republican star make? What kind of traditional family values does he reflect?

Sordid, that's what kind.

And I'm not talking about just the violence, although that's what he's best known for: blood spurting, body parts flying, murder, mayhem, disfigurement, and corpses strewn from the screen to the popcorn machine.

In one of his "Terminator" movies, he barged into a police station and blew away every cop in the place. Mowed them down like empty bottles on a fence. Was there any compassion for the family values of the policemen—their weeping widows and wailing offspring? No, Arnold coolly stepped over their lifeless bodies and went looking for someone else to shoot.

But does Dan Quayle, in his crusade against Hollywood, say anything about that? When asked about Arnold's mayhem during a TV interview, Quayle's lips trembled, his hands fluttered, and he burst into tears and screamed: "Don't ask me about Arnold because I am afraid he will crack my head like a walnut."

(Actually, I'm not sure about that because I dozed off during the interview and maybe I dreamed Quayle said it. But it's probably what he felt in his quivering soul.)

As I said, though, the violence is only a part of it. There is also the issue of illegitimate children, which got Quayle into his great spat with the fictitious TV character Murphy Brown.

Now, remember, all Murphy Brown did was have a one-night fling with her ex-husband, get pregnant, and have the child. (And she didn't even apply for welfare or take much maternity leave from her job, which should have been some comfort to Quayle.)

But consider what happened in a couple of Arnold's movies.

In *Twins,* Arnold's mom was inseminated with the sperm of nine brilliant men. I'm not sure how it was done. Maybe they mixed it all up in one of those milkshake machines.

So what kind of family values were those? Arnold and Danny DeVito, his twin, being illegitimate and having not one, but nine fathers? Genetic engineering? Test-tube parenting? Is that in the Republican platform?

I'll be interested in hearing Quayle's response if, during his debate with Al Gore, he is asked: "And, Mr. Vice President, how do you feel about Arnold Schwarzenegger, the chairman of your commander in chief's fitness program, playing the role of the offspring of a woman who was inseminated with the seed of nine men? Is that the kind of family value you would recommend to your fellow Hoosiers, hey?"

And there was similar hanky-panky in the "Terminator" movie. There a man comes back from the future to the present and makes the female star of the movie pregnant. (Although we don't actually see the deed, it is assumed that he does it the old-fashioned way, rather than through test tubes.)

He wasn't even the young woman's ex-husband. She hardly knew the fellow. One day he comes popping out of the future. A day or two later, they are having what used to be known as a "quickie."

This is the key to the movie's plot, since the illegitimate tyke will grow up to be a great hero in the future and fight the forces of evil who are taking over the world, which is why the forces of evil send the Terminator back into the past to kill her and prevent the pregnancy, so that the great hero is never born and can't fight the forces of evil.

Well, fighting the forces of evil is a worthy cause, I suppose, and even the most prim Republicans would probably forgive the future hero's mom her indiscretion if it preserves life, liberty, and the pursuit of happiness.

But how does Dan Quayle know that Murphy Brown's tot won't grow up to be a great hero and fight the forces of evil? And if that happens, won't he feel silly? Quayle, I mean, not Murphy Brown's kid.

Anyway, if Quayle is going to wage war on Hollywood's warped view of family values, he should have a heart-to-heart talk with the chairman of the president's fitness and sports commission.

Quayle might ask him: "Nine fathers? Arnold, what kind of sport is that?"

November 27, 1992

He Could Fill Book with Pithy Phrases

A flattering invitation recently arrived. It was from Joseph Neely, an author in Michigan, who wrote:

"I am compiling a book which features the favorite saying of successful persons such as you. This book is intended to inspire people and to give them some insight into the philosophies which help certain people to accomplish significant tasks.

"Essentially, I am looking for a saying which has given you comfort, kept you focused on your goals, or inspired you during your life. The saying can be one which you composed or it can be from some other source.

"As of this date, I have received contributions for this book from a diverse group of persons, including former NATO commander and White House Chief of Staff Alexander M. Haig Jr.; minister and author Norman Vincent Peale; Dr. Deborah McGriff, the first African-American woman to serve as superintendent of a major urban school system; and Notre Dame's head football coach Lou Holtz, to name just a few."

That's an impressive group, and I'd like to be in it. But I've never had one favorite saying that inspired, comforted, or focused me throughout my life. And I don't have any that would be likely to inspire someone else to lead a better life.

At different times, a variety of sayings have helped me in one way or another.

Like most young men of my generation, I believed in the saying our mothers passed on to us: "Always wear clean underwear, so if you get in an accident and go in the hospital, you won't be embarrassed." That's still a good idea, although I would add, "and no pastel colors."

As a lad, I abided by a saying in my neighborhood that went: "Don't go on the other side of Chicago Avenue, because the Italian kids there will always jump a Polack." The one time I became careless, a group of young men surrounded me and demanded my name. I said: "Rocko Rico Royko," which I thought was a clever ruse.

But they jumped me anyway.

That experience led me to believe in the saying that is familiar to many Cub fans: "You win some and you lose some, but mostly you lose some."

Then there was my grandfather's favorite saying: "Never trust a Russian." He said that long before the Cold War began. So I asked my grandmother what he meant by it, and she provided me with another saying: "Never trust your drunken grandfather."

Later, when I was in the military, I placed great faith in the popular saying: "Don't never volunteer for nothing." But it didn't make much difference, because if you didn't volunteer, they made you do it anyway.

Early in my newspaper career, a wise old reporter passed along a saying that helped me become thrifty. He said: "Always stash away some (deleted) money, so if you got a boss you hate, you can say, '(Deleted) you' and quit." I'm still saving.

And another mentor had a saying I tried to follow: "Be nice to the copy boy, even if he's a mope, because he might grow up to be your boss some day." And sure enough, several mopes did.

Some coworkers once tired of hearing me complain about not having anything to write about. So they put an inspirational plaque on my wall that showed a little sailboat with limp sails and a man pulling some oars. It bore the words: "When there's no wind, row."

But I've since taken it down and replaced it with a sign that says: "When there is no wind, book a cabin on a cruise ship, sit by the pool, order a cool drink, and look at the babes."

Several of my friends have had sayings that I like, although I'm not sure what they mean.

For example, Studs Terkel always ends his radio show by saying: "Take it easy, but take it." I once asked him if that was something he learned when he went to law school, but he denied it.

The late Marty O'Connor, a Chicago reporter, used to say: "Only suckers beef." He said it was an old South Side Irish expression. While it sounds manly, it wouldn't make sense today, when the most successful special-interest groups are those that beef the loudest and most often. Now the saying should be: "Only suckers don't form an organization, compile a list of unreasonable demands, and hold a crabby press conference."

I used to be impressed by the line John Wayne uttered in so many of his western movies: "A man's got to do what a man's got to do." But when feminists heightened my social sensitivities, I realized it was a sexist saying. After all, the feminists pointed out, we could just as well say, "A woman's got to do what a woman's got to do." For that matter, a puppy's got to do what a puppy's got to do. That's life, which is a favorite saying of Frank Sinatra. Or maybe Mike Ditka.

So I guess I won't qualify for Mr. Neely's book of inspirational sayings. Unless he would consider using one of my friend Slats Grobnik's lines.

Slats always tosses off this salutation when saying goodbye to friends: "Stay out of the trees, watch out for the wild goose, and take care of your hernia."

When I ask what it means, he shrugs and says: "Just do it; you won't go wrong."

He's right, but I'm not sure it's something to live by. Unless you have a hernia.

Anyway, I appreciate Mr. Neely's kind invitation. Although I haven't been able to contribute to his book, he did give me something to write about.

As I always say: "Another day, another dollar."

December 1, 1992

Parents, Not Cash, Can Enrich a School

I hate statistics, but when Chicago's school tests are published, as they were yesterday, I wade through and find my old grammar school. The scores were depressing.

Then I look up the school where my two older sisters went. The scores were just as bad.

After that, it's the grammar school my kid brother attended. Oh, his was even worse.

There was a time when all three schools would have done well, if they had conducted tests in those days. If not excellent, at least adequate.

I'm confident, because the kids in my class could all read and write, some quite well; my sisters were voracious readers by the time they graduated, and my brother's fundamentals were good enough to get him to college and a successful business career.

So what's changed? Why were we able to get the basics out of these inner-city schools, as they are now called, but today's kids are barely learning to read a street sign?

Money? That's the first thing that will come to many minds. The children going to those schools today are from poor families. And that's true.

But it was true when we were in the same schools. My sisters graduated at the height of the Great Depression, when relatives and neighbors borrowed coal from those lucky enough to work, when the only welfare was called "relief" and it meant standing in line for a box of groceries.

My brother and I had it a little better, but by today's standards, we were close to or below the poverty level. So were the families of many of our classmates.

But there was a difference, although it can't be found in any of the statistics, including how much each community spends on students.

It's called family. The families weren't perfect. For perfection, there were the "Andy Hardy" movies, which wasn't the way life was in the cold-water flats around Humboldt Park.

But in most of the flats, there was some semblance of a family life, even if the parents spoke broken English or none at all.

And if you look hard enough, that's what those long tables of statistics tell us.

You have to skip beyond the obvious. Sure, in the wealthy suburbs, where they spend $9,000 or $10,000 a year per pupil, compared with Chicago's $6,000, the results are excellent. But should that be a surprise?

So forget the wealthy suburbs. Look at the middle-class, working-class suburbs, where there are as many blue collars as white collars, where they aren't spending any more on each student than Chicago does. In many, they spend even less.

Yet they get results. Most are at the state and national averages or above.

Eldon Gleichman is superintendent of an elementary school district in Des Plaines, which is seldom compared with, say, the affluent Lake Forest.

He has 3,360 pupils. "This year, one-third of our kindergartners don't speak English. . . . In fact, 58 percent of our kids don't speak English at home."

But despite being more fluent in Spanish, Polish, and Russian, the kids scored above average.

It isn't easy, Gleichman says. "Parents are busier and busier in their lives. It's getting harder and harder, but we get the parents involved. Parental involvement—that's really where it's all at. The key is whatever goes on in the classroom and whatever goes on in the living room. It's a team effort."

Or the superintendent of a district in a southwest suburb, who said: "The parents are here. They listen to kids read, they get involved in our reading contests—book weeks—where children read to parents who must verify their children are reading.

"The parents are an extension of the school, just as we here at school are an extension of the parent. We have similar expectations, and the children know it.

"But one thing to keep in mind about spending. Yes, we don't spend any more [than Chicago], but we have the luxury of spending directly on the kids. We don't have security guards. We don't need building security or money to clean up vandalism or fix broken windows."

Just about every suburban school superintendent or principal says the same thing. From the principal of a middle-class district in the western suburbs:

"When we have an open house, it's packed. Parents give visible support for what their kids are involved in. Parents give their time to be at the school, to call the teacher, to be with their kids.

"You can't focus on how much we spend on students. Just looking at the simple numbers doesn't tell the whole story."

Exactly. And crying out for more money for Chicago's schools isn't the answer, unless the money is spent in a way that will get results.

But how do you use money to replace a family structure that isn't there? If you know the answer to that question, then pass it along to the eighth-grade teacher at a West Side school who wearily told me:

"I try to teach, but it isn't easy when my smartest student is a girl who is already pregnant with her second child."

So when you hear the educational experts talk about the problems of Chicago's schools, tossing programs and plans in every direction, unless they use words like "family" and "parents," tune them out.

And get ready for next year's bleak statistics.

December 3, 1992

Old Story Is News to Baby Boomers

The sobbing came from the next booth. Glancing over, I saw an attractive couple, tears streaming down their cheeks and dripping on their veggie lunch plates. And I spotted the source of their grief.

On the table was the latest copy of *Newsweek,* with a cover story revealing the shocking news that countless Baby Boomers have reached or are now approaching middle age. This issue of the magazine has traumatized many of those born in the fifteen years after World War II.

"It's so cruel and unfair," the woman gasped.

"Yes," said the man. "I don't know if I can cope."

Then they saw me staring and the woman shrieked: "Look, it is an old person, an ancient."

The man indignantly said: "Hey, you have frightened my companion. The least you can do is cover your face."

Draping a napkin over my head, I apologized for intruding and asked if I could be of any assistance in their time of sorrow.

"No," he said, "there is nothing you can do or anyone else. As incredible as it may sound, I am going to turn 40 in a couple of days. And she will do the same next month."

That admission brought on another fit of sobbing. When it subsided, she sighed and said: "And just when we're getting through that, we pick up this magazine and discover that some day we'll have to become 50. It says so right on the cover. How much bad news is a person expected to endure?"

But we all go through it. I once turned 40.

They stared suspiciously. "I don't believe that," she finally said.

It's true. Did you think that the rest of us were always middle-aged or elderly?

"As a matter of fact, yes," she said. "Weren't you born that way? I mean, as far back as I can remember, people like you have looked old. Are you trying to say you were once young?"

Sure. Did you think yours was the first generation to experience aging?

He nodded. "We thought this was some sort of new disease that was infecting only Baby Boomers. I was going to write my congressman and demand to know why the government isn't spending more money to find a cure. But you say it actually happened to you once? Turning 40?"

Absolutely. Happened about a year after I turned 39, as I recall. Back in 19-something or other. Way back before the CD, the PC, and even the VCR. But it was after the LP, FM, and TV.

Leaning forward, he said: "Tell me, what was it like? How did it feel? How did you cope?"

Don't remember.

"Ah-hah, it was so painful an experience that you have blocked it out of your memory."

No, I simply forgot it like most other birthdays.

"That's impossible," he said. "How could you possibly forget something like that?"

Easy. You see, there was a time when turning 30, 40, or 50 was no big deal. Sixteen was a big deal because you could get a job. And 21 was a very significant milestone because it meant you could order a drink without worrying about being carded. But 30, 40, or 50 just quietly happened to people. Magazines didn't put it on the cover like it was a national crisis. And every columnist who turned 40 didn't write about his or her new age of enlightenment. You just got up and went to work, or went outside the cave to fight a dinosaur.

The woman said: "Are you trying to tell us that this sort of thing has been going on for a long time?"

Oh, sure, for centuries, since before recorded history.

Becoming angry, she said: "Then why hasn't anything been done about it? How could you just sit there and let it happen?"

But there isn't anything that can be done. You're born, you have birthdays, you turn 30, 40, 50, and so on, if you're lucky. And then, phfft.

"Phfft?" he said. "What do you mean 'phfft'?"

I mean, phfft: The bell tolls, we have our exits and our entrances, the long sleep, adios amigos. You know, phfft, and it's all over.

He looked shocked. "You mean actually dying? Like in the movies and on TV shows, but for real?"

That's it. Happens all the time, and in the best of families, too.

She waved the magazine at him and said: "Was there anything about that in here?"

He shrugged and said: "I didn't get that far."

"Well, isn't that a fine kettle of tofu," she said. "How can a person make vacation plans?"

They were silent for a moment, then he grinned and said: "You're just trying to scare us, aren't you? A real kidder."

I'm afraid not. But don't worry. You have a lot of time left. With modern medicine and diet, you're a good bet to make it to 80.

His eyes narrowed in deep thought, then he took out his portable wallet-sized computer, called up a spreadsheet, punched in some numbers, studied the results and said: "He's right. Eighty is 40 plus 40, so we've used 40 but we have another 40 left. Not bad."

She looked relieved and said: "Then we can plan that vacation."

"Yes," he said, hitting more keys, "and it looks like we'll have time to pay off the credit cards."

Having eased their concerns, I paid my check and left.

While walking away, I heard him chuckle and say: "You know, I still think he's just a kidder."

She said: "Who?"

October 7, 1993

(Mike wrote this column the day Michael Jordan announced his retirement—not a permanent one, it turned out—from the Chicago Bulls.)

A City in Full-Court Depression

"I'm really depressed," said Slats Grobnik, tears dripping into his beer.

Me, too.

"You're not as depressed as me."

Believe me, I am.

"Then how come you ain't blubbering like I am?"

It is early. Give me time. Before long, I will be wailing like an infant.

"How could he do this to us?"

He says he has lost his zest.

"Hey, I lost my zest thirty years ago."

Me, too.

"You ain't lost as much zest as me. I'm running on minus zest these days."

Me, too.

"Stop saying, me, too."

I'm sorry, but I'm too depressed for an original thought.

"Maybe he don't understand."

Understand what?

"What he means to this town. To guys like me."

Me, too.

"You did it again."

Sorry.

"Do you remember way back when we got hooked on the Cubs?"

Almost to the day.

"We got in just when they stopped being a power and turned into world-class schlumps for almost fifty years."

It has been a rather long ordeal.

"Same with the Bears. We signed on just when they stopped being the Monsters of the Midway and became the Mopes of the Midway."

Be fair, the Bears won a couple of titles along the way.

"That ain't much for a lifetime of stupid loyalty."

Yes, but if our teams have been lacking, we have been blessed with some great individuals. Banks, Williams, Santo, Sandberg, Minoso, Appling, Allen, Thomas, Hull, Mikita, Butkus, Sayers, Payton, Hampton, Ditka, Weigel.

"Weigel?"

Best little left fielder my softball team ever had.

"Maybe you are more depressed than me."

I'm getting there.

"OK, we had some great guys, but nobody like him."

There's never been anybody like him, in any sport, anywhere, any time. He was simply the best.

"You're getting me even more depressed."

It's the least I can do.

"After all those loser years, when the only thing we got to cheer for is crooked elections, he comes along: a skinny kid in baggy shorts, and he makes this town stand tall."

You have been on that bar stool so long, I don't remember you standing tall or short.

"OK, I sat tall. But he gave this town a jolt. Made us all proud to be from Chicago. No matter where I traveled, to foreign places like Wisconsin, Indiana, even Iowa, they would all talk about how great he was. And that made me feel great. And that's what else I don't understand. Why should what some basketball player does make me feel so good?"

Well, someone once said that his performances were among the few pure things from which we can derive joy.

"Yeah, pure. Straight up, legit."

And we got it about 100 times a year. There aren't many pure things from which we can derive that much joy that often.

"Especially at my age."

So as sports nuts, I guess we should be grateful for what he gave us.

"I'm grateful. But I still don't know why a guy would walk away when he is the best there is, the best there was, and maybe the best there will ever be. Nobody quits when they are the best."

Maybe it's because being the very best is a hard standard to maintain. He knew that if his skills slipped ever so slightly, the media jackals would be upon him. Remember, when Babe Ruth was a star, there was no TV. The Babe could have howled at the moon in his underwear and even the tabloids would have ignored it. Today, a golf course bet becomes a national scandal.

"It's like that movie, *The Gunfighter,* when all the young guns are out to get the fastest gun there is."

Like that. Or the other great western, *Shane.*

"Yeah, where Shane rides in from nowhere and takes care of the bad guys."

Yes, in this case the Pistons and the Knicks.

"Then, when he has done in the bad guys, Shane gets on his horse and rides off into the sunset."

Exactly.

"And he keeps riding, even when that little kid is yelling: 'Come back, Shane, we love you.' "

You got it.

"Excuse me. Something I have to do."

What?

"I'm going outside and yell, 'Come back, Michael, we love you.' "

November 30, 1993

Politically Incorrect, But Right on Target

I have run across what appear to be several classic examples of political incorrectness and insensitivity by a major political figure.

So shocking are they that I hesitate even repeating them here for fear that they might cause widespread shrieking and fainting on the part of the politically proper.

Consider this statement:

"There is nothing more painful to me at this stage of my life than to walk down the street and hear footsteps and start thinking about robbery. Then [I] look around and see someone white and feel relieved."

Or this observation about street danger in the cities:

"This killing is not based upon poverty; it is based on greed and violence and guns."

Let us examine what might be considered wrong with these remarks.

First quote: It could be viewed as racist for someone to say he hears footsteps, fears robbery, looks over his shoulder, sees that it is only a white person, and feels relief.

Second quote: Greed? Plain nastiness? That flies in the face of the belief that only social conditions cause our widespread street violence. And that society at large is at fault.

You could be run off many college campuses for such simplistic offenses. Most public radio producers would hyperventilate if a guest uttered such heresies.

But these statements came from one of this country's best-known public figures. A man, in fact, who sits in the United States Senate.

Guess who?

No, it isn't Sen. Jesse Helms or any other red-nosed right-winger.

Would you believe Rev. Jesse Jackson, the nonvoting shadow senator from the District of Columbia?

Yes, it was Jackson, talking about crime in the black community last Saturday at a meeting of Operation PUSH.

He said a lot more too. Such as it's a waste of time to expect government to reduce or put an end to urban mayhem.

". . . We've got the power right now to stop killing each other. . . . There is a code of silence, based upon fear. Our silence is a sanctuary for killers and drug dealers. There must be a market revolt. The victim has to rise up."

And about making heroes of gang killers who are in prison and trying to get them out so they can become "leaders."

"When we are on the offensive arguing about getting killers out of jail, there is no moral authority in that."

But are these words really politically incorrect or insensitive?

They might be described that way if I or any other white commentator said them.

That shouldn't be. In Chicago, the majority of murders involve blacks killing other blacks. Many are kids. And black-on-white crime is more common than the opposite.

And while I believe that poverty and other socioeconomic conditions are a big factor in crime (come on, how many street gangs are shooting it out in Lake Forest?), a Nobel-winning economist makes a good argument that profit is also a basic crime motive. Drug pushers don't win Nobel prizes, but they'd surely agree.

But since these words were delivered by Jackson to a black audience, it's not politically incorrect. He was talking reality. Specifically: The biggest physical threat to a black is another black. As it is commonly called, black-on-black crime.

Jackson has been talking about crime for a long time, but he gets surprisingly little news coverage.

For reasons I don't understand, but find embarrassing, the people in my business are quicker to give prime time coverage to a goof like Al Sharpton, who seems to blame most black woes on Korean shopkeepers or the nearest white guy with a badge.

Meanwhile, Jackson is saying things that sound so . . . well, so middle class, that I suspect white media liberals are a bit appalled.

That might be why Jackson seems to have done a media fade. For a long time—longer than most people realize—he's been talking about individual responsibility and black community action. He has attacked drug use, teenage pregnancy, gang membership, and dependence on government.

What he seems to be saying is: In mounting crime, poor education, and collapsing family structure, we have deadly problems, so don't wait for white professors with their tedious studies, government bureaucrats, or anyone else to solve them. We have to do it ourselves.

If that's what he's saying, he's right.

During the 1950s through the 1970s, the civil rights movement had clear, heroic goals. It was inspiring, and Jackson was a major part of it.

But something happened. I don't know what, exactly. Grand hopes that were unfulfilled. The loss of unskilled but decent-paying jobs. The rise of a sort of to-hell-with-it attitude. Whatever it was, the movement was derailed.

On one hand, there was victory. The black middle class grew. Considering the time span, an incredible number of racial barriers fell.

On the other hand, the black lower class became more isolated, dejected, and violent. A threat to themselves and anyone else in range.

And that's what Jesse has focused on. Black-on-black suicide and genocide. He's saying what others are afraid to say. Or have said and have been burned for it.

Right now, he's only making the inside pages and is being ignored by the networks.

That's because Jesse, as he's been in the past, is so far ahead of the parade that he's almost walking alone.

But if he keeps it up, they'll catch up.

And when they do, it might be his finest moment.

February 1, 1994

We Love Her, We Love Her Not, We Love . . .

In my business, people are expected to take firm positions on public issues and not sit around wringing our hands and being wishy-washy.

But I have to admit that I have never bounced from one side to the other as often as I have in the case of Tonya Harding, the ice skater.

When the story first came out that her bodyguard and two other yahoos had plotted the attack on rival skater Nancy Kerrigan, my harsh response was: "That's it—it is a disgrace and she should be barred from competing in the Olympics."

But then I remembered the basic principle of law and fairness—we are all innocent until proven guilty. And I quickly reversed myself and said: "Let her skate."

Then her live-in ex-husband admitted that he had been part of the plot, and I became stern and said: "If he knew about it, she had to know about it. Cast her into the darkness."

But when she pleaded ignorance, I quickly reconsidered. There are many things husbands do that wives don't know about. Thousands of bartenders will attest to that.

So I decided that she should be given the benefit of the doubt. Just because her husband is a creep doesn't mean that she is a creepette. "Let her have the chance for the glory she has worked so hard to attain since she was a mere tyke," I said.

But in a twinkling her ex-husband established that he is both sleazy and lacking chivalry when he said she knew what was going on right from the beginning.

And this forced Tonya to admit that, yes, after Kerrigan was whacked in the leg, she knew that her crowd had done it.

"That," I said, "finally clinches it. If she knew and didn't say anything, lying to the cops and the cameras, she is unworthy and should be banished."

But then I remembered her sad, deprived childhood. A mean, self-centered mother, who seemed to be trying to make the *Guinness Book of World Records* for most husbands. Kind of a weak father. Living in dumps. A creepy half-brother. A struggle for survival since she was a tot.

And somehow having the spunk not only to overcome her bleak surroundings, but also to achieve great heights as an athlete.

The part of my brain that harbors latent social worker instincts said: "She was the victim of the evil actions of others. We must take her entire life's experience into consideration: the lack of maternal love, the domination of a manipulative husband, the hunger to rise from Dickensian squalor and to be somebody. Can we not forgive? Yes! So let her skate."

But then I thought: "Wait a minute. She's an adult. All she had to do was go to her coach, who is good, kind, and wise, and say: 'Holy cow, coach, you know what that bozo ex-husband of mine did?'" The coach would have surely said: "We blow the whistle." But she didn't. She just kept lying.

Forget it. I wouldn't let her skate in my ice-clogged driveway.

And that was my final position.

For about half a day. Then I heard a learned woman on the radio talk about how Tonya was a classic female victim of male domination. Yes, it was true. Her husband, a sneaky male person. The bloated bodyguard, a male hulk. The getaway driver, another of the bestial male persuasion.

Was I so lacking in sensitivity that I could not recognize a muddled little female who was nothing more than a prisoner of loutish male clods?

So let the kid strap on the blades and do her triple klutz, or whatever those twirls are.

And that became my final position.

For maybe an hour. Then I remembered that this was not some young Mary Tyler Moore we are talking about. Tonya has been around the block more than once. What we have here is a female Dead End Kid. If she were a man, she'd be a world-class barroom brawler or maybe a tattooed arm-wrestling champ.

She admits she knew about the attack after the fact, and my hunch is that she knew about it in the planning stage.

That has brought me to my final position, which I will not change.

And that is to let her skate in the Olympics.

Like everything else today—politics, crime, news, and the lifestyle of anybody besides hermits—the Olympics are show biz. What could be better show biz than the really mean and nasty girl competing against the really sweet and good girl?

Most of us don't know a triple klutz from a double putz.

Most men who watch figure skating are far more interested in perky buns.

But this time we'll be staring at the TV as a rare drama unfolds: Goodness and honesty being challenged by the forces of darkness and sleaze.

Even if neither wins a gold medal or any medal, it will still be the highlight of the Olympics.

And if it happens and the judging is legit, I know who will come out the winner.

My money will be on Tonya.

Why should ice skating be any different from just about everything else in the world?

March 9, 1994

Whitewater Almost Too Far Out There

You probably don't realize it, but most of us live in a place called "Out There."

The land of Out There is huge. It sprawls from the warm tip of Florida to the frigid Canadian border, and from New York to Los Angeles.

In fact, it includes everything in this country except Washington, D.C., and the surrounding suburbs where the politicians, bureaucrats, and newspeople make their homes.

This much tinier community of Washington is known as "Here."

I've become aware of this geographic distinction by watching the various Washington-based TV shows that feature big-time news pundits who discuss the great issues of the day.

On most of these shows, one of the pundits will say: "Is this something that they care about *out there* or is it something that only we care about *here?*

The idea is that if the people who live Out There don't care, then the issue might be less important than those who live Here realize.

An example is the Whitewater affair, which has just about everybody of importance in Washington in a tizzy.

But when Whitewater is discussed on TV, the question is still asked: Does anyone Out There really care?

As a lifelong resident of Out There, I think I can answer that question: Yes, no, maybe, and who knows?

Most of us who live here, which means Out There, are not as obsessed by the Whitewater affair as those who live there, which means Here.

For one thing, most of us Out There don't understand what it is all about. We are waiting for those who live Here to explain it to us.

But that's a problem because those who live Here, which means there, don't seem to understand it too well, either.

As far as I can tell, there is a suspicion that back in their Arkansas days, the Clintons did something unethical and now they are trying to cover it up.

But what they did isn't clear, except that they invested in a bum real estate deal in Arkansas with a banker-friend who turned out to be wild and crazy with other people's money. He is no longer the Clintons' friend and has become kind of a seedy local kook. That's life in the fast lane.

There are also questions about lawyer Hillary serving on boards of big corporations that gave money to her husband's political campaigns, handling legal matters that put her on both sides of the fence, and maybe fudging on income tax.

So how do most of us Out There, which means just about everywhere, feel about this?

Well, in Chicago, which is part of Out There, most people are less concerned with this issue than they are over whether Michael Jordan should keep trying to hit a baseball, or come back and rescue the Bulls from total collapse.

They are also concerned about their schools, children, cars, paychecks, and mortgage payments; their cholesterol level, sodium intake, and pains in their joints, chest, and sinuses; the arrogant bully who is their boss; and whether they should splurge on a new set of heel-toe weighted irons.

It's not that they are indifferent to the great issues of the day that send TV's McGoofy Group into a tizzy. But most people lead normal lives, which means that they don't hang on every word uttered at every Washington press conference. While C-SPAN has a devoted following, it can't compete with Oprah or even Geraldo.

Then there is the shock factor. And so far Whitewater doesn't have it.

Most people Out There know that Clinton is a lawyer and has spent most of his adult life in politics. Hillary was a big-time corporate lawyer and political wife in Arkansas.

Is anyone going to gasp and collapse at the thought that a pair of successful lawyer-politicians might have engaged in practices that were . . . eek . . . unethical? Of course not. It is assumed that politicians and lawyers are capable of being unethical, or why would they embarrass themselves and their loved ones by taking up these trades?

If anyone ran for office by saying, "I have never done anything unethical or dishonest or fibbed in my whole life, and I never will, honest to goodness, cross my heart and hope to die," he would immediately be branded a shameless liar and a fraud and would suffer a crushing defeat.

No, most of us who live Out There have become almost shock-proof. A new serial killer has trouble crashing the front page, so who gets bug-eyed about details of a failed real estate development on an Arkansas trout stream?

During his campaign, it came out that Clinton had been a draft-dodger and quite possibly was a chronic bed-hopper. That was so shocking that he was elected president of the United States.

Since the election, his old Arkansas bodyguards have told lurid stories of Clinton sneaking out of the governor's mansion for late-night hanky-panky in, among other places, school parking lots.

And that was met by a national yawn.

So why should anyone expect the great population Out There to be excited over murky ethical, legal, and financial questions that most lawyers and CPAs would have trouble understanding?

I've said it before and I'll say it again: What Washington needs is its own baseball team. It would give the McGoofy Group something to think about.

June 29, 1994

EEOC Is Lacking in Wisdom Teeth

A Chicago corporation recently received an ominous letter from the Equal Employment Opportunity Commission.

The letter said: "You are hereby notified that a charge of employment discrimination has been filed against your organization under the Americans With Disabilities Act."

It told the corporation to submit "a statement of your position with respect to the allegation contained in this charge, with copies of any supporting documentation. This material will be made a part of the file and will be considered at the time that we investigate this charge. Your prompt response to this request will make it easier to conduct and conclude our investigation of this charge."

Then came the specific allegation, which was made by a woman:

"On or about April 28, 1994, I applied for the position of Benefits Representative at the above referenced Respondent. On or about April 28, 1994, I was interviewed by the Respondent for the position.

"During the interview, I advised the Respondent that I have a microchip embedded in one of my molars and that it speaks to me and others.

"I believe I have been discriminated against because of my disability in violation of the Americans with Disabilities Act of 1990, in that I am qualified for the position.

"After explaining to the Respondent that I have a microchip embedded in my molar, I was not hired."

Now, imagine for a moment that you are a federal bureaucrat at the Chicago office of the EEOC, and someone comes in and says something like this:

"I just applied for a job and I was turned down because of discrimination."

You would probably ask what form the discrimination took.

"I have a microchip embedded in one of my molars."

Ah, a microchip in your molar.

"Yes, the microchip speaks to me and to others."

Ah, the microchip in your molar speaks to you.

"Yes, and that is why they didn't hire me."

I see. They didn't hire you because a microchip in your molar speaks to you. Well, well. An interesting problem.

Assuming you are a reasonable person, how would you respond to such a complaint?

Well, you might ask the woman to go and get a statement from a physician or dentist verifying that she has a microchip in her molar that talks to her.

Or you might suggest that she ask her dentist to remove the microchip from her molar.

You might even ask her how and why the microchip found its way into her molar and what it talks to her about.

Actually, I've had considerable experience in such matters. Anyone who works on a newspaper long enough—especially the night shift—will eventually talk to people who receive personal messages through fillings in their teeth, bedsprings, light bulbs, TV sets, or voices that ride the winds.

So do desk sergeants in police stations and those who answer 911 calls.

Sometimes the strange messages come from outer space, fiendish neighbors, a nasty relative, Elvis, or the president.

But when a caller says she is getting messages through fillings or microchips in her teeth, the cops don't send out a detective to peer into her mouth. Newspapers don't assign a reporter to press an ear against the molar to listen in on the messages.

Yet, here we have a federal agency that takes a talking molar seriously.

Some EEOC investigator actually took down the information and guided the woman through the complaint procedure.

Then the appropriate forms were filled out, a higher-up signed the complaint, and the file and investigation were officially opened.

Now an official at the accused corporation is required to formally respond to the federal complaint, supplying "any supporting documentation" as to why the corporation wouldn't hire a woman who said she had a microchip embedded in her molar that talked to her.

I don't know what the corporation's response will be. How do you answer a charge of this sort?

Maybe you could say: "Our company policy forbids employees receiving personal calls through microchips embedded in their molars on company time."

Or maybe: "At this time, we did not have a need for someone with a talking microchip embedded in her molar. However, should such a position open . . ."

The most appropriate response would be to dash off a note saying: "Hey, do you bureaucrats have microchips embedded in your heads? Is this what we're paying taxes for? Bug off."

But that wouldn't be smart. If offended, the EEOC might very well order the company to make amends by hiring a dozen people who receive messages through their teeth. Nothing the EEOC does would surprise me. Or any of the businesses they torment.

We asked a spokesperson for the EEOC whether the laws require the agency to investigate any and all discrimination complaints—even those from people who claim to have microchips in their molars.

No, the law doesn't require it, the spokesperson said. It is an office policy.

"You have to remember," she said, "what's crazy to you might not be crazy to someone else. . . . Besides, you're always calling us heartless bureaucrats. Do you really want us heartless bureaucrats making the decision about what cases to take?"

I'll have to think about that question. Or maybe I'll get the answer through one of my teeth.

August 30, 1994

Not His Kind of Photog, Ferguson Is

It was once my privilege to be challenged to a public duel by Frank Sinatra.

He was upset because I questioned the wasteful assignment of several Chicago cops to guard his hotel suite while he performed in this city.

In doing so, I made a fleeting reference to what appeared to be his splendid hairpiece.

Angered by the suggestion that his tresses had been purchased, he sent a lunk over with a letter in which he called me a pimp and offered to let me pull his hair.

The deal was, if the hair moved, he would pay me a large sum of money. But if the hair held firm to his scalp, he would punch me in the mouth.

The challenge was intriguing. Even if I lost, I could probably charge admirers of Ol' Blue Eyes a fee to examine or photograph my split lip. And if he knocked out one of my teeth, I could sell it to a collector for a small fortune.

But I declined because I thought that a bout of hair pulling and mouth punching would not be dignified behavior by two supposedly mature persons. And if he punched me in the mouth, I probably couldn't resist asking for his autograph, which would be even less dignified.

However, I did auction off his signed letter to the highest bidder and turned the proceeds over to a worthy charity, so some good came out of the foolish flap.

As a proud veteran of a Sinatra tiff, I believe it is my duty to defend him in his most recent altercation with the press.

If you are a reader of a sleazy tabloid called the *Globe,* you know about this incident. But if you read the *Globe,* it's unlikely that you read a respectable paper, so I'll tell you about it.

The big headlines shrieked "Ol' Blue Mouth," and "Screaming Sinatra threatens GLOBE photog with a big stick—and here's the pictures to prove it."

A sequence of pictures did indeed show Sinatra losing his poise. They showed Sinatra and his wife coming out of a restaurant; the wife gesturing for the photographer to go away; Sinatra getting angry; Sinatra looking in a dumpster for a weapon; and finally Sinatra glaring at the photographer while brandishing a piece of broomstick.

The story said that Sinatra told the photographer: "Come here, you (bleep) rat (bleep). I'll break your (bleep) camera, you low-life bleep (bleep) scum."

Then, the account said, Sinatra flung the broomstick at the cameraperson before his wife and daughter persuaded him to get in the car so they could go home.

And what was this photographer's reaction to the incident? Had he been honest, he would have said something like this:

"I was thrilled out of my shoes by Sinatra's furious reaction. I knew that if I just kept clicking, I would have a spread of sensational photos for this cheap, sleazy tabloid, and my sleazy editors would be delighted and might give me a bonus for my sleazy efforts. Had Sinatra just smiled and waved at the camera, I would have been crushed. Who needs friendly photos, for Pete's sake? But he rose to the bait. What a great guy."

Instead, the photographer, Mike Ferguson, was quoted as saying: "If the scene wasn't so laughable, it would have been tragic. Here's a 78-year-old man threatening me with a broomstick. It was pathetic."

What ingratitude. What an ungracious remark. Pathetic? I will tell this camera-clicker what strikes me as being pathetic.

We live in an incredible world, full of amazing sights. The sun rising over snow-capped mountains. Beautiful birds flitting through exotic trees. The tragedy of war and famine, crime and punishment, the miracle of birth, the sadness of death.

All these sights and thousands of others waiting to be captured on film by a sensitive and courageous photographer.

But what does this bozo do with his journalistic talent? He spends an evening lurking outside a Hollywood restaurant so he can stick a camera in the face of a seventy-eight-year-old show business legend and irritate him into cranky behavior. Now that is pathetic.

I'm sure this photographer was once a newborn baby, as most

of us were. And his proud parents looked at him with joy and wondered, as parents will, what he would do with his life. Become president, a hero, a great athlete, or artist?

How would they have reacted if that little tot had looked at them and gurgled: "I am going to grow up to be a photog for a sleazy supermarket tabloid, and I am going to skulk outside of Tinseltown restaurants and pop flashbulbs in the faces of an elderly singer, his wife, and daughter after they have finished dinner, hoping he will get angry and threaten me. It is my destiny."

Why, they surely would have thrown that baby out with the bath water, and who could fault them? Then they could have sold the story to the *Globe*.

January 26, 1995

Don't Bet on a Guilty Verdict for O. J.

After hearing the opening statements, my bets would be on O. J. Simpson walking out a free man.

It isn't that the prosecution doesn't have an arsenal of persuasive evidence—trails of blood DNA samples and a portrait of Simpson as a jealous and violent stalker.

And it's possible that when all the testimony is over, the majority of people watching TV will be persuaded that he is guilty.

But it won't matter what you or I and all the other spectators think. We're just part of the world's biggest gapers' block.

It will take only one person—a member of that California jury—to dig in his or her heels and say: "I don't believe it." And hold to that view. If that happens, it's a hung jury, and the prosecutors will have to decide whether to go through the whole thing again.

Something in Johnnie Cochran's opening pitch makes me believe that he and the defense team will be able to plant enough doubt in at least one juror's mind to prevent a guilty finding.

That something is Mark Fuhrman, the eager-beaver Los Angeles detective who was involved in so much of the early Simpson investigation and seemed to have an uncanny knack for coming across important clues and evidence.

He was also in on one of those past domestic squabbles between O. J. and Nicole.

But most important, the defense believes it has evidence that Fuhrman said things in the past that indicate he is a racist.

If he is, that shouldn't be much of a shock. Many cops are racists. So are many other Americans in other jobs.

But Fuhrman isn't just any cop or any American. And that's why Cochran made a point of mentioning Fuhrman in his opening remarks.

It's a safe guess that Cochran is going to try to put Fuhrman on trial. The goal will be to try to establish that he is a racist cop who didn't like seeing a black man become a big success and marry a gorgeous white woman.

And that Fuhrman's dislike of Simpson was nasty enough to prompt him and possibly others to plant evidence—the bloody glove, for example—to hang Simpson for crimes someone else committed.

Does that sound implausible or even far-fetched? It depends on your background.

If you have lived most of your life in a friendly small town or a quiet comfortable suburb, yes, it might be unthinkable that your nice Officer Friendly would try to railroad an innocent person.

But if you are a black person, you might say: "So what else is new?"

Few blacks, especially in big cities like L.A., would be shocked by the suggestion that a white cop might find it in his heart to try to frame or railroad a black person.

And there are valid reasons for their feeling that way. Blacks have indeed been framed by racist cops and prosecutors. If not framed, then pushed around and deprived of a fair shake. There's nothing new in that. It is part of our legal heritage.

I doubt if there are many adult blacks who haven't had bad experiences with cops. And few who can't talk about someone they knew being given a bad deal in a courtroom or a police station.

We don't know a lot about the twelve Simpson jurors. But we do know that eight are black, and all but one of the others are Hispanic or Native American.

It's possible, I guess, that those eight black jurors are unique, that they have had amazingly carefree lives, somehow sheltered from the tensions and nitty-gritty of a multiracial society that isn't always friendly and filled with brotherly love.

Sure, it's possible. It's also possible to draw three cards to an inside straight.

It's far more likely that one or more of those eight black jurors already believe that white cops are capable of railroading a black man. If they know that J. Edgar Hoover and his FBI waged a campaign to malign Martin Luther King Jr., why should they have faith in the honesty of some L.A. cop with a possible history of using the N-word?

Yes, all of those jurors promised that they have open minds and would consider only the evidence and testimony. That's what jurors always say.

But no lawyer believes that. To the contrary, a good trial lawyer is looking for jurors who will lean in the direction of his client, whatever the evidence shows. If they wanted someone impartial and influenced by only the evidence, testimony, and law, they'd ask for a bench trial and take their chances with the judge.

So Cochran will try to show that there was a bad cop—maybe more than one—out there, trying to nail an innocent man. Such things have happened.

And all it will take is for one juror to believe that it is happening again. Don't bet against it.

February 24, 1995

Horrors of the Past Are G-Rated Today

While walking through the video store, the seven-year-old boy stopped and gawked at a display of movie tapes.

"Wow," he said, "what are those?"

His father said: "Never mind. You don't want to watch those movies."

"Why not?"

"They are old horror movies. And they'll scare you, give you nightmares."

The boy began reading the titles of the video boxes aloud. "*The Wolf Man.* Wow. *Frankenstein. Dracula.* Wow. *Frankenstein Meets the Wolf Man. The Mummy's Tomb.* Wow, what's a mummy?"

The father explained. "A mummy is a very scary guy. They are all very scary."

"Did you ever see them?" the boy asked.

"Yes, all of them, a long time ago when I was a kid."

"Did they scare you?"

"I was so scared that I crawled under the seat in the movie theater and hid. People in the audience screamed and fainted."

"Cool, let's rent one."

"I told you. They are just too scary. You won't be able to sleep. And you might be the only kid in your class with gray hair."

"C'mon, please. Pleeeese."

They discussed it for a while, as modern families do, and finally negotiated a deal. The boy agreed that if he became too terrified, and closing his eyes and putting his head under a sofa cushion didn't protect his psyche, the father could switch the film off.

They walked out with three tapes—*Dracula,* for Friday night; *Frankenstein,* for Saturday night, and *Frankenstein Meets the Wolf Man,* for Sunday night.

"Can't we get that mummy movie too?" the boy asked.

"Your mother will kill me as it is," the father said.

He wasn't far off. "Are you crazy?" she said. "Those three movies over the weekend? By the time he gets back to school Monday, he'll be afraid to go to the bathroom alone."

"Don't worry. If it's too much for him, I'll hit the zapper."

"Why are you doing this?" she asked. "It's sadistic."

"No, it was his idea. Maybe he'll learn a lesson, that you should be careful about what you ask for."

That night they watched *Dracula.*

When the ship carrying the vampire's coffin arrived in England, and all the crew members were mysteriously dead, the boy asked: "What killed them?"

"Count Dracula. He got their blood."

"Why didn't we see that?"

"They didn't show stuff like that."

"Oh."

Later, a leering Dracula leaned slowly toward a sleeping woman's throat. But the scene ended.

"What happened?" the boy asked.

"Dracula bit her on the neck and got some of her blood."

"Why didn't they show it?"

"Because they didn't show that kind of stuff."

"Huh."

When the movie ended, the boy said: "Hey, what happened to Dracula?"

"Professor Van Helsing found the coffin where he sleeps and pounded a stake through his heart and killed him."

"When?"

"Just before the end."

"I didn't see that."

"No, they didn't show it."

"Why not?"

"I guess it's too scary."

A few minutes later, he heard the boy say to his mother: "It was kind of boring."

The next evening, they watched *Frankenstein.*

It reached the memorable scene when the monster has croaked the nasty hunchback, escaped from the castle, and tossed a girl into a stream.

"What happened to her?" the boy asked.

"She drowned."

"Couldn't she swim? She was only a few feet from the shore and it didn't look very deep."

"I guess not."

"Huh. Anybody can do the dog paddle."

The angry villagers were finally marching, torches aloft, to find the monster.

The man glanced at the boy. He was sleeping soundly.

In the morning, the boy said: "What happened to the monster?"

"He died."

"Yeah, I figured that would happen."

The mini-festival ended Sunday night with *Frankenstein Meets the Wolf Man.*

"How come there's never any color in these movies?" the boy asked.

"Because it is scarier in black and white."

"Oh."

When Larry Talbot (Lon Chaney Jr.) grimaces at the full moon and slowly turns into a hairy-face, the boy said: "Hey, cool."

But a few minutes later, he said: "What happened there?"

"He kills people by biting them on the neck."

"Why didn't they show that?"

"I told you, they didn't show graphic stuff like that."

The movie abruptly ended with a dam bursting and the flood-waters sweeping both creatures to wherever wet monsters and werewolves go.

The boy yawned and said: "Too bad. That Wolf Man was really a nice guy."

Then he said: "When you were a kid, you didn't really crawl under the seat in the movie theater, did you?"

"Uh, no, not really, unless I was looking for a lost glove."

"Yeah, I knew you were kidding."

"Yeah, sure I was."

October 17, 1995

Look, Up in the Sky, It's a Bird . . .
It's a Plane . . . It's Mike!

This is going to be a diary. A very short diary. It is being written with trembling fingers on a laptop computer.

Sunday, 9:40 A.M.: For the last twenty minutes, I have been strapped into a seat in a large metal tube. This tube is about five miles above the state of Colorado. It is moving in an easterly direction at about the speed of a bullet.

In other words, I'm in a commercial jet airliner, and I don't belong here.

That's because I don't fly. I have a phobia. Several, in fact. I'm a control freak, and I fear heights, confined spaces, and terrorists, both domestic and foreign.

The last time I got on one of these things was about twenty years ago. But that doesn't count because some friends poured an afternoon's worth of vodka into me and I thought I was on a fast bus.

But this time I did it without even one drink. Which shows that sobriety is overrated.

So what am I doing way up here, thousands of feet from the surface of the planet I love and already desperately miss?

It's the fault of the sadistic blond woman sitting next to me, calmly reading a magazine. She loves flying, and she bullied, cajoled, and shamed me into getting on this thing with her.

By the time I changed my mind and decided to leave and catch a night train out of Denver, it was too late. We were already along the ground and hurtling into the sky.

My life didn't flash before my eyes because I had my hands over them.

When I opened them, I nudged my wife and said: "Look at that poor guy. He either fainted or died of fright."

"No," she said, "he started taking a nap as soon as he got on."

"Then he must be that lunatic Chuck Yeager."

Sunday, 10:05 A.M.: It still hasn't crashed. But, then, there is always a calm before the storm.

The stewardess came by and asked if I wanted something to drink. I said yes, some scotch, and leave the bottle. My wife said: "He'll have coffee."

When the stewardess brought the coffee, I told her I would like to speak to the pilot. She asked why. I said I wanted to see his driver's license. She chuckled. I don't know why she thought that was funny. The pilot is an absolute stranger. How do I know what his qualifications are?

Sunday, 10:30 A.M.: Neither of the wings has fallen off yet. I asked my wife to look out of the window and keep her eyes peeled.

"For what?" she asked.

"Birds. All it takes is one dumb goose or even a sparrow flying into an engine and we've all had it. I don't want to end it that way, screaming the Lord's Prayer as we plunge toward a Nebraska cornfield. I want to go out with dignity in my own bed, surrounded by my loved ones and watching their faces when I tell them they've been cut out of my will."

Sunday, 10:45 A.M.: My wife said: "You don't have to keep your safety belt on for the whole flight."

"Like hell I don't. If the door accidentally pops open, I don't want to be sucked out. I still can't understand why we aren't issued parachutes."

Sunday, 11 A.M.: The door to the cabin has opened and a man comes out and talks to the stewardess.

"There's the pilot," my wife said.

"My god," I said. "Who's flying the plane?"

"The copilot."

"What, some rookie kid? That's outrageous. If we make it alive, I'm going to write to the FAA."

Sunday, 11:20 A.M.: The plane dips to one side. Then it starts to lose altitude. In my steadiest hysterical voice, I tell my wife: "I knew it. We're going down. We're doomed. Forgive me for not being a better husband. Or don't forgive me. What's the difference now. I'm about to become a charred lump."

"Shhh, relax, we're just landing," she said.

"Oh, boy, that's when it always happens."

"We're fine. Look, you can see O'Hare."

"What are those cars doing on the runway? This is insane."

"That's the toll road, silly."

"I hope the pilot knows it."

Sunday, 11:40 A.M.: There is a tiny thump.

"We've had it," I moaned.

"We've landed," she said.

I open one eye. Then the other. She's right.

The napping guy on the other side of the aisle yawns, stretches, and rubs his face. So I yawn, stretch, and rub my face. It's a guy thing.

Sunday, noon: We're in a cab. The driver asked: "How was your flight?"

"Smooth as silk," I said. "Slept most of the way."

The blond snickered and said: "Should I call a travel agent tomorrow?"

"Why not? It's a small world."

October 18, 1995

Eloquence and Gall on Washington Mall

Take your pick. The enormous gathering of black men in Washington—the Million Man March—was moving and inspiring. Or it was depressing. It provided hope for the future. Or pessimism and worry.

Or maybe all of the above.

The sight of hundreds of thousands of men getting together to pledge themselves to fatherhood, marriage, family life, hard work, and other virtues should be inspirational, whatever color they might be.

But it means even more when black men express devotion to these values, since our most serious domestic problems begin with the no-father black family. When daddy is a no-show, it leads to illegitimacy, chronic welfare, child neglect, drug use, black crime, and so many other social migraines.

However, there is a slight problem. It's not easy to be a dutiful family man when there's no paycheck because you can't find a decent job or even a crummy one.

With businesses possessed by the downsizing spirit—the 1990s' cool way of saying "take a walk, you're fired"—it's hard to see where these jobs are going to come from. Especially for the young blacks who are coming out of the big-city warehouses that we call schools.

But maybe Newt or Bill will think of something.

Many of the speeches at the great rally were truly eloquent. There was emotional talk about shunning guns and drugs, treating each other with respect, pooling resources, starting businesses, rebuilding neighborhoods, and other good works.

Fine. Wonderful. But the most gripping, eloquent speaker of them all was Louis Farrakhan, one of the few men in America who can talk for two hours without putting anyone to sleep.

I have to admit that I enjoy a Farrakhan speech. It has rhythm, style, pacing, graceful transitions, soft phrases rising to thunderous crescendos. It's very much like a fine musical composition, which isn't surprising, since Farrakhan used to be a professional calypso singer.

Unfortunately, it's not music. It's words. And no matter what kind of soft-spoken con job he tries to feed Larry King on TV, Farrakhan just can't resist playing the Jew-baiting, honky-hating, history-twisting demagogue when he has a live and receptive audience.

So there we had hundreds of thousands of black men, pouring into Washington in a show of solidarity, brotherhood, and praiseworthy expectations. They were joined by some of black America's most respected leaders.

Which was inspiring and should be a cause for hope.

But who got them together? Who was the big drawing card? Who got the biggest cheers and most adulation?

Louis (the Lip) Farrakhan, black America's most influential hate monger.

If that's not depressing, you'll never need Prozac.

Farrakhan even had the gall to speak fondly of Malcolm X while reciting a list of outstanding black men who have been victimized by white America.

Apparently he thinks we've all forgotten that Malcolm X was murdered in public, not by white racists, but by black hit men from the very same Black Muslim organization in which Farrakhan was a rising star.

Yet the big Washington rally provided hope that was so obvious that most of us could have overlooked it.

The speakers included black men who hold high political and governmental positions and wield considerable political power. The audience included black men who work in the professions and the news media, run their own businesses, live in solid middle-class communities, and attend fine universities.

Just think back only thirty years and the way things were.

I was in Alabama, where Martin Luther King was leading marches so blacks could be allowed to vote. Redneck thugs with badges were riding them down with horses, crushing their skulls with clubs, and shooting them dead from ambush.

In other parts of the South, black homes were being burned, civil rights workers—black and white—were being murdered. White politicians were bellowing about how niggers would be kept in their place and would be wise not to get uppity. Black students needed military bodyguards to enter some universities.

If anyone had told me the following: Within a few generations, the biggest cities in America would elect black mayors, major corporations would have black executives, the finest universities would be chasing after black students, the black middle class would dramatically expand, and laws would have prohibited just about all forms of housing, political, and educational discrimination.

And that the polls would show that the leading potential candidate for president would be a distinguished retired Army general who happens to be a black man from New York.

If anyone had promised those things when I was dodging Klansmen in Alabama, I would have said that I hoped to live long enough to be part of that utopian society.

And I've made it.

So how come I'm depressed?

January 26, 1996

And It's One, Two, Three Strikes . . . You're Sued

The news business, especially the radio and TV babblers, remains obsessed with O. J. Simpson and the poor fellow's endless legal troubles. They can have Simpson. I'll take the unusual case of Johnny (the Arm) Lupoli.

Johnny is the defendant in a personal-injury lawsuit. He is accused of really messing up a woman's face.

What makes his case unusual is that Johnny is only nine years old. This makes him the youngest person I've heard of being sued for anything.

How did he damage the woman's face?

Last summer, he was at a Little League park in Connecticut warming up on the sidelines while waiting for his game to start.

He's a pitcher, but apparently he has a slight problem with control, which is not uncommon for nine-year-old athletes. As a result, one of his tosses missed a teammate's glove.

It struck the face of Carol LaRosa, who was sitting nearby on the grass. She was there because her son is on the same team as Johnny.

Mrs. LaRosa left the ballpark and went to a hospital to have her face treated. And nothing more was heard of the incident until a couple of days before Christmas.

That's when little Johnny happened to find a document addressed to him stapled to the front door of his home.

The kid can read. And what he read was a copy of the lawsuit. He found himself accused of the following acts, among others:

He "failed to warn the plaintiff that he was throwing the baseball to her . . . threw the baseball at a dangerous speed . . . was inattentive and failed to keep a proper lookout while throwing a baseball."

Reading further, he found that Mrs. LaRosa wanted at least $15,000 from him for her injuries (the suit said she required 60 stitches), pain and suffering, and the rest of the usual miseries lawyers toss into a lawsuit.

Johnny's parents and lawyer say he was quite shaken, which is understandable. Imagine how you would have felt at age nine if you found yourself being sued for $15,000. That's a lot of weekly allowance.

I have a friend who still feels nervous when he goes near a public library, because when he was about ten, he lost a library book and got a stern letter that made him fear he would go to prison.

Todd Bainer, who is Johnny's lawyer, says: "I think it stinks. He is the only defendant, not the Little League, not the coaches. I think it takes a certain type of human being to sue or cause to be sued a child.

"I have adults who have no familiarity with the legal process, and when they are sued for anything, they are extremely apprehensive. Imagine how it would affect a nine-year-old kid."

Mrs. LaRosa and her lawyer declined to discuss the suit. The lawyer says he feels that he has been wronged by sportswriters who have written about it.

Without judging the merits of the lawsuit, some things do sound puzzling.

For example, the allegation that Johnny was "inattentive." Are there any nine-year-old boys who aren't "inattentive"? The typical nine-year-old boy spends most of his time in another mental galaxy.

And that he threw the ball "at a dangerous speed." If that's true, Johnny's parents should get him over his trauma, hire some coaches, and get ready for that first multimillion-dollar contract.

But what makes this lawsuit interesting is that it raises simple questions about our litigation-crazed society:

Doesn't anything qualify as a plain old accident? Does any mishap that requires more than a Band-Aid have to land in front of a judge and jury?

One of the dictionary definitions of "accident" is "lack of intention; chance."

As Johnny's mother said: "He's just a normal boy who was playing baseball. He didn't mean to hurt anybody."

Right. And one might argue that if you are going to sit around where nine-year-old boys are tossing baseballs, you might be guilty of being "inattentive" if you happen to get conked.

This is the kind of lawsuit that gives all lawyers a bad name. They argue that tort reform is terrible because lawsuits protect us all from evil corporations and devil-may-care doctors. And there is some truth to that.

But then you get a nine-year-old kid being sued for what amounts to just being a nine-year-old kid.

Incidentally, LaRosa's husband also has put in a claim as part of the suit. He says that his wife's injuries caused him a loss of "consortium." That means . . . well, I'm sure you know what that means.

Something like that could cause even further confusion for Johnny. If he had any sex-education courses in school, he probably asked his parents: "Hey, didn't they say that the ball hit her in the face?"

April 10, 1996

Rostenkowski's Sin Was Not Changing with the Times

Her name was Mary, and she was middle-aged, worked as a domestic, had little money and no medical plan, and was in need of some serious and expensive life-saving surgery.

But she had lived in her Northwest Side neighborhood for most of her life. And she knew somebody who knew somebody who knew a politician of considerable importance.

Some calls were made, the most important coming from the office of the politician.

The result was that Mary went to a good hospital, was treated by skilled physicians, was cured, and went home with a bill of $0.00.

How the politician arranged this, I don't know. I assume that the hospital and the doctors owed him favors. That's the way things have always worked in Chicago, which can be good or bad. In this case, it was good.

And it wasn't the only time the politician did something like that. Using his political muscle to help people out was part of his trade. That's the good side of what used to be called machine politics.

I like to think of the late alderman Vito Marzullo, who usually placed one or two young lawyers in city or county patronage jobs. And one night every week, the lawyers came to Vito's ward office and handled legal chores for low-income people from the neighborhood. Free, of course.

In Mary's case, the politician who took care of her medical needs was Rep. Dan Rostenkowski, whose career in public service has just ended in a most tragic way—pleading guilty to illegal use of federal funds.

Before anyone leaps for the phone, stationery, or e-mail device, let me say that Rostenkowski and I are not pals. Far from it. We've never particularly liked each other, and our longest conversation has been about two minutes.

Many years ago, we sat together at a banquet honoring up-and-coming young Chicagoans in various fields. He was the young politician with a future and I was the young columnist.

He was aloof and wary of talking to someone who just might stick it to him down the line. Which shows he was smart, because I later did exactly that.

That was a pity, really, because we had a lot in common besides our ethnicity. We came from the same neighborhood. My family once owned a tavern within a short walk of Rostenkowski's house. And his precinct captain never once hustled us for a fast buck.

We have mutual friends and share some of the same bad habits. But when he was grabbed for DUI in Wisconsin some years ago, he had the good sense to be polite to the cops.

We share having had kid problems, which can be agonizing for any parent. And if you're in public life, the minor foibles of your kids wind up in the newspapers while the neighbors of Joe the Bricklayer don't even know his kid was mugging old ladies.

Being a public figure, he is held to a higher standard. And sometimes, it isn't exactly fair.

What I'm stumbling into saying is that nobody should be taking pleasure from Rostenkowski's misfortune. Not unless you have never, ever, broken even a minor law and gotten away with it, fudged a bit on your taxes, or violated any of the Ten Commandments.

Only a few decades ago, none of this would have been happening. That's because the rules changed. Most of the things he was nailed for would have been legal and common or, at worst, nickel-dime offenses when he began his career in Congress.

That's the way it is in our society. The rules keep changing. Things we could once say or think are now taboo. And acts that were once considered gosh-awful are now embraced.

Rostenkowski's mistake was not changing. Maybe he didn't notice. Or maybe he didn't see the danger.

The danger was that he was a big political fish—the kind of trophy that an ambitious federal prosecutor loves to stuff and hang on his wall.

There is no one in our society more powerful—judge, governor, mayor, legislator, or even president—than a prosecutor. Local or federal.

At the federal level, they have a compliant grand jury and all the investigative tools they need: the agents of the FBI, the Internal Revenue Service, and every other federal agency. Plus eager assistants who will send their own grannies up the river to enhance their careers.

And the most dangerous and ruthless are those prosecutors who have political ambitions that are most easily fulfilled by hanging a well-known public figure.

That's what did Rostenkowski in, a federal prosecutor's personal ambitions. If I could put those federal headhunters on a lie box and ask, "Do you really believe that what he did was a terrible crime?" and they said "Yes," the needle would clang when it went past the marking for "liar, liar, pants on fire."

So now Rostenkowski goes to prison for a year or so. And the TV cameras go on the Chicago streets and ask people what they think.

And without having read one word of evidence, some glassy-eyed mope says: "Well, he did wrong and he gotta pay for it, right?"

Lord, please let a hard-nosed cop grab that mope the next time he runs a red.

May 16, 1996

Clinton's Big Lead Easily Explained
in Age of Indulgence

Why would anyone be surprised that President Clinton has a huge lead in all the popularity polls and would win by a landslide if the election were held today?

The answer is so simple and obvious, and it has nothing to do with political ideology or executive capabilities.

The glib, youthful Clinton is almost the perfect man for these fast-paced times and the future. But the grim, aging Bob Dole is a carryover from a past that to many Americans is gone, except in the grainy films shown on the American Movie Classics channel.

We know that television is the most powerful of all political tools. Clinton was born into the TV age. He knows when to be softly serious, when to grin and chuckle, when to be bold and play the statesman, when to feel our pain, and when to whip off a crisp commander-in-chief salute.

And he can do any of the above in a snappy ten-second sound bite, nibble, or hickey—whatever the script requires. He can even play rock on his sax and gyrate his hips with considerable soul.

He would make a masterful daytime talk-show host, possibly the equal of Geraldo or Oprah.

In contrast, Dole was already a grown man and a heroic war casualty before TV began shrinking the national brain. He has never bothered to learn the art of the ten-second bite, much less the nibble or the hickey. I can't think of one industry that would hire him to sell its product on the tube. Well, maybe hernia trusses. If he dances, it has to be a dignified fox trot.

Then there are their voices. Clinton's voice is high-pitched. Dole's is much deeper.

Does that matter? You bet it does. Clinton has a voice for today. Just listen to popular rock music. All of the singers have high-pitched, eunuch-like voices. It's almost impossible to tell the men from the women, if there is any difference.

There was a long-gone time when a baritone such as Perry Como or a bass such as Vaughn Monroe topped the hit charts; when a deep-voiced singer would bellow: "Old Man River, that Old Man River . . . he don't plant taters, he don't plant cotton."

But today, the lyrics would have to be changed to "Old Person

River, that Old Person River . . . he or she does not plant potatoes or cotton because the work is demeaning."

And today's deep-voiced singers are found only in the country music field, self-pitying losers groaning about their two-timing women going honky-tonkying and leaving them with a sink full of dishes and not one beer in the fridge. Their fans will be too hung over to vote.

If anything should have delighted the Clinton backers, it is a couple of nontraditional political polls that were widely reported.

One asked who people would trust to baby-sit their kids. The other asked which candidate they would ask to choose the top-pings for their pizza. Clinton easily outdistanced Dole in both polls.

This tells us that most American parents are indulgent and wouldn't want someone such as Dole telling their kids: "Sit down, shut up, turn off the TV, eat your vegetables. I will tell you a story about the government bureaucrat in wolf's clothing that ate chil-dren who didn't finish their dinners." They would prefer someone who would gently say: "I feel your pain, I feel your diapers, have another Twinkie."

It also tells us that most Americans don't know much about pizza if they would trust a guy from Arkansas to pick their toppings.

These silly polls were brought to my attention by an angry Dole supporter who said: "Why doesn't someone do a poll in which they ask people this question: 'Who would you ask to walk down to the OK Corral with you—Clinton, the slick draft dodger, or Bob Dole, the pain-wracked World War II combat soldier?' "

Nice try, but a poll that asked such a question would be in-conclusive.

That's because this is 1996, and most of the answers would be something like:

"I'm not asking anybody to go there with me because I have no intention of walking down to the OK Corral. It is not my fight, and I'm not going to get involved. And if anyone tries to involve me, they will hear from my lawyer."

A far better measure of true voter sentiment would be a poll in which people were asked: "If you wanted to borrow money from someone with no intention of ever paying it back would you bring your hard-luck story to Bill Clinton or Bob Dole?"

It would be a landslide.

January 10, 1997

Arrghh! Disney Walks the Plank for Politically Correct

A heated debate has taken place in Southern California over whether political correctness has stuck its pointy nose into one of the oldest and most popular features of Disneyland.

It was decided recently that a change had to be made in the sexist behavior of the mechanized creatures who provide the entertainment in the Pirates of the Caribbean exhibit.

Those who have seen this display in either the California or Florida Disney park know that pirates from a big sailing ship have shelled and overrun a town and are behaving as we have been conditioned to believe pirates did in their heyday.

They are boisterously looting, drinking, eating, singing, swaggering, and chasing the town's womenfolk.

But there has long been a subtle difference in the Florida and California shows.

At Orlando's Disney World, the women being chased are carrying food. Those who are inclined to give the pirates the benefit of the doubt could believe that the buccaneers are after a hearty meal rather than a roll in the hay.

But at California's Disneyland, the fleeing women don't have food. So a spectator who analyzes the scene might conclude that the pirates are intent on doing "it."

This is apparently the conclusion that was drawn by some spectators, presumably of the feminist persuasion. And they brought their views to the people who run the Disney park.

So it was decided that while the pirates exhibit was closed for renovation, a change would be made.

The fleeing ladies would be equipped with platters of food, making them appear to be waitresses, barmaids, cooks, or something of the sort.

Then the pirates might be assumed to be after the food rather than the female bods.

The change was greeted with cheers by feminists and sneers by those who are less sensitive.

Although I have been in both Disney parks more than once—the fate of those of us who can't stop rearing kids—I have to admit that I never noticed the fleeing women were carrying food.

If I had thought about it, which I don't recall doing, I would have assumed that the pirates were pursuing the women because they had sex on their minds.

After all, they were low sorts—thieves and cutthroats—who had been cooped up with other men on a ship for who knows how long.

Let us be honest. We all know what pirates were like when it came to women. And accountants, lawyers, carpenters, tree-trimmers, and journalists, too.

So what we were seeing in the Disney exhibit was a bunch of scruffy criminals with—let us not mince words—sexual assault on their minds. If they had minds. But of course, being mechanical creatures, they didn't.

I'm sure that Walt Disney, a square sort, wasn't thinking about rape when he personally supervised creation of the pirate exhibit. In his day, the Hollywood pirate was always singing yo-ho-ho and pinching or ogling females—or wenches, as the ladies were called.

But we are in a different era with different standards. About the only way you can see pirates act that way is to watch old films on the American Movie Classics channel.

If you switch over to the up-to-date cable movie channels, there is little pinching or ogling. They don't waste time. The females fling off their clothing and spring atop the compliant male for a few filmed minutes of joyous moaning, writhing, and grimacing.

So by today's entertainment standards, the behavior of the me-chanical pirates is restrained.

But that doesn't mean that the protesting feminists were wrong. I can understand how a woman might feel, taking her little daugh-ter through the show and hearing her ask: "Mommy, why are those men chasing the ladies?" What does the parent say? "Oh, they want to propose marriage or living together for a while to see if they are on the same page"?

On the other hand, if zealots wanted to make a big deal out of the pirates' conduct, they could question why they are shown guz-zling what is obviously booze.

Do we want the kids to see the glorification of drunken bums? Could this not offend those who are going through the pains of a twelve-step program?

And if the pirates are assumed to chase the women for the food on their platters, doesn't this make a humorous statement about

the serious problem of gluttony? Are those with weight, cholesterol, and blood pressure problems supposed to be amused?

So if we start demanding that it be too realistic — or not realistic
enough — who knows where these paths might lead?

Remember, these pirates are men who spend long periods of
time in the company of other men.

So would it be unreasonable to wonder if some of the pirates
might not prefer the company of other men? In more ways than
singing yo-ho-ho together?

If so, would not gay men be justified in asking the Disney
people to acknowledge them by maybe having a few of the pirates
hold hands and do a bit of smooching?

Sometimes life in these strange times is just one can of worms
after another.

March 21, 1997
(This is the last column Mike wrote.)

It Was Wrigley, Not Some Goat,
Who Cursed the Cubs

It's about time that we stopped blaming the failings of the Cubs
on a poor, dumb creature that is a billy goat.

This has been going on for years, and it has reached the point
where some people actually believe it.

Now a beer company, the Cubs, and Sam Sianis, who owns
Billy Goat's Tavern and the accused goat, have banded together to
lift the alleged curse that was supposedly placed on the Cubs in
1945 — the last time they were in the World Series.

As the story goes, the late Bill Sianis, founder of the old tavern,
tried to take his pet goat into Wrigley Field and was turned away
because the goat smelled.

That's when the curse was placed on the Cubs, and they haven't
been in a World Series since.

It's an entertaining story, but is only partly true.

Yes, blame for many of the Cubs' failings since 1945 can
be placed on a dumb creature. Not a poor, dumb creature but a
rich one.

I'm talking about P. K. Wrigley, head of the chewing gum company and the owner of the Cubs until he died in 1977.

In many ways, Wrigley was a nice man—shy, modest, and very good at selling chewing gum. He was a lucky man, inheriting the thriving gum company and a fine baseball team from his more aggressive father.

In baseball, what P. K. Wrigley was best known for was preserving day baseball long after all other franchises were playing most of their games at night.

A myth grew that Wrigley believed baseball was meant to be played in sunshine and, as a matter of principle, kept lights out of his park.

The truth was that he planned on lights very early. But when World War II began, materials necessary for lights were needed in the war effort. So he shelved plans for the lights, and when the war ended, he didn't bother to revive them.

The only other baseball feat he was known for was running the worst franchise in baseball.

And a big part of that can be blamed on racism. If not Wrigley's, then that of the stiffs he hired to run his baseball operations.

After World War II ended, the best players available were being discharged from the military and returning to the teams on which they had starred a few years earlier.

But Wrigley had a unique manpower problem. His best players had remained home during the war because they were 4-F for one physical defect or another or too old to have served.

So as other teams quickly got better, all the Cubs' 4-F team did was get older and more enfeebled.

Because he had a second-rate minor-league system, there were few good young prospects moving up.

But all of that could have been overcome in 1947—two years after the Cubs' last World Series and the end of the war.

That was when Branch Rickey of the Brooklyn Dodgers knocked down the racial wall in baseball by signing ex-Army officer Jackie Robinson.

Although he went on to a fabulous career, Robinson was not nearly the best available black ball player at the time. Rickey chose him because Robinson had the education and character to endure the racial abuse heaped on him by fans, press, some of his own teammates, and opposing players.

The old Negro League was loaded with outstanding players. When they played off-season exhibition games against white all-star teams, the blacks won as often as they lost.

By 1947, the year Robinson broke in, the Cubs were already pathetic doormats.

Had Wrigley followed Rickey's lead, he could instantly have had a competitive team. And depending on how many black players he could have tolerated, maybe a great team.

He didn't. His players had made their feelings clear, voting not to play if the other teams boycotted Robinson. And his team's front office wouldn't listen to those who urged them to sign black players.

It wasn't a momentary hesitation. It was not until September 1953—nearly seven full seasons after Robinson arrived—that Wrigley signed two black players.

By then, the Dodgers, with Robinson, Roy Campanella, Junior Gilliam, Don Newcombe, and Joe Black, and the New York Giants, with the amazing Willie Mays and clutch-hitting Monte Irvin, had become dominant teams.

Who did Wrigley ignore? Besides some of the names above, there was Larry Doby, who became an American League home run leader; slugger Luke Easter; Minnie Minoso; the great Satchel Paige; and Hank Aaron, who broke Babe Ruth's lifetime home run record. During the years Wrigley snubbed black players, the black players who were in their late twenties or early thirties when Robinson broke in had aged past their primes.

By the time Cubs management got over their racial fears, the black league was getting ready to fold. Fewer players were available and better teams competed for them. Other sports, college and pro, began going after black athletes.

So what might have been, wasn't. It had nothing to do with a goat's curse. Not unless the goat wore a gabardine suit and sat behind a desk in an executive suite.

Yes, I know, so don't grab your phone: The corporation that owns this paper has owned the Cubs since 1981. So why, you ask, haven't they made it to the World Series?

Because they haven't been good enough. But I do know that if they thought a three-legged green creature from another planet could hit home runs or throw a 95 m.p.h. fastball, they'd sign it. And we'd cheer.